tom smith's cricket umpiring and scoring

The internationally recognised definitive guide

to the interpretation and application of the laws of cricket

tom smith's cricket umpiring and scoring

The internationally recognised definitive guide

to the interpretation and application of the laws of cricket

Introduction by

Richie Benaud

New and completely revised edition

Includes the 2003 changes to the
2000 Code of the Laws of Cricket

WEIDENFELD & NICOLSON

Contents

All communications should be addressed to
THE ASSOCIATION OF CRICKET UMPIRES AND SCORERS
PO. BOX 399, CAMBERLEY
SURREY, GU15 3JZ

First published in Great Britain by J.M. Dent, 1980
This 6th edition, completely rewritten, revised and redesigned, published by
Weidenfeld & Nicolson, 2004

Official Laws of Cricket © Marylebone Cricket Club, 2003
Definitions, additional text and graphics © Association of Cricket Umpires and Scorers, 2004
Introduction © Richie Benaud, 2004

A CIP catalogue record for this book
is available from the British Library.

Printed by Legoprint, Italy

WEIDENFELD & NICOLSON
The Orion Publishing Group Ltd
Orion House
5 Upper Saint Martin's Lane
London, WC2H 9EA

www.orionbooks.co.uk

Umpires and Scorers at all levels,
at all times, owe it to the players,
the clubs, the supporters,
the governing bodies and themselves
to be and to remain as highly trained,
highly qualified, competent
and professional as possible.

ACU&S

Introduction

by Richie Benaud

It was difficult to believe there was any sport busier than cricket as we edged our way into the first five years of the 21st century. Controversy abounded in regard to the players, it surged when we started considering different countries and whether or not they would care to play against one another. Technology made life easier for some and more difficult for others, with ideas constantly being produced to have umpires off the field play a greater part in the game. It is certainly a fact now that umpires, as has always been the case, need to have their wits about them, their concentration must be fierce but calm, and their judgement well in advance of others watching the game in question.

Through all this there remains one outstanding and comforting aspect of the game, the MCC Official Laws of Cricket. They have always been as concise as possible even though new challenges arrive almost daily, often through the medium of television which is increasingly able to take the match, the umpires, the captains and the players to watchers at home. In the 2000 Code of the Laws a Preamble was added involving the Spirit of Cricket. The Preamble was well written and well presented, it was concise, with its main thrust that total responsibility lies with the captains and that captains and umpires together must set the tone. It was a timely reminder and this 2004 edition of *Tom Smith's Cricket Umpiring and Scoring* will continue to be one of the more important items I take with me to every cricket ground and have near me every time I am watching a match on television.

There are plenty of heroes in cricket today, not all of them the outstanding players who gain most publicity. There are many others making up the team without whom the stars would be unable to function and there are thousands upon thousands of others around the world who make sure the game is played and loved. Umpires have a joyous task which sometimes can be thankless as well; scorers sometimes see their matches from the most uncomfortable of places and are still expected to miss nothing, and see and record everything. It has been so over the past several hundred years whether being done by notching a stick or pressing a computer key. Unsung heroes abound and Tom Smith is one of them. In 1953, the year I first came to England under Lindsay Hassett's captaincy, Tom founded the Association of Cricket Umpires, an event 51 years ago which hardly merited a raised eyebrow, because people had no idea if such a modest organisation would flourish or simply wither. In the year 2004, there are almost 8,000 members of the Association and more than 250 affiliated organisations. One of the reasons there are so many people interested in the Laws of

Cricket and the Association of Cricket Umpires and Scorers is that Tom Smith's book based on the Laws is, in itself, thoroughly interesting.

Three times the book has been of immense value to me, twice 'live' at a ground when working on television and the third time when watching a replay of a controversial incident of a bowler being no-balled for a front-foot infringement. These were major occasions as far as I was concerned because the first two, involving Dean Jones and Mark Waugh, needed instant opinion and the third, the no-balling of Shaun Pollock in a match in India, required a quick answer to a question. The Dean Jones matter was when he was given out run out in Georgetown, Guyana, when he had left the crease after being caught at the wicket off a no ball. Ian Chappell and Clive Lloyd were commentating at the time and I was able to confirm Chappell's opinion that he couldn't be out when the West Indian fieldsman broke the wicket. It had already happened in a match in Australia during my playing days and Smith's page, note 5 in Law 27, Appeals, was the valuable wording. *'The umpires shall intervene if satisfied that a batsman, not having been given out, has left his wicket under a misapprehension that he has been dismissed.'* Then in Adelaide, in early February 1998, there was the Mark Waugh incident when he was hit on the forearm and eventually his bat fell against the stumps; he was given not out after consultation between the umpires Cowie and Randell. Tom Smith's note to Law 35 was quite clear, *'Only if the striker breaks his wicket whilst making a stroke or in setting off for a run immediately after the completion of his stroke, should he be given out under this Law.'* Equally clear is his wording on the no ball Law which was the contentious one in a match in India when television showed that Pollock's foot had clearly landed behind the batting crease and then had slid forward. Smith's notes stated, *'The landing of the back foot begins the delivery stride, the delivery stride is completed when the front foot lands. As with the back foot, any subsequent movement should be ignored.'*

The book is both informative and eminently readable. Many people know the Laws of the game but it takes considerable expertise in writing to add to them and catch the attention of the reader, and Tom Smith, and those who have followed him after his death in 1995, have managed that in splendid fashion. To do this it was necessary to have both expertise in writing and authority. One of the problems in cricket in its modern style is that players, for whatever reason, have taken to challenging the decisions umpires make on and off the field, sometimes verbally, sometimes in a more physically aggressive manner. There is a theory that the introduction of a third umpire, and now a fourth, plus whiz-bang television replays, actually make the task of the umpire considerably easier. Although that may be true in the case of run outs and stumpings, it is not necessarily so when you take into account the many disputed matters involving catches, boundaries and lbws. Players sometimes give the impression that because machines have taken away some of the umpire's authority there is no need to show as much respect for those in charge on the field. Some of this will be taken care of by the Preamble to the Laws and the Spirit of Cricket and I shall continue to applaud any improvement in on-the-field behaviour that comes about because of this written word. Fortunately there are many whose names will endure in cricket despite its recent and current problems. Tom Smith and those who have followed him will be high on my list and, I believe, on the lists of many others who have been brought up to love the game and what it stands for.

The Author – Tom Smith

The late TOM SMITH, after many years as a player, football referee and cricket umpire, founded the Association of Cricket Umpires in 1953; he served continuously as General Secretary for twenty-five years and upon his retirement was appointed a Life Vice-President. Well known and respected in every cricket playing country of the world, Tom was recognised as an authority and umpire arbiter on the Laws of the game and the technique of cricket umpiring. For some years he wrote regularly for *The Cricketer* on field umpiring and problems of cricket Law.

During 1956–7 Tom Smith spent many long periods at Lord's assisting the late Colonel Rait Kerr with the preparation of the Association textbook; and in 1961, at the request of the late author, he took over the revising of the book until 1979. The 1980 Code of Laws brought the need for the production of a complete new up-to-date book.

For services to cricket, Tom Smith was awarded an MBE and honoured by the MCC with election to Honorary Life Membership – a distinction awarded to only a small group of people who have carried out special services for cricket – and in 1980, HRH the Duke of Edinburgh presented him with the National Playing Fields Association's Torch Trophy Award for outstanding services to cricket. He served a term as a member of the Test and County Cricket Board Cricket Committee, from its inception, as a member of the MCC Laws Committee, and at one time Chairman of the National Cricket Association Cricket Committee. He also served for several years on the National Association Management Committee and specialist Working Parties as well as the Surrey County Cricket Association Committee.

During 1974, Tom was appointed by the MCC to assist Mr S.C. Griffith, former MCC Secretary, in revising and redrafting the 1947 Code of Laws at the request of the International Cricket Conference.

During the years between the preparation of the new draft and final presentation to the International Cricket Conference, Cricket Council and other representative bodies, Tom Smith was appointed by the MCC to a special Redrafting Committee set up to produce the final draft of the new code, after giving careful consideration to all the suggestions and recommendations from the United Kingdom and overseas.

Tom Smith gave a lifetime of devoted service to umpires and umpiring and, under his leadership and inspiration, the Association of Cricket Umpires and Scorers, has grown from a small beginning to become a recognised international association with over 8,000 members and 200 affiliated organisations.

He died on 14 December 1995. His legacy will long be remembered.

Preface to this Jubilee Edition

Since Tom Smith assisted Colonel Rait Kerr in the 1950s in bringing this book to the light of day, it has subsequently been revised and rewritten by Tom in the 1960s and again for the 1980 Code. Since then other revisions have been published in 1989, 1993 and 1996. These editions have taken his original work forward as the Laws have been revised by the MCC.

With the passing of Tom in 1995, the subsequent revisions and rewrites have been undertaken by others, each following the ideals Tom established to make his book the most widely read publication on the subject throughout the world. When the millennium Code of Laws 2000 was introduced, members of the Association of Cricket Umpires and Scorers rewrote the book to reflect these changes.

As the game developed into the new century, more demands than ever have been placed on both umpires and scorers to get it right; demands brought about by the increasing examination of decisions scrutinised by the eagle eye of the television camera. This should not be seen as a negative thing; rather it has a benefit, by highlighting, more often as not, the excellent decisions made by umpires at that level.

The book sets out to assist umpires and scorers to guide them as they develop their knowledge of the Laws and their fieldcraft, to ensure the players enjoy their game. After all, it is a players' game: it is the players that spectators come to watch, not the umpires. If the umpires remain virtually invisible in a match, they know they have had a good game.

This edition has been produced not only to acknowledge the contribution Tom made to the game, but also to celebrate the founding, by him, of the Association in 1953. It also seeks to celebrate and acknowledge the many thousands of umpires and scorers around the world who each make their own contribution to the game.

The book remains, as Tom would have wished, an easy to read and understand account of the Laws and their official interpretation. It is not just for umpires and scorers. It is also for the players and spectators worldwide who enjoy the game with their own passion. It does not delve into esoteric points or into unlikely situations. Such matters are better left for the after-match function.

Acknowledgements

Gratitude must be expressed and thanks given to the MCC, the holders of the copyright, for their kind permission to print herein the Laws of Cricket, complete with the 2003 amendments. We also owe much to the continuing support of MCC in all matters connected with the laws.

We are also grateful to Richie Benaud for his warm introductory comments. We thank too the members of the Editorial Review Committee, comprising senior members of the Association, for their valuable advice as this edition progressed.

Our thanks also go to Weidenfeld & Nicolson our publishers, and to the Post Office for their generous sponsorship of our Association and this work.

On a personal note the authors were, without exception, honoured to be entrusted with the task of preparing this ACU&S Golden Jubilee Edition. We consider it a privilege to be asked and we each have to acknowledge so many people, instructors, colleagues and officials who have contributed to our own knowledge and love of the game. Thank you.

Thank you, too, to the umpires, scorers and players who have granted permission to use photographs of them in this edition.

Hilary Faulkner receives our grateful thanks for relieving us of the problems of indexing.

Finally, we acknowledge the contribution of the members and officers of the Association, for their contributions to our efforts and their confidence in us to complete the book that is now in your hands.

If you, the reader, gain as much from the Jubilee edition of *Tom Smith's Cricket Umpiring and Scoring* as we have in writing it, our efforts will be amply rewarded.

GC; CJE.

PART 1

Umpires and Scorers

1. THE ASSOCIATION OF CRICKET UMPIRES & SCORERS (ACU&S)

The Association of Cricket Umpires (ACU) was founded in 1953, by Tom Smith, and its main aim was to help educate umpires, not only in the area of Law but also in fieldcraft. At that time Scorers were not included in the remit of the umpire training programme but this was corrected as the training of umpires progressed. By the 1970s the role of the scorer was recognised, officially, when they were added to the Association's name – hence the name, The Association of Cricket Umpires & Scorers (ACU&S).

While the Association has grown during the last fifty years into a body that even Tom Smith would not have envisaged, its main objective remains as it was in 1953: to educate umpires and scorers so that they can fulfill their roles within the game to their best ability. Training methods have changed radically over the years and the massive expansion of computer technology during the 1990s has meant that training now takes place on a scale that was hitherto unforeseen. Multimedia presentations can now be prepared at relatively small cost and the benefits to all aspiring, as well as experienced, umpires and scorers cannot be overstressed. The problems faced on the field can now be brought directly into the classroom where they can be dissected and discussed at leisure.

However, there will always be a place in the area of training for a definitive explanation of the Laws, umpiring fieldcraft and scoring techniques in book form. Cricketers, be they players, umpires, scorers, spectators or commentators on the game, need an easy reference to the Laws and that is where this edition of *Tom Smith's Cricket Umpiring and Scoring* takes its place among the legion of books written on the wonderful game of cricket.

2. QUALIFICATIONS

As with any training programme there have to be benchmarks against which any individual is measured. The learning process differs from individual to individual and, while some may readily take to examinations, others find them much more of a problem. The ACU&S recognises this and has tried to format its examinations to cater for all requirements. However, it still remains that a series of qualifications have to be available to all members so that the required training can be provided – thus giving everyone the opportunity to attain their preferred level within the umpiring and scoring fraternity. Not everyone will reach their target, but the fact remains that the Association provides all the necessary training to enable everyone to try to fulfill their ambitions.

The ACU&S provides various levels of training, examination and grading and all members are given precise details of this qualification/grading process when they join.

Not all the qualification/grading processes are examination based. Once the formal examinations are over the umpire or scorer must satisfy the Association that their ability on the field matches their ability in the classroom. To this end the Association undertakes 'on the job' assessments of umpires and scorers. These assessments help the Association to have a clear picture of an individual's ability while providing him with the opportunity to talk to and seek guidance from an experienced colleague.

3. PERSONAL ATTRIBUTES NEEDED TO UMPIRE

Anyone taking up umpiring requires a blend of the following skills and attributes, some of which are fairly self evident, others less so. They are in no particular order because each one is as important, in its own way, as the others. Some will come naturally, others will require the umpire to work hard to achieve the necessary level of competence.

CONCENTRATION

Matches/sessions of play vary in length but it is not uncommon for any particular session of play to last for three hours or more. A full game may well occupy the best part of the day, eight hours, and an umpire must be able to give the game his full concentration for this length of time. Any lapses in concentration could result in an error that could seriously affect the outcome of the game. While players will accept errors made by their teammates they do not take kindly to umpiring errors, especially when they are the result of a lack of concentration on the part of the umpire.

GOOD EYESIGHT

This is essential since an umpire must, initially, judge events by what he sees. Anything less than good eyesight, be it with or without spectacles or contact lenses, is not acceptable for a person as important as the umpire.

GOOD HEARING

While eyesight is the main sense that an umpire uses, the sense of hearing must also be used to good effect. Hearing is used to back up what the eyes have seen and the two senses together are more effective than either used alone when it comes to the umpire making a decision.

PHYSICAL FITNESS

Standing, walking and swift movement over a short distance are all part of the umpire's role and he needs to be physically fit in order to undertake these parts of his job. An umpire's poor positioning will soon show up any lack of mobility and this undermines his credibility with the players.

MENTAL FITNESS

An umpire must be able to withstand constant appealing and be strong enough to maintain his composure under duress from players and spectators. This requires confidence in his own knowledge/ability and not be afraid to express it. He must have the courage to give the correct decision even though it may not, at the time, seem to be the popular one.

SENSE OF HUMOUR

An umpire must have the ability to laugh with the players and to be able to laugh at himself when the occasion arises.

FIRMNESS

An umpire must always be polite yet firm in his decisions.

HUMILITY

An umpire must be able to carry out his duties with firmness and authority without being officious and overbearing.

FAIRNESS

An umpire must always be fair with his decisions.

IMPARTIALITY

An umpire must remain totally impartial on all things. The umpire is an independent arbiter and must be seen to be such. Any action that indicates that he is favouring one side must be eliminated.

AUTHORITY

An umpire has to exude an air of authority throughout the game. What is said, and the way it is said, and the way that he conducts himself during the game, will go a long way in achieving this. An overbearing, officious umpire who constantly brings himself, unnecessarily, into the game is not going to be highly regarded by the players. An air of quiet authority will give the umpire a much better chance of being accepted, while an umpire who is constantly seeking to be the centre of attention will only be rewarded by disdain and derision by the players.

ACCEPTANCE OF RESPONSIBILITY

Many umpires are very keen to umpire until something unpopular happens. The good umpire will accept the unpopular parts of his job as well as those that are more enjoyable. The job has serious responsibilities and the umpire must ensure that he embraces all aspects of his role.

GOOD JUDGEMENT

To a certain extent good judgement is a talent that some possess in greater measure than others. The ability to judge a very quick piece of stumping, or a run out, or to detect a fine snick that carries to the wicket-keeper who is standing up to the stumps, is something that cannot be taught in a classroom. However, it can be improved by practice, just as batsmen and bowlers spend hours in the nets honing their skills. The more exposure an umpire gets at making close decisions the better he will become.

CONSISTENCY

The most common complaint levelled at umpires is that of inconsistency. Players like to know where they stand and if the umpire keeps moving the goalposts during a game they get very confused. For example, the judgement of a wide ball must be the same in the last over as it was for the first over of the game. To change the criteria just because the game has reached a crucial stage is wrong. This applies to any situation where the umpire's judgement is called upon.

STAYING CALM UNDER PRESSURE

An umpire must not lose control of his decision making abilities by allowing the frenzied state of the game to get to him. If things are getting rather fraught, the umpire should take a deep breath and remain calm – this in itself will allow clear thinking and logical thought.

MAN MANAGEMENT SKILLS

People respond to things in different ways and an umpire's ability to recognise this will stand him in good stead throughout the game. An umpire needs to talk to players in a way that will achieve the required response. There are many useful books on the subject of man management. Suffice to say that if umpires talk to players in the manner in which they themselves would like to be addressed they will not go far wrong.

CONFIDENCE

An umpire must always come across as being very confident in what he is doing. An umpire who appears intimidated or hesitant is going to experience a very hard match because some players will try to exploit this weakness.

BODY LANGUAGE

In any area where authority needs to be shown, body language plays an extremely important part in the acceptance of a decision. Players are more likely to accept a decision if it is made with an air of authority. The umpire needs to conduct himself in a way that demonstrates to others that he is both confident and assured of his own ability. It is not necessary for him to go around telling everyone that he is in charge – the way that he walks and conducts himself will say that for him.

19

SOUND KNOWLEDGE OF THE LAWS

In any walk of life, where a person has to adjudicate on the actions of others, that person must know the rules by which such adjudications have to be made. And so it is with cricket umpiring. Knowledge of the Laws is paramount to an umpire's ability to maintain order during a match. A full knowledge of the Laws and how to administer them will stand the umpire in good stead at any level of cricket. It is a fallacy to claim that the lower the level of the game the less the umpire needs to know. All matches should have the benefit of umpires who are fully trained in their art and it is this that drives the ACU&S to improve its extensive training programmes.

It is written within The Preamble (to the Laws) – The Spirit of Cricket that the players should have 'respect for the role of the umpires'. Whilst agreeing wholeheartedly with this it should be pointed out that any respect for the umpire, as an individual, has to be earned. The respect for his role within the game should never be in question, but the individual respect that players, spectators, commentators etc. have for the person in that role is something that every umpire has to work extremely hard to obtain. It is only by developing the skills/attributes above that this respect can hope to be earned and maintained.

4. DRESS AND EQUIPMENT

A significant part of an umpire's credibility rests in his appearance. While this may sound superficial it is, nonetheless, a fact of life. An umpire who is poorly dressed will not inspire confidence. The first impression that an umpire gives at a match is the one that stays throughout the day. If that impression is poor, based on his appearance, he will put himself at a great disadvantage for the rest of the day. The ACU&S is very keen that their members are dressed appropriately when officiating. With the advent of coloured clothing for players and the modern approach towards casual clothing for officials in other major sports, the ACU&S has introduced a range of umpire's clothing that reflects this trend. However, it is appreciated that not all members may wish to take this modern approach and to take this into consideration more tradi-tional guidelines on formal clothing are offered.

CASUAL ON-FIELD ATTIRE

- **Dark trousers or skirt** (black or navy).
- **Umpires shirt**: this is a long sleeve shirt, mainly white with coloured collar and sleeves with coloured piping. It also features the ACU&S logo. It is suitable for either male or female umpires. It is meant to be worn as the outer layer of clothing with thermal wear being worn underneath in cold weather.
- **Umpires windcheater**: this has the same colour scheme as the shirt and is worn

during inclement conditions as the outer layer of clothing. These two items are only available from the ACU&S and are restricted to members.

TRADITIONAL/FORMAL ON-FIELD ATTIRE
- **Dark trousers or skirt** (black or navy).
- **White (or pastel coloured) shirt or blouse**
- **Tie**: standard for male umpires. Female umpires should wear some type of formal neck wear. When adopting the formal approach to dress it is preferable that umpires wear a tie. Should they wish to be less formal then the casual approach, as detailed above, is recommended.
- **White umpire coat**: it is now accepted that this is optional and it is not uncommon, in hot weather, for umpires to stand without coats. Any coat worn should be laundered frequently to maintain the overall formal impression.
- **Pullover**: any pullover worn under the coat should be of a cricketing nature i.e. white or cream. It is not desirable for dark colours to be worn under the coat.

GENERAL ITEMS
- **White shoes or boots**: these should be comfortable bearing in mind that the umpire will be standing for long periods of time. The shoes should be cleaned regularly especially after prolonged use during wet weather. A cushioned sports sock that gives extra support is recommended
- **Sunglasses**: it is now fully recognised that good quality sunglasses do help an umpire to see better in bright conditions and reduce the problems associated with glare off the pitch.
- **Hats**: from flat cap to panama, some would say that a hat is essential. Provided that they are of a cricketing nature (i.e. not baseball caps) and white most styles are acceptable.

EQUIPMENT
In order to undertake the many duties that umpires have to perform it is necessary for them to carry certain items onto the field. The following list, while not exhaustive, highlights the essential ones:
- **Match ball**: the balls for the match should be in the possession of the umpires before the match.
- **Spare balls**: a selection of spare balls should be made available to the umpires so that any replacements needed during the match can easily be accessed. The umpires can either leave these in a readily accessible place (e.g. the scorebox) or they can each take one onto the field in their pocket. The important thing is that the spares are available when needed.

- **Bails:** although some ground authorities provide bails it would be unwise for an umpire to expect this service at every match they attend. It is better for the umpire to have his own set of bails. Whoever provides the bails, the umpire must take them onto the field at the start of each session of play.
- **Spare bails:** bails may get broken during the course of play and in order to save time looking for spares in the pavilion, the umpire must carry at least one spare bail with him while on the field. Some umpires prefer to carry a matching pair.
- **Counters:** the umpire needs to count the number of balls in the over and some sort of counting device is recommended. There are several patented devices available commercially. Others prefer to use coins, stones or marbles. Whatever system is employed, the chosen device should become an integral part of the umpire's on-field equipment. If single items, such as coins, are used it is advisable to have a spare available in case one of the originals is lost.
- **Bowler's mark:** these can be purchased commercially or home-made items and should be flat so that they do not cause a potential danger to players. Umpires should remember to collect any markers at the end of the innings/match so that they don't become lost or entangled in the groundsman's mower at a later date.
- **Run (tally) counter:** such a device is available commercially and is used to record every run scored during a single innings. The umpire uses it as a check against the scoring record total and by doing so can easily detect variations between the scoreboard total and his own.
- **Notebook:** used to record events that need to be referred to during or after the match.
- **Overs card:** these are primarily used in limited-overs matches to record the bowlers' overs so that they do not exceed their allocation. Available commercially, many such cards incorporate areas for recording other information such as number of overs bowled per innings, fall of wickets, details of intervals. They can also be used in place of a notebook.
- **Pen or pencil**
- **Towel or other drying material:** all umpires should carry a drying cloth of some description onto the field of play. There are many occasions when the ball needs wiping/drying and it saves time if the umpires carry a cloth with them.
- **Scissors or knife:** it is often helpful to have such implements handy in case they are needed.
- **Watch:** this should be syncronised with the master timepiece, the other umpire's watch and the scorers' watches.
- **MCC Laws of Cricket:** while it is not advocated that the umpire be constantly referring to this during play it is often helpful to have it available during the match. The size of the book means that it can fit into most trouser pockets but if

the umpire does not wish to take it onto the field, it should at least be readily available in the pavilion.

- **Competition Regulations**: these must be available, either on the field or easily accessible in the pavilion. Any umpire who stands in a match covered by Competition Regulations who does not have them to hand is storing up problems for himself.
- **Special Directives issued by Governing Body**: these could include directives relating to juniors and to fielding, bowling and batting restrictions. While not applicable in every country or even every match they should be available for reference where they do apply.

Essential equipment for the scorer is covered in Part 3 – Scoring.

PART 2

The Laws of Cricket
with interpretations

The Preamble – The Spirit of Cricket

The Laws are reproduced with the permission of the Marylebone Cricket Club. They are those of the 2000 Code amended at their AGM in May 2003 to take effect from 1 October 2003. Copies may be obtained fromMarylebone Cricket Club (MCC Book Shop), Lord's Cricket Ground, London NW8 8QN.

THE PREAMBLE – The Spirit of Cricket

Cricket is a game that owes much of its unique appeal to the fact that it should be played not only within its Laws but also within the Spirit of the Game. Any action which is seen to abuse this spirit causes injury to the game itself. The major responsibility for ensuring the spirit of fair play rests with the captains.

1. THERE ARE TWO LAWS WHICH PLACE THE RESPONSIBILITY FOR THE TEAM'S CONDUCT FIRMLY ON THE CAPTAIN.

RESPONSIBILITY OF CAPTAINS
The captains are responsible at all times for ensuring that play is conducted within the Spirit of the Game as well as within the Laws.

PLAYER'S CONDUCT
In the event of a player failing to comply with instructions by an umpire, or criticising by word or action the decisions of an umpire, or showing dissent, or generally behaving in a manner which might bring the game into disrepute, the umpire concerned shall in the first place report the matter to the other umpire and to the player's captain, and instruct the latter to take action.

2. FAIR AND UNFAIR PLAY

According to the Laws the umpires are the sole judges of fair and unfair play. The umpires may intervene at any time and it is the responsibility of the captain to take action where required.

3. THE UMPIRES ARE AUTHORISED TO INTERVENE IN CASES OF:

- Time wasting
- Damaging the pitch
- Dangerous or unfair bowling
- Tampering with the ball
- Any other action that they consider to be unfair

4. THE SPIRIT OF THE GAME INVOLVES **RESPECT** FOR:

- Your opponents
- Your own captain and team
- The role of the umpires
- The game's traditional values

5. IT IS AGAINST THE SPIRIT OF THE GAME:

- To dispute an umpire's decision by word, action or gesture
- To direct abusive language towards an opponent or umpire

- **To indulge in cheating or any sharp practice, for instance:**
- **to appeal knowing that the batsman is not out**
- **to advance towards an umpire in an aggressive manner when appealing**
- **to seek to distract an opponent either verbally or by harassment with persistent clapping or unnecessary noise under the guise of enthusiasm and motivation of one's own side**

6. VIOLENCE

There is no place for any act of violence on the field of play.

7. PLAYERS

Captains and umpires together set the tone for the conduct of a cricket match. Every player is expected to make an important contribution to this.

The players, umpires and scorers in a game of cricket may be of either gender and the Laws apply equally to both. The use, throughout the text, of pronouns indicating the male gender is purely for brevity. Except where specifically stated otherwise, every provision of the Laws is to be read as applying to women and girls equally as to men and boys.

If players follow the Spirit of Cricket, they have nothing to fear from the Laws, indeed they can ensure they have an enjoyable match and the camaraderie that their participation deserves. The umpires and scorers too have the right to enjoy their participation in the game, but they should always remember the order of the first four Laws:

- Law 1 refers to the players
- Law 2 refers to the substitutes
- Law 3 refers to the umpires
- Law 4 refers to the scorers

The compilers of the Laws have made it quite clear: cricket is a game for players. Within this Preamble, the role of the umpires is clear. They are the sole judges of fair and unfair play and are required to intervene in the match either by invitation, when an appeal is made, or when required to do so under the Laws.

Cricket has a history and reputation for fair play and it is incumbent upon all participants that this be maintained. The continued popularity of the game depends on future generations taking up the sport and this will only happen if the sportsmanship, historically attached to the game, is nurtured and built on.

Law I The players

I. NUMBER OF PLAYERS

A match is played between two sides, each of eleven players, one of whom shall be captain.

By agreement a match may be played between sides of more or less than eleven players, but not more than eleven players may field at any time.

This clause formalises the requirement that a match is played between two teams, each consisting of eleven players. It permits a match to be played with fewer than eleven players, provided that this is agreed between the two captains before the toss; it also permits a match to be played with more than eleven players. However, in the latter case it is only permissible to field eleven players at any one time. The fielding captain may seek to 'rotate' his fielders so that everyone has an opportunity to field. However, if this is not agreed before the toss and the umpires are not informed, there could be problems during the game if one side suddenly objects to the practice.

The Law does not give a minimum number of players that will comprise a team, only a maximum that may field. On occasions, match regulations will state a minimum number of players that have to be present in order for the match to start, and umpires will have to be aware of any such provision. There may also be a provision stipulating a time after which a late player may not take part in the match. For the purposes of this clause, there is no such stipulation.

Prior to calling Play both umpires should count and confirm that the correct number of fielders are on the field.

This clause also states that one of these players must be elected or appointed as captain. The captain is the person the umpires discuss matters with when decisions are required to be made during the match.

2. NOMINATION OF PLAYERS

Each captain shall nominate his players in writing to one of the umpires before the toss. No player may be changed after the nomination without the consent of the opposing captain.

Here the Law states that players must be nominated prior to the toss. Such nomination must be given, in writing, to one of the umpires before the toss.

The importance of this team nomination list cannot be overstressed. Umpires must know which players are part of the nominated team. This is particularly important at the start of the match when the players take the field. The umpires must be told if any nominated player is not present and, if applicable, give permission for a substitute to field until the nominated player arrives. Only by checking the team nomination list will they be able to assure themselves that they have the situation under their control.

Recognising the vulnerability of young players, and with a desire to protect them from potential injury when batting, fielding or bowling, some countries have introduced directives which limit the activities of players under 19 years of age. The umpires must know the age group to which each young player belongs. Then they can monitor his contribution to the game and ensure that it does not exceed the limitations laid down within the directives.

Team Sheet

_____ XI

v. _____ XI

ECB

Umpires: _____ & _____

(together the "Umpires")

Helmet Consent Form held (tick)		Under 18 on day of match (tick)	Age Group* for Fast Bowlers
	Capt		
	Wk		
	3		
	4		
	5		
	6		
	7		
	8		
	9		
	10		
	11		
	12		

*Note:
Age Group is based on age at midnight on 31 August the previous year. The Fast Bowling Directives apply to players in the Under 19 age group and younger.

To be completed by the person responsible for the team and provided to the Umpires before the toss takes place:

I confirm and undertake on behalf of _____

that: _____ (the "Club" / "School") Please tick

Either - (a) There are no players under eighteen years of age in today's team ☐

Or - (b) In line with Club/School policy, all players under eighteen years of age in today's team will wear a helmet with a faceguard when batting or when standing up to the stumps when keeping wicket ☐

Or - (c) The Club/School has received, in writing, a parental consent form allowing those players in today's team holding such consent, as shown on the reverse, to bat or to stand up to the stumps when keeping wicket without wearing a helmet, and the Club/School accepts responsibility for accepting this consent in line with the England and Wales Cricket Board (ECB) safety guidance ☐

And - The ECB Fast Bowling Directives apply to the players in today's team as shown on the team sheet.

I confirm that I am an authorised signatory on behalf of the Club/School and that I have read and understood the ECB safety guidance and the ECB Fast Bowling Directives.

I agree that prior to the toss I have discussed with the Umpires the policy adopted by this Club/School with regard to the wearing of helmets and the age group of the young players taking part in the match.

The Club/School hereby agree to indemnify the Umpires from and against all actions, costs, claims and demands (including reasonable legal fees) and any other damage suffered or incurred arising from any confirmation contained in this document relating to the provision of parental consent forms being incorrect.

Signed _____

Print name _____

On behalf of _____

Address of Club / School _____

Date _____

The card shown is the one issued by the ECB for cricket in England and Wales and is two sided. It must be completed, signed and handed to the umpires prior to the toss being made.

Once nominated, a player cannot be changed without the consent of the opposing captain who, if he chooses, may decline. If permission is granted, the replacement player may take a full and active part in the game without restrictions of any kind. A replacement may be requested at any time during the match.

Should a replacement be approved, the scorers must be informed as soon as possible.

3. CAPTAIN

If at any time the captain is not available, a deputy shall act for him.

(a) If a captain is not available during the period in which the toss is to take place, then the deputy must be responsible for the nomination

of the players, if this has not already been done, and for the toss.
See 2 above and Law 12.4 (The toss).
(b) At any time after the toss, the deputy must be one of the
nominated players.

The key element of this clause is that one of the nominated team must be appointed as **captain**, and if he is not available at any time then a deputy must act for him.

While **on the field**, should the umpires require a decision to be made relating to either the giving up of the drinks interval or the suspension of play for adverse conditions they will ask the batsmen at the wicket to make a decision. The batsmen deputise for the actual captain in these circumstances in order to avoid protracted delays while trying to locate the captain himself.

Should the captain not be available when the teams are nominated, a **deputy** must undertake this duty.

During the period up to the scheduled (or rescheduled) time for the toss, the deputy need not be a nominated member of the playing team. However, once the toss has been made, any decisions that have to be made in the absence of the captain must be made by a deputy who must be one of the nominated team. This includes the decision taken resulting from the toss i.e. whether to bat or to field.

Play should not be held up if a captain is unavailable at any time. If necessary the deputy must fulfil all the absent captain's duties.

The scorers must be kept informed of events, to enable them to complete their records.

In youth grades it is not uncommon for a coach or parent to assume the role of off-field captain. A prudent umpire accepts their role in the game.

4. RESPONSIBILITY OF CAPTAINS

The captains are responsible at all times for ensuring that play is conducted within the spirit and traditions of the game as well as within the Laws. See The Preamble – The Spirit of Cricket and Law 42.1 (Fair and unfair play – responsibility of captains).

On occasions, player behaviour may present a problem. This clause requires a captain to ensure his team follows the Laws as well as the Spirit of Cricket.

Law 2 Substitutes and runners; batsman or fielder leaving the field; batsman retiring; batsman commencing innings

1. SUBSTITUTES AND RUNNERS

(a) If the umpires are satisfied that a player has been injured or become ill after the nomination of the players, they shall allow that player to have

(i) a substitute acting instead of him in the field.

(ii) a runner when batting.

Any injury or illness that occurs at any time after the nomination of the players until the conclusion of the match shall be allowable, irrespective of whether play is in progress or not.

(b) **The umpires shall have discretion, for other wholly acceptable reasons, to allow a substitute for a fielder, or a runner for a batsman, at the start of the match or at any subsequent time.**

(c) **A player wishing to change his shirt, boots, etc. must leave the field to do so. No substitute shall be allowed for him.**

2. OBJECTION TO SUBSTITUTES

The opposing captain shall have no right of objection to any player acting as a substitute on the field, nor as to where the substitute shall field. However, no substitute shall act as wicket-keeper. See 3 below.

3. RESTRICTIONS ON THE ROLE OF SUBSTITUTES

A substitute shall not be allowed to bat or bowl nor to act as wicket-keeper or as captain on the field of play.

4. A PLAYER FOR WHOM A SUBSTITUTE HAS ACTED

A player is allowed to bat, bowl or field even though a substitute has previously acted for him.

It is important that umpires fully understand the difference between the terms 'replacement' and 'substitute', and how the difference can have an important influence on the game .

A **replacement**, a term not used in Law, is commonly used when, after the nomination of the team, a nominated player is unable to take part in the match and permission is given for another to take his place. This could occur through an injury sustained prior to the game starting, or the player being called away for an emergency (he might be a doctor or fireman) or for a domestic matter.

If this happens, that player's captain may request that a replacement be permitted to take the original player's place. If the opposing captain grants the request, the replacement may take a full part in the game and can undertake any role his captain wishes.

If the opposing captain refuses the request, which he is quite entitled to do, then the doctor or whoever remains one of the nominated players. Any person coming onto the field to field for him in his absence is only a **substitute** and is subject to the restrictions applicable to substitutes.

To summarise:

- a **replacement** takes a **full part** in the game, whereas
- a **substitute** is only allowed on the field to act as a **fielder** during the absence of a nominated player.

RESTRICTIONS PLACED ON THE USE OF A SUBSTITUTE DURING A MATCH

The umpires must carefully monitor the use of a substitute. They will allow a player to be substituted only if certain conditions have been met:

- the player being substituted must **be injured, ill or unable to field for** a **wholly acceptable reason**
- the above will only be acceptable criteria if they occur between the times when the teams are nominated and the end of the match.

The word 'injured' covers not only new injuries sustained after the nomination of players and during the game itself, but also any recurrence of an injury previously sustained. In cases of old injuries being aggravated all the umpires need to decide is whether or not something happened in the current game to cause the injury to become worse. Provided they are satisfied that the aggravation was caused during the current match, a substitute should be allowed.

Note that if a player has an ongoing physical condition or disability, his participation should be encouraged without unreasonable and additional restrictions.

The phrase 'wholly acceptable reason' is open to interpretation as it can cover any reasonable excuse offered by the player concerned. The umpires have discretion to decide if the reason given is 'wholly acceptable'. The opposing captain, players or team officials cannot influence their decision in any way.

The understanding of the time span is important since it includes any interval or interruption that takes place during the course of the day's play as well as any overnight interval and rest day. It is possible, therefore, for a player to injure himself during a rest day or during the evening of a playing day and not be able to play the following day. In such circumstances, he would be allowed to have a substitute act for him until he had recovered.

Should a player wish to leave the field to change boots or any item of clothing he may do so, but a substitute is not permitted.

It can be seen how important it is for umpires to be informed why a player leaves the field. If a player fails to tell an umpire the reason for his absence, the umpires must find out from either the player or his captain.

When the use of a substitute has been granted by the umpires, the opposing captain can object neither to who the substitute is nor to where he fields. The fielding captain can call upon anyone he likes to undertake the role, and they can field anywhere he directs. Note, however, the restrictions below regarding the roles that a substitute can undertake:

- a substitute cannot act as captain (Law 1 states that one of the nominated players must be captain and, since a substitute does not have to be named at any time, it follows that he cannot fulfil this criterion). If the substitute appears to be acting as captain the umpires must immediately step in and prevent him from doing so. A substitute may offer advice to the captain or his deputy, and that advice can be accepted, but he must not be seen to be openly captaining the side

- a substitute cannot bat or bowl
- a substitute cannot act as wicket-keeper (this is the only restriction on where a substitute can field).

To summarise, a substitute is only there to **field the ball** – he cannot otherwise influence the progress of the game.

It can be seen that these clauses are primarily directed at fielders, but they are also applicable to batsmen who may become ill or injured during an innings. If a batsman is able to bat and is physically unable to run, he is allowed to request a runner. Details of the restrictions placed upon the runner are given in clause 7 below.

An injured or ill player may resume his part in the game when he is able to do so and is allowed to bowl (subject to certain conditions) and bat if required.

Whenever a substitute is used, the scorers must be informed. Traditionally the names of substitutes are not entered in the scoring record. Should they take a catch, it is recorded as 'Caught sub'. This is changing, however, and more scorers are adding the name in brackets so that a more complete record is made.

5. FIELDER ABSENT OR LEAVING THE FIELD

If a fielder fails to take the field with his side at the start of the match or at any later time, or leaves the field during a session of play,
(a) the umpire shall be informed of the reason for his absence.
(b) he shall not thereafter come on to the field during a session of play without the consent of the umpire. See 6 below. The umpire shall give such consent as soon as is practicable.
(c) if he is absent for 15 minutes or longer, he shall not be permitted to bowl thereafter, subject to (i), (ii) or (iii) below, until he has been on the field for at least that length of playing time for which he was absent.
  (i) Absence or penalty for time absent shall not be carried over into a new day's play.
  (ii) If, in the case of a follow-on or forfeiture, a side fields for two consecutive innings, this restriction shall, subject to (i) above, continue as necessary into the second innings but shall not otherwise be carried over into a new innings.
  (iii) The time lost for an unscheduled break in play shall be counted as time on the field for any fielder who comes on to the field at the resumption of play. See Law 15.1 (An interval).

6. PLAYER RETURNING WITHOUT PERMISSION

If a player comes on to the field of play in contravention of 5(b) above and comes into contact with the ball while it is in play
  (i) the ball shall immediately become dead and the umpire shall award 5 penalty runs to the batting side. See Law 42.17 (Penalty runs). The ball shall not count as one of the over.

(ii) the umpire shall inform the other umpire, the captain of the fielding side, the batsmen and, as soon as practicable, the captain of the batting side of the reason for this action.
(iii) the umpires together shall report the occurrence as soon as possible to the Executive of the fielding side and any Governing Body responsible for the match, who shall take such action as is considered appropriate against the captain and player concerned.

Before looking at the restrictions placed on a bowler who leaves the field it must be understood that when **any** player wishes to leave the field of play or does not take the field at the start of any session the **umpires must be informed.** It is vital that both umpires are aware when a player is not on the playing area since his absence from the field may well place restrictions on when he may bowl upon his return.

If either umpire notices that a player is leaving the field it is his duty to find out why from the player or his captain. The umpires are not going to stop the player from leaving the field, but they do need to record the time, the player's name and his reason for leaving so that they can deal with any problems arising out of his absence. The reason given will also dictate whether or not a substitute will be allowed. If an umpire sees a player leaving the field, or the captain tells only one umpire that a player is leaving, that information must be conveyed to the other as soon as possible.

Equally important is the situation when the player wishes to **return** to the field, which he can do only with the consent of the bowler's end umpire.

On most occasions the player will wait on the boundary, at least until the over is finished, before returning. Even then he must ask permission from the bowler's end umpire before doing so. However it is not necessary for him to wait until the end of the over before seeking this permission. Provided he is near to where he would field the umpire may recall him to the field when the ball is dead i.e. between deliveries. If the returning player is likely to have to cross to the other end of the field in order to take up his position and the umpire believes that his return would result in time wasting, the umpire may withhold consent until the end of the over.

When the fielder returns the umpire must ensure that both his colleague and the batsmen know that he has returned:
• Play must not be allowed to resume without informing everyone that the fielding side is back to full strength
• Both umpires should note the time and calculate the duration of his absence as this information may be needed at a later stage should he wish to bowl
• Both umpires should recount the number of fielders to ensure that no more than eleven members of the fielding team are on the playing area.

RETURNING TO THE FIELD WITHOUT PERMISSION
The penalty for returning to the field without the permission of the bowler's end umpire is quite severe if the player subsequently touches a ball that is in play. The act

of returning to the field without permission is not, in itself, grounds for invoking the penalty. It is only when the player in question makes contact with the ball, in play, that a 5 run penalty is awarded. In addition to this penalty the delivery in question does not count as one of the over.

If the umpires notice a fielder return to the field, for example at the end of an over, without first asking permission, it is extremely poor umpiring if the umpires, having observed this occurrence, say nothing and wait to penalise the player when he eventually makes contact with the ball – which could be several overs later. A prudent umpire will immediately advise the captain of his obligations and politely request that, in future, permission be sought before one of his players returns.

If a player returns without permission and comes into contact with the ball in play, the Law has been breached and the appropriate action must be taken.

Player returning to the field without permission

If the player returns without permission and touches the ball in play

Action	Inform
• Award 5 penalty runs to the batting side (the ball becomes dead automatically).	• Colleague.
	• Batsmen at the crease.
	• Fielding captain.
	During the next interval:
• This ball does not count as one of the over.	• Batting captain.
	• Scorers (of the reasons why an extra delivery was bowled).
	• Report to the Executive of the fielding side.
	• Report to the Governing body responsible for the match.

The runs scored will depend on where the batsmen were at the instant the fielder made contact with the ball.

Any runs completed before the offence are scored as is the run in progress provided that the batsmen had crossed **prior** to the fielder's contact with the ball. (This principle is similar to that of overthrows and illegal fielding; this method of calculating the number of runs scored appears several times in the Laws, full details of which are dealt with under Law 18.11.)

EXAMPLE 1
The striker hits the ball and the batsmen complete 2 runs. They cross on their 3rd run when a player returns to the field without permission and makes contact with the ball.
RUNS SCORED: 2 (completed ones) + 1 (for run in progress since the batsmen had crossed) + 5 penalty runs = 8.
RECORDED AS: 5 penalty run extras and 3 runs to the striker.

EXAMPLE 2
The striker misses the ball, as does the wicket-keeper, and the batsmen complete 2 runs.

They turn to start their 3rd run when a player returns to the field without permission and makes contact with the ball.

RUNS SCORED: 2 (completed ones) + 5 penalty runs = 7.

Since the batsmen had only started their third run they have not crossed, so cannot be credited with the third run.

RECORDED AS: 5 penalty run extras and 2 runs as Byes.

The 5 penalty runs are always entered in the Penalty run section of the scoring record. The other runs are recorded as appropriate, either to the striker, No ball extras, Wides, Byes or Leg byes.

The batsmen must be directed to the ends that they were nearest to when the errant fielder first touched the ball. If the batsmen have crossed they will continue to the ends to which they were running, otherwise they must return to the ends they have left.

PLAYER BOWLING AFTER RETURN FROM ABSENCE

If a player does not take the field at the start of the match or the start of a session or leaves the field during a session then, upon his return, should he wish to bowl he is subject to certain restrictions:

- provided the absence is for **less than 15 minutes**, no bowling restrictions apply and he may resume bowling whenever his captain wishes. He does not have to make up any time for the period he was absent
- if, however, a fielder is absent from the field for **15 minutes or more** then he has to be back on the field for the same length of playing time that he was absent (for brevity this will be called 'penalty time').

EXAMPLE 3

A fielder is off the field from 12.00 p.m. until 12.27 p.m.

On his return he would have to be back on the field for 27 minutes' playing time before he may bowl again: 12.54 p.m. would be the earliest that he could bowl.

This restriction applies not only to when he leaves the field and comes back on during the same session, but also to when he fails to return to the field of play after an interval.

EXAMPLE 4

A fielder leaves the field 10 minutes before lunch and does not return until 10 minutes after the game has restarted.

Since he has failed to return from an interval he has been absent from the field for 20 minutes and would have to serve 20 minutes' penalty time.

A player is not penalised for the time taken for any **interval**, scheduled or not, since everyone benefits from this break. This period of absence is not playing time so a fielder cannot be penalised for not being on the field during that time.

EXAMPLE 5

A fielder leaves the field 20 minutes before lunch and does not return until play resumes immediately after lunch.

He only has to wait 20 minutes before he may bowl – the interval for lunch is not added to his penalty time. Neither can he use the lunch period to 'work off' his 20 minutes of penalty time.

If the bowler leaves the field more than once during an innings, each period of absence is treated separately – they are not added together. Any occasion that is less than 15 minutes is not penalised and no sanction is incurred, no matter how many of these absences there may be. However, each period of absence of 15 minutes or more will require penalty time to be served.

EXAMPLE 6

A fielder leaves the field for 25 minutes and then returns and serves 20 minutes of his penalty time before he is forced to leave the field again, this time only for 10 minutes.

On his return he only has to serve the remainder of the original 25 minutes' penalty time, i.e. 5 minutes, before he can bowl again. The second period of absence is ignored because it was less than 15 minutes.

EXAMPLE 7

Same scenario as above but this time the second period of absence was 30 minutes.

Now when he returns he has to wait 35 minutes before he can bowl. He has to finish the penalty time for the first period of absence (5 minutes) and also has to serve a further 30 minutes due to his second period of absence, which exceeded 15 minutes.

In the situation where a player has left the field and while he is off an **unscheduled break** occurs, any penalty time he has accumulated is affected by the action he takes when play resumes. There are two possible scenarios:

*   The player is allowed to count any time off the field during this unscheduled break as penalty time provided that he returns to the field immediately play resumes
*   If he does not return immediately he has failed 'to take the field with his side' and therefore cannot count the time of the unscheduled break as part of his penalty time

EXAMPLE 8

A fielder leaves the field at 11.30 a.m. and is still absent from the field when it starts to rain and the match is suspended at 11.55 a.m. Play resumes at 12.30 p.m. and the fielder returns with the rest of his team ready to restart play.

He can bowl whenever his captain wishes. Since he has returned immediately following this unscheduled break he is allowed to count the unscheduled break as part of his penalty time. As the break was for 35 minutes and he was off the field for only 25 minutes' playing time, the time spent off the field during the unscheduled break clears all of his penalty time.

EXAMPLE 9

A fielder leaves the field at 11.30 a.m. and is still absent when play is suspended for rain at 11.55 a.m. Play resumes at 12.30 p.m. and the fielder fails to return for the restart of play. He returns to the field at 12.35 p.m.

He cannot bowl until he has served his penalty time of 30 minutes i.e. 1.05 p.m. Since he did not immediately return to the field when play resumed he cannot count the 30 minutes of the unscheduled break as penalty time.

This scenario differs slightly from Example 6 above, in as much as the 5 minutes for which he was off the field after the resumption of play does not count as a 'second period of absence' because he failed to return to the field after his first absence. As he did not return at the resumption, the 5 minutes between 12.30 p.m. and 12.35 p.m. is a continuation of his first absence.

If he was not able to return immediately after the break then he would not have been able to do so between 12.00 p.m. and 12.30 p.m. during the interruption. However, since there was this interruption, he is lucky. He is not penalised for the break of 30 minutes (everyone was off the field at that time so no advantage was gained by him) but he is penalised for failing to return immediately by having the 5 minutes included and added to his penalty time.

If there is a **follow-on** or **forfeiture**, a bowler's unserved time from the first innings is carried over into the next innings.

EXAMPLE 10

A fielder has been absent for 50 minutes when a change of innings takes place requiring his team to field again. The fielder returns to the field 20 minutes after the start of the new innings.

His total penalty time is 70 minutes. As a change of innings is a scheduled interval, the 10 minutes between innings is neither deducted from, nor added to, his penalty time. Therefore he must make up his entire penalty time of 70 minutes before being permitted to bowl.

However, carrying over any part of this remaining penalty time into the next day is not required and any such penalty time yet to be served at the end of a day's play is cancelled.

EXAMPLE 11

A fielder leaves the field at 5.00 p.m. and is still absent when the batting side is all out at 5.45 p.m. His captain enforces the follow-on. The fielder comes on to the field at 5:55 p.m. at the start of the new innings. Play is due to end for the day at 6.30 p.m.

Since he was absent for a total of 45 minutes he will serve out as much of his penalty time as he can during the current day's play. In this case it will only be possible for him to serve 35 minutes of it – 5:55 pm to 6:30 pm. The remaining 10 minutes are cancelled and he may bowl at the start of play again first thing next day if his captain wishes. Since a change of innings is considered a scheduled interval, the 10 minutes between innings is neither deducted from, nor added to, his penalty time.

EXAMPLE 12

A player leaves the field 35 minutes before the end of play on day two, not to return that day.
He does not have to serve any penalty time on the morning of day three and, provided he
arrives on the field within the first 15 minutes of the call of Play, he can bowl immediately. The reason is that he has not gained any advantage by being off the field for those
35 minutes as all players have had the same overnight rest during which to recover.

If a bowler arrives 15 minutes or more late for the start of play on any day of a
match, the same restrictions apply as when a player leaves the field during a session.
If the bowler is less than 15 minutes late in arriving on the field he can bowl
immediately. If he is 15 minutes or more late in arriving then he cannot bowl until
he has served his total penalty time.

PLAYER BATTING AFTER RETURN FROM ABSENCE

There are no restrictions in Law, though there may be in some competition regulations, on when a player can bat in the batting order when he has been off the field
while his side was fielding.

EXAMPLE 13

A fielder leaves the field at 3.00 p.m. and is absent when the batting side declares at 3.50 p.m.
Penalty time does not apply, he may bat at any time his captain chooses. He does not
have to serve any penalty time as this only applies to a player when his side is fielding.

As always, as the recorder of all events on the field, scorers should note the departure
and return of any player.

7. RUNNER

**The player acting as a runner for a batsman shall be a member of the
batting side and shall, if possible, have already batted in that innings.
The runner shall wear external protective equipment equivalent to
that worn by the batsman for whom he runs and shall carry a bat.**

8. TRANSGRESSION OF THE LAWS BY A BATSMAN WHO HAS A RUNNER

**(a) A batsman's runner is subject to the Laws. He will be regarded as a
batsman except where there are specific provisions for his role as
a runner. See 7 above and Law 29.2 (Which is a batsman's ground).**
**(b) A batsman with a runner will suffer the penalty for any
infringement of the Laws by his runner as though he had been
himself responsible for the infringement. In particular he will be
out if his runner is out under any of Laws 33 (Handled the ball),
37 (Obstructing the field) or 38 (Run out).**
**(c) When a batsman with a runner is striker he remains himself
subject to the Laws and will be liable to the penalties that any
infringement of them demands.**

Additionally, if he is out of his ground when the wicket is put down at the wicket-keeper's end, he will be out in the circumstances of Law 38 (Run out) or Law 39 (Stumped) irrespective of the position of the non-striker or of the runner. If he is thus dismissed, runs completed by the runner and the other batsman before the dismissal shall not be scored. However, the penalty for a No ball or a Wide shall stand, together with any penalties to either side that may be awarded when the ball is dead. See Law 42.17 (Penalty runs).

(d) When a batsman with a runner is not the striker

(i)   he remains subject to Laws 33 (Handled the ball) and 37 (Obstructing the field) but is otherwise out of the game.

(ii) he shall stand where directed by the striker's end umpire so as not to interfere with play.

(iii) he will be liable, notwithstanding (i) above, to the penalty demanded by the Laws should he commit any act of unfair play.

This part of the Laws is not always understood and may require explaining to an inexperienced captain or player. Although not an everyday occurrence, on-field umpires must be able to handle any situation that might arise. Provided that the umpire understands the principles of the Law he can apply them to any given situation and arrive at the correct decision.

For the purpose of explaining this Law the following terms are used:

Injured player: the person who, for whatever reason, cannot run and requires assistance in the form of a runner. When referred to as the **injured striker** he is facing the bowling. When referred to as the **injured batsman** he is **not** facing the bowling.

Runner: the designated person who is on the field solely to run for the injured player.

Non-striker: the other batsman who is on the field running with the runner. When on strike he is referred to as the **striker.**

FUNDAMENTALS OF THE LAW

Whenever an injured player is allowed a runner to run for him he may call upon one.

All the relevant points about this statement are covered in clause 1 of this Law. Suffice to say that provided the umpires are satisfied that the reason is valid – i.e. he has suffered an injury or has become ill after the nomination of players – then a runner will be allowed. This is a decision solely for the umpires to make - no other player or official may influence it and no member of the opposing side can object.

The Law makes it very clear that the runner must fulfil certain criteria before he is allowed to act on behalf of the injured player:

• **He must be a nominated member of the batting side**

He cannot be a spectator or a friend who is keen to help out. It is only fair that he should be taking part in the game.

• **He must, if possible, have already batted**

He must not be the next man in as he would gain an unfair advantage in being able to accustom his eyesight to the prevailing weather conditions as well as observing the bowling. This is obviously unfair on the fielding side. The only occasion when the runner cannot already have batted is when no wicket has fallen in the innings. Here, the umpires must insist that a lower order batsman act as runner.

Although not specifically mentioned within the Law, it would be within the spirit of the game to expect that, once elected, the runner would not be changed during the course of the innings of the injured player. Unless the runner himself is injured or becomes ill, or wickets fall and the time approaches when the runner will be required to bat, the umpire should not readily agree to a change of runner.

- **He must wear similar external protective equipment as the injured player for whom he is running including a helmet if applicable**

External protective equipment that must be worn includes pads, batting gloves and, if visible, forearm guards as defined in Appendix D. External protective equipment does not extend to items of clothing – if the injured player is wearing a pullover it is not necessary for his runner to wear one too. The wearing of a helmet is, of course, only possible if there is one available – if there is not one for the runner to wear then the umpires must use their discretion, accepting the situation until a helmet becomes available. Any internal protection such as a box or thigh pad is not included in this clause.

- **He must carry a bat**

Having agreed that the runner fulfils these criteria the umpires must allow the runner to take part in the game.

'CONTRACTUAL' RELATIONSHIP BETWEEN BATTING AND FIELDING SIDE
It is at this point that the batting side and fielding side enter into a 'contract'. It is not a contract in the legal sense but in a sporting one. By considering it in this light it becomes easier to follow its terms and conditions.

CONDITIONS OF THE 'CONTRACT'
1. For the fielding side's part, they 'accept' the runner on to the field to do all the injured player's running for him. In return for this concession the runner may be out by certain of the conventional methods and, by doing so, the injured player will be out.
2. For the batting side's part, their obligations in the 'contract' are much more complex. They are permitted to have this extra person on the field to run for the injured player but in return they have to undertake that:
a) the injured player will keep within the Laws applicable to any batsman
b) the injured striker only has safe ground, at all times, at the wicket-keeper's end
c) the injured striker cannot add to his score by physically running himself. He can only directly add to his score by hitting boundaries. For any other runs, he is totally reliant on his runner
d) the runner is only there to run for the injured player

e) the runner is also subject to the following Laws: Run out, Obstructing the field, Handled the ball and to any acts of unfair play.

PENALTIES FOR BREAKING ANY PART OF THE 'CONTRACT'

Since this is a 'legally' binding contract (legal in as far as these are the Laws of Cricket) there are penalties for any breaches by either party to it.

3. For the fielding side the penalties are the same as when dealing with any batsman. That is, any penalty suffered by the fielding side under normal circumstances still apply.

4. For the batting side the penalties are more severe since they have more to gain from the 'contract'.

PENALTIES – THE INJURED PLAYER

a) if while the ball is in play the injured striker is out of his ground, for any reason at all, and the wicket at the wicket-keeper's end is fairly put down, then on appeal he is dismissed. It does not matter where the runner or non-striker are when this happens as the fact that the injured striker is out of his ground overrides the position of the other two.

b) if the injured striker is dismissed in this fashion no runs are scored, even though the runner and non-striker may have legally completed runs. (The statement that no runs shall be scored refers to runs made by the runner and non-striker from running. It does not include any penalty runs given away by the bowling side such as the penalty run for bowling a No ball or a Wide or the 5 penalty runs given away through unfair acts.) Since the runs have been disallowed the non-striker must be returned to his original position and the incoming batsman must be directed to replace the batsman who was at the wicket-keeper's end.

c) when the injured batsman is not facing the bowling he is temporarily out of the game and can be ignored. However, if he handles the ball or obstructs the field he will be considered to have brought himself back into the game and, on appeal, must be dismissed. He is also liable to any penalty demanded by the Laws should he commit any act of unfair play e.g. if he showed dissent over an umpire's decision he would be reported as detailed under Law 42.18. Although not dismissed for such an act, he would still suffer the consequences of having committed it.

PENALTIES – THE RUNNER

The runner is on the field to run for the injured player and if he is out
• Run out or
• Handled the ball or
• Obstructing the field
the injured player is also out. The method of dismissal will be recorded against the injured player as though he had himself been responsible for the infringement.

POSITIONING

Having established the 'contractual' requirements of each side it is important that the participants stand where directed by the umpire on the field of play. Everyone needs to be aware of their respective positions to ensure that there is no confusion. It is difficult enough for the umpires to watch everything that can occur when a runner is on the field and the situation is not helped if the umpires do not have the right people in the right place at the right time.

STRIKER'S END UMPIRE

When there is a runner on the field, the runner will normally be directed to stand at square leg and run on that side of the pitch. The umpire will therefore move over to the **off side**. This is so that he has everyone – runner, injured striker and non-striker – within his field of vision. If he has the runner next to him at square leg, he would not only potentially obstruct the runner when running but also, more importantly, run the risk of having the runner running behind him.

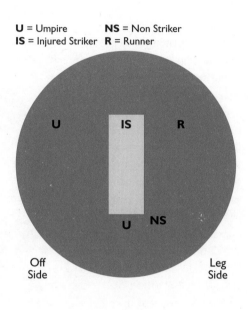

BOWLER'S END UMPIRE

Under circumstances where there is not an injured player, the bowler's end umpire normally moves to the side best suited to the shot played by the batsman. When there is a runner acting for an injured striker the umpire must restrain this normal instinct and move to the side opposite that of the runner and non-striker. This will probably be the off side since the runner and non-striker will be running on the leg side. If the umpire follows

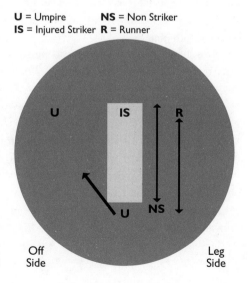

the ball to the wrong side, then he will have the runner running behind him and will be unable to adjudicate on run out appeals.

Where the non-striker and runner are on different sides of the wicket (e.g. a left arm over the wicket bowler would have the non-striker on the opposite side of the wicket to that of the runner) the umpire must ensure that his final position is well to the off side. To achieve this he will have to move very quickly to get past the non-striker's position in order to have both batsmen running in front of him.

INJURED BATSMAN

When not facing the bowling the injured batsman must stand where directed by the umpires, in a position where he is unlikely to affect any action on the field. In theory, the best place would be off the field altogether; in practice, it is best to have the injured batsman standing alongside the striker's end umpire, thus forming one 'obstacle'. If the injured batsman is positioned on the opposite side of the field to the umpire the fielding side would have two obstacles to deal with.

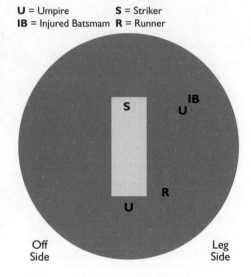

U = Umpire   **S** = Striker
IB = Injured Batsmam   **R** = Runner

The positioning of the umpire (and injured batsman) will usually be at square leg, in his normal position. Should the umpire wish to move to the off side then he must remember to take the injured batsman with him.

While standing in this position the injured batsman is out of the game and provided that he does not handle the ball or obstruct the field the only way he can be dismissed is if his runner runs him out.

RUNNER

When the injured striker is facing the bowling the runner is stationed where directed and this would usually be at square leg, on the opposite side of the pitch to the umpire. It has already been established, above, that the striker's end umpire would be at point for this delivery, with injured striker, runner and non-striker all in his view. When the injured batsman is not facing the bowling the runner occupies the normal non-striker's position.

GENERAL COMMENTS ABOUT POSITIONING OF UMPIRES AND BATSMEN

The ideal positions given above do not always present themselves on the field and umpires must be flexible in their handling of the various scenarios they may face. Law 3 details instances where the striker's end umpire may wish to move to the off side but, in reality, it does not matter which side of the pitch the umpire stands provided that he applies the following:

- when the injured striker is facing the bowling, the runner will always be on the opposite side of the pitch to the striker's end umpire

- when not facing the bowling the injured batsman will always stand next to the striker's end umpire.

The umpire will then always be in control of the situation and able to ensure that the players are in the correct positions.

EXAMPLES

For the sake of clarity it is assumed that the umpires are in the positions already described and are, therefore, not shown on the diagrams.

R = Runner   **WK** = Wicket-keeper
IS = Injured Striker   **NS** = Non Striker

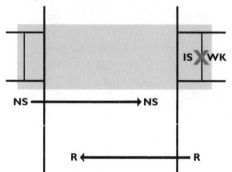

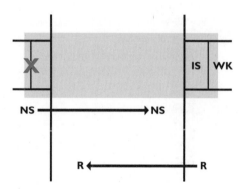

EXAMPLE 14

- *Injured striker hits ball to off side and stays behind popping crease*
- *Runner runs*
- *Non-striker runs*
- *Wicket broken at the wicket-keeper's end (**X**) appeal*

Non-striker is Run out because he has not made good his ground.

Incoming batsman goes to the wicket-keeper's end.

EXAMPLE 15

- *Injured striker hits ball to off side and stays behind popping crease*
- *Runner runs*
- *Non-striker runs*
- *Wicket broken at the bowler's end (**X**) appeal*

Injured striker is out Run out because runner has failed to make good his ground.

Incoming batsman goes to the bowler's end.

R = Runner   **WK** = Wicket-keeper
IS = Injured Striker   **NS** = Non Striker

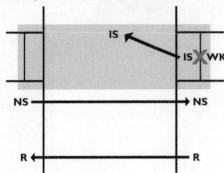

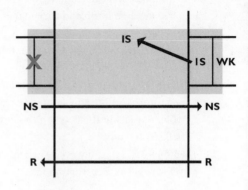

EXAMPLE 16

- *Injured striker hits ball to off side and, forgetting himself, sets off for a run*
- *Runner runs*
- *Non-striker also runs*
- *Wicket broken at the wicket-keeper's end (**X**) appeal*

Injured striker is out Run out because he has left his ground at wicket-keeper's end.

Positions of non-striker and runner are immaterial.

Non-striker is returned to his original end.

No runs are scored except No ball, Wide or penalty runs.

Incoming batsman goes to the wicket-keeper's end.

EXAMPLE 17

- *Injured striker hits ball to off side and, forgetting himself, sets off for a run*
- *Runner runs*
- *Non-striker also runs*
- *Wicket broken at the bowler's end (**X**) appeal*

No one is out – runner has made good his ground at bowler's end.

Position of injured striker is ignored – he is not supposed to run.

R = Runner   **WK** = Wicket-keeper
IS = Injured Striker **NS** = Non Striker

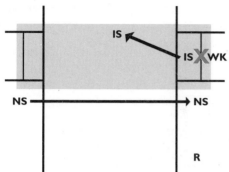

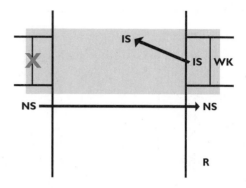

EXAMPLE 18

- *Ball is hit to the leg side*
- *Injured striker runs*
- *Runner stays in his ground*
- *Non-striker runs*
- *Wicket broken at the wicket-keeper's end (**X**) appeal*

Injured striker is out Run out because he has left his ground at wicket-keeper's end.

Positions of non-striker and runner are ignored.

Non-striker is returned to his original end.

No runs are scored except No ball, Wide or penalty runs.

Incoming batsman goes to the wicket-keeper's end.

EXAMPLE 19

- *Ball is hit to the leg side*
- *Injured striker runs*
- *Runner stays in his ground*
- *Non-striker runs*
- *Wicket broken at the bowler's end (**X**) appeal*

Non-striker is out Run out.

Since the runner has not left his ground the non-striker's ground is at the bowler's end. The injured striker is ignored as the wicket was not broken at the wicket-keeper's end.

Incoming batsman goes to the bowler's end.

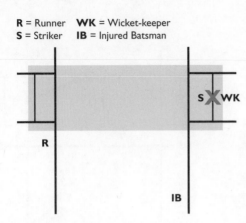

R = Runner   **WK** = Wicket-keeper
S = Striker   **IB** = Injured Batsman

EXAMPLE 20

- *Striker misses the ball and stays in ground*
- *Injured batsman is standing in front of popping crease*
- *Wicket broken at the wicket-keeper's end (**X**) appeal*

No one is out. The injured batsman is not the striker and so the fact that he is in front of the popping crease is ignored. The striker is in his ground and is therefore Not out.

To summarise:

When the injured striker is facing the bowling and runs are attempted:

- if the injured striker stays in his ground **ignore** him. It is the positions of the runner and non-striker that determine if there is a run out
- if the injured striker is out of his ground and the wicket at the bowler's end is broken **ignore** him. It is the positions of the runner and non-striker that determine if there is a run out
- if the injured striker is out of his ground and the wicket at the wicket-keeper's end is broken **he is out**. Ignore the positions of the runner and non-striker.

9. BATSMAN LEAVING THE FIELD OR RETIRING

A batsman may retire at any time during his innings. The umpires, before allowing play to proceed, shall be informed of the reason for a batsman retiring.

(a) If a batsman retires because of illness, injury or any other unavoidable cause, he is entitled to resume his innings subject to (c) below. If for any reason he does not do so, his innings is to be recorded as 'Retired – not out'.

(b) If a batsman retires for any reason other than as in (a) above, he may only resume his innings with the consent of the opposing captain. If for any reason he does not resume his innings it is to be recorded as 'Retired – out'.

(c) If after retiring a batsman resumes his innings, it shall be only at the fall of a wicket or the retirement of another batsman.

10. COMMENCEMENT OF A BATSMAN'S INNINGS

Except at the start of a side's innings, a batsman shall be considered to have commenced his innings when he first steps on to the field of play, provided Time has not been called. The innings of the opening batsmen,

and that of any new batsman at the resumption of play after a call of Time, shall commence at the call of Play.

This section of the Law focuses on the batsman and deals with the situations that occur when he has to leave the field. It is logical to reverse the sequence of these two clauses by considering first the start of a batsman's innings then what happens if he retires or leaves the field.

COMMENCEMENT OF INNINGS

At the start of a side's innings the opening batsmen's individual innings commence on the call of Play. If the players have cause to leave the field before Play has been called then it is permissible for either or both batsmen to be changed upon the resumption. As Play has not been called, the innings has not started.

If a new batsman commences his innings immediately after an interval or interruption his innings starts on the call of Play. If Play has not been called and the players have cause to leave the field this batsman may be changed upon the restart. Since Play has not been called the interval or interruption has not concluded.

If a new batsman commences his innings during a session of play his innings commences as soon as he steps over the boundary on to the field of play – not when he reaches the wicket, nor when he has taken guard, nor when he has received his first ball. If the players have cause to leave the field after this batsman has crossed the boundary he cannot be changed on the restart as his innings has commenced.

RETIREMENT OF A BATSMAN

The following applies to any batsman who has commenced his innings. The circumstances of when this occurs are immaterial, since these points apply to all batsmen.

RETIREMENT OF A BATSMAN – GENERAL POINTS

A batsman may retire at any time during his innings and if he does so he must inform the bowler's end umpire of the reason. This is particularly relevant should he later wish to return to resume his innings. The umpire should inform his colleague and both must note the batsman's name and reason for retiring. While not strictly relevant it is advisable for umpires to note the time and/or the over at which it occurs.

The scorers must note the retirement in the scoring record for the purposes of calculating partnerships. The details of the entries required are contained in the Scoring section of this book.

RETIREMENT OF A BATSMAN THROUGH INJURY, ILLNESS
OR ANY OTHER UNAVOIDABLE CAUSE

A batsman may retire and leave the field of play due to illness, injury or any other unavoidable cause. Although a substitute cannot be used to take his place as a batsman, the batsman is allowed to continue his innings, by right, if he recovers and wishes to do so. However, he is not permitted to interrupt the innings of another batsman just because he has recovered. He must wait until either a wicket falls or another batsman retires. If a batsman wishes to resume his innings under these circumstances, the fielding captain has no right of objection.

If he is unable, or is not required, to resume his innings, he is recorded in the scoring record as Retired – not out. The innings is deemed Not out when his averages are calculated.

RETIREMENT OF A BATSMAN DUE TO ANY OTHER REASON
A batsman is permitted to leave the field for any other reason but, under these circumstances, may only resume his innings with the consent of the opposing captain. The fielding captain is under no obligation whatsoever to give this consent – he may withhold it if he so wishes. The umpires have no right to influence his decision one way or the other. If consent is given the batsman may resume his innings at the fall of a wicket or retirement of another batsman.

If consent is not given, or the batsman does not seek to return, he is recorded as Retired – out. The innings is then deemed completed when his averages are calculated.

Scorers must record the time each batsman starts his innings and the time of his dismissal. Should he retire, the time of retirement and, should he return, the time he resumes his innings should also be recorded. Only in this way is it possible to record the duration of his innings.

Law 3 The umpires

1. APPOINTMENT AND ATTENDANCE
Before the match, two umpires shall be appointed, one for each end, to control the game as required by the Laws, with absolute impartiality. The umpires shall be present on the ground and report to the Executive of the ground at least 45 minutes before the scheduled start of each day's play.

DUTIES PRIOR TO THE MATCH
This is the most important time for umpires because it enables them to resolve any potential problems before the game starts. Having discussed and agreed all relevant matters with both captains and the scorers; familiarising themselves with their surroundings – the playing area and beyond; and developing the rapport with each other, they become better able to deal with all the eventualities and situations that could develop during the game.

This time should be used to clarify all extraneous issues and any subsequent problems can be dealt with expediently and efficiently without undue stress.

These pre-match duties are explained below and it will be seen how a little preparatory work before the game can save a lot of headaches later. It is also during this time that the players, especially the two captains, will form their initial impression of the umpires and of their mental strength. A firm and decisive manner demonstrates to them that here is someone who knows what he is doing and is not going to be pressurised into any rash or incorrect decisions. In short, it gives them confidence in the umpires. On the other hand if the umpire appears timid, shy and lacking self confidence this will be immediately apparent and players may attempt to exploit that during the game.

It must be stressed, however, that it is not necessary to be overbearing and officious to achieve this goal – simple firmness and an assured presence is sufficient. A sound knowledge of the Laws and match regulations, along with ample preparation, gives umpires the confidence necessary to do their job well, and gain the confidence of the players.

ARRIVAL

The Law states that the umpires should arrive at the ground at least 45 minutes prior to the start of the game. This should be considered an absolute minimum, rather than a maximum, time allowance because there are a number of duties the umpires must complete during this pre-match period. If rushed, important matters can often be overlooked and these can lead to mistakes later in the day.

If an umpire is unfamiliar with the ground he should arrive at least an hour before the match in order to acclimatise himself to his unfamiliar surroundings. If the umpire is familiar with the ground – it may be his home ground – then he must always bear in mind that his colleague for the day may not be so familiar with it. A good host will always be on hand, ready to offer any assistance and guidance that is necessary to complete all pre-match duties.

By arriving early the umpires may also be able to clarify any unexpected problems that the groundstaff have in preparing the pitch and playing area.

MEETING BETWEEN THE TWO UMPIRES

It is beneficial for the two umpires to get to know each other before the match. Since they will be working together for some time it is vital that, before the match starts, they talk to each other and develop the rapport necessary to gain confidence in the other. Early team building with each other and with the scorers is essential.

MEET THE GROUNDSMAN

During the match he can be of great assistance to umpires. His knowledge of his ground's playing and drying properties, and his cooperation, can be invaluable.

Although the umpires are in charge of the playing area after the toss has been made, they would be foolish to totally ignore the groundsman's role both before and during the game. There is a history of co-operation between umpires and groundsmen that must be kept alive.

TOUR OF THE GROUND

The early tour of the ground is the most vital walk the umpires will undertake each day. While walking the umpires have a quiet time together, not only to get to know each other, but also to learn of any peculiarities of the match venue. Things to look for are:

- **boundary** – how is it marked? The boundary may be marked in different ways around the ground – by means of rope, painted line, boundary boards, flags and imaginary straight lines, wall, fence, building, advertising boards. The umpires need to know how these markings vary at any given part of the ground.
- **sightscreens** – are they inside the playing area? It is essential that the umpires make a note of where the sightscreens are in relation to the field of play. If the sightscreens have been positioned within, or partly within, the marked playing area, the umpires must ensure that the boundary at this point is re-marked so that the screens are **outside** the playing area. The boundary must go around the front of the screen(s) and must allow for the screen(s) to be moved during the match without changing the boundary.
- **trees, bushes and shrubbery** – are any overhanging the playing area? It must be made clear to the captains that, should the ball come into contact with the over-hanging part of the tree/bush/shrubbery, a boundary will be scored. A boundary will also be scored should a fielder, who is in contact with the ball, touch any part of the overhanging vegetation. The reason for this is that in order to overhang the boundary the item concerned – be it vegetation, a wall or even electricity pylons and cables – will be in contact with the ground beyond the boundary. This means that **every** part of the object is grounded beyond the boundary.

Umpires need to know the answers to all the above so that the correct decision and allowances can be made in any given circumstance.

Moving from the boundary to the pitch, the umpires should also check:
- **pitch** – is the pitch for the match identified?
- **pitch** – is the prepared area in accordance with the Law i.e. 22 yards (20.12 m) long and 10 ft (3.05 m) wide? See Law 7, page 85, for a full explanation of why this is important.
- **crease markings** – are they correctly marked out? See Law 9, page 90.
- **wickets** – are they pitched correctly? See Law 8, page 87.

All these questions require satisfactory answers before the toss. Should it be found that any of these matters are not correct, particularly the crease markings, the umpires should endeavour to have them corrected promptly. If this is not possible, the umpires should inform both captains and seek their agreement to play the game as things stand. Such matters should never be permitted to pass unmentioned possibly to become subject of later debate. Better to discuss them when noticed during the pre-match meeting with the captains. Prevention of a problem will save the umpires having to cure it at a later stage.

- **stumps** – are they the correct size and height for the grade of cricket being played?
- **condition of the outfield** – are there any dangerous rabbit holes, goal post holes or water hydrants etc. that are not properly covered? They would be a danger to the fielding side or a source of a possible lost ball. The umpires must, if possible, get these matters rectified before the game starts.
- **obstacles within the field of play** – old rollers, seats etc. These should be cleared if possible – if they cannot be moved then the umpires must agree what happens if the ball comes into contact with them – first, between themselves and then inform both captains and the scorers of their decision.
- **provision of covers and sawdust** – although not always needed when the game starts they may be needed later and so their accessibility should be noted before the game begins.
- **official timepiece** –this is usually the pavilion clock if there is one. Umpires should synchronise their watches with it and also nominate a back-up timepiece, in case it breaks down – this will usually be the watch of one of the umpires. In such an event the back-up timepiece becomes the official one. The scorers must be informed of both timepieces and they will usually synchronise their timepiece with the official one.

It should not be necessary to remind umpires or players that umpires are appointed to control the match in a neutral and impartial manner. It may be that a club appoints an umpire but from the moment he arrives at the ground he is required to be absolutely neutral. Umpires are appointed one for each end, **not** – as some players may wish to believe – one for each side. An umpire must adjudicate on matters within his jurisdiction. He is also required to offer support to his colleague whenever requested or required.

2. CHANGE OF UMPIRE

An umpire shall not be changed during the match, other than in exceptional circumstances, unless he is injured or ill. If there has to be a change of umpire, the replacement shall act only as the striker's end umpire unless the captains agree that he should take full responsibility as an umpire.

Umpires are appointed for the duration of a match and should not normally be changed. However there may be circumstances that could cause an umpire to be replaced – illness, injury or some other exceptional circumstance. Should this occur, the remaining umpire must approach both captains advising them of the situation and the requirements of this clause. If an umpire is changed the replacement may only officiate at the striker's end, unless both captains agree otherwise. If such an agreement is made the replacement umpire will replace the absent one and will undertake a normal umpiring role.

Neither captain is permitted to instigate a change of umpire.

3. AGREEMENT WITH CAPTAINS

Before the toss the umpires shall
(a) ascertain the hours of play and agree with the captains
    (i)   the balls to be used during the match. See Law 5 (The ball).
    (ii) times and durations of intervals for meals and times for drinks intervals. See Law 15 (Intervals).
    (iii) the boundary of the field of play and allowances for boundaries. See Law 19 (Boundaries).
    (iv) any special conditions of play affecting the conduct of the match.
(b) inform the scorers of the agreements in (ii), (iii) and (iv) above.

4. TO INFORM CAPTAINS AND SCORERS

Before the toss the umpires shall agree between themselves and inform both captains and both scorers
    (i)   which clock or watch and back-up time piece is to be used during the match.
    (ii) whether or not any obstacle within the field of play is to be regarded as a boundary. See Law 19 (Boundaries).

Before the match the two umpires and both captains are required to meet and agree on several matters relating to the game about to be played. Many of these points are covered by competition regulations and so it may not be necessary for umpires to dwell on them. However, inexperienced captains may seek clarifications of them and the umpires must be available to offer guidance when asked. Some matters can often be easily dealt with since they are common to all matches played within that competition. However, if it is a competition that is not played very often, or the clubs concerned have not previously played in it, or the Regulations have some unusual elements, it is appropriate for the umpires to discuss them with the captains.

These discussions are of vital importance in the run-up to the game. It not only gives the umpires a chance to meet the two people who are responsible for their team's conduct, but also gives them a chance to settle possible points of contention that they have discovered during their tour of the ground. It also grants the captains an opportunity to establish a rapport with the umpires outside the cut and thrust of the actual match.

All the items listed below must be covered in one way or another – either by regulations or through verbal discussion and agreement.

In agreement with the captains the umpires must resolve the following:

- **format of the match** – is the match limited by time or overs? If limited by overs, how many per side?
- **hours of play** – fairly obvious, but it is surprising how often in a friendly game the two captains never consider this. It is often left to the umpires to get them to make a decision.
- **meal intervals** - these need to be confirmed. What intervals are there going to be, when will they start, and how long will they last?
- **drinks interval** – are there going to be any and, if so, at what time(s)? For example, should these be at particular times or when a specified number of overs have been bowled? It is often necessary to remind captains that the scorers also require refreshments; this is particularly relevant if the scorers are stationed some distance from the pavilion.
- **provision for new balls in the match** – if it is a competition match the Regulations usually regulate the number of new balls that may be used, but in the absence of such a regulation the umpires must ensure that all parties agree to when and how any new balls may be taken.
- **boundaries** – these need to be discussed if there is a problem with differing allowances at different parts of the ground. Any matters relating to these, found by the umpires during their walking tour of the ground, must be discussed at this point.
- **local customs** – these could include anything that is not covered in the Laws but are peculiar to that ground.
- **special regulations or playing conditions** – these could be directives, usually issued in printed form by the Governing body, or any
- **competition regulations** – these must be discussed and any special issues clarified. Also, the umpires may need to explain how they are to be applied and interpreted during the game. For example, overs limitation per team and bowler; one-day wides, etc.

The umpires must inform the two captains of the following:

- **the official clock or watch used** – everyone must know which timepiece is the official one, and whose watch is the official back-up timepiece.
- **obstacles within the field of play** – the umpires, as they walk around the ground, must decide whether any obstacle within the field of play is to be regarded as a boundary. They will inform the captains of their decision and, if it is to be a boundary, agree with them the allowance or allowances to be made.

Although not specifically covered in this Law, the umpires should also check the following matters that are contained in other Laws:

- **pitch to be used** – this may be obvious, however there have been occasions where two adjoining pitches have been prepared and marked out at the match venue. The umpires must ensure that the pitch for their game is clearly identified before the toss takes place since captains and umpires need to know which one to check.

- **provision and use of covers** – any relevant agreement regarding the use of covers must be made before the toss.
- **nomination of players** – teams must be nominated prior to the toss, and a written list of names given to one of the umpires. It assists the scorers if they are afforded the opportunity to copy this or to be given their own copy.
- **result of the toss** – which captain won and did he decide to bat or to field?
- **any other relevant points** raised by the umpires or captains.

UMPIRES TO INFORM SCORERS

It is important to remember that the scorers are part of the **team of officials** and as such must be included in the arrangements for the match. Having discussed and agreed all the above, the umpires must meet with the scorers and inform them of all points of agreement.

- **format of the match**
- **hours of play**
- **start time**
- **boundaries**
- **the official clock or watch used** – ensure that the scorers know which timepiece is the official one, and whose watch is the official back-up. They should adjust theirs as required.
- **meal intervals** – scorers need to know when the sessions are scheduled to finish and how long each is to last. A scorer has to perform various balancing checks of the scoring record at all intervals and they need to know how long they have in order to achieve this. Umpires should bear the scorers' needs in mind at all times.
- **drinks interval** – umpires should always ask the captains (or match manager) to provide the scorers with drinks at the drinks break. Because of their specialised duties, they may need to use this time to complete the balancing processes. Events during a match can cause the hours of play and the timing of intervals to be varied and on occasions eliminated altogether. The umpires are required to inform the scorers of all such changes.
- **obstacles within the field of play** – the umpires, having decided on these, must ensure the scorers are informed.
- **special regulations** – particularly if these effect the scorers.
- **competition regulations** – the scorers must be informed of all relevant matters e.g. overs limitation per team and bowler etc.
- **nomination of players** – although not the umpires' direct responsibility they should ensure the scorers have a copy of each team list.
- **result of the toss** – the scorers record this in the scoring record.

There are several other matters that need to be decided between the umpires and scorers. These include:

- **display of the score** – umpires need to discuss how often the scoreboard is going to be updated. This is best done by someone other than the two scorers since their responsibility is to ensure that the scoring record is correct. However, in practice the scorers will often undertake this task so how and when this is done needs to be discussed. If runs cannot be shown as they are scored then an arrangement can be made that the scoreboard will be updated at the end of each over. Towards the end of the match it may be desirable that the scoreboard be updated after every run in order that the players and umpires are kept fully aware of the situation.

- **display of the overs** – the same applies here as it does for the score. Umpires should agree upon a sensible timing for updating the overs bowled throughout the game – the same criteria apply to this as to the displaying of the score. The display of the overs **during the last hour**, however, must be updated after each over has been bowled. Umpires should request that the overs be displayed as they are completed, that is work up from 1 to 20, not down from 20 to 1. This method is the more appropriate of the two if more than 20 overs are bowled in the last hour.

- **acknowledgement of all signals** – scorers must clearly and promptly acknowledge all signals made by the umpires and the umpires must not permit play to resume until each separate signal has been acknowledged. While it should be easy for scores to see the umpires 'in the middle' wearing white coats, the reverse is not always possible with the scorers situated inside a dark score-box. A suitable item, for this acknowledgement, is a white or brightly coloured card, or table tennis bat painted a fluorescent colour. A light that is switched on every time a signal is acknowledged is excellent, but does have its drawbacks. Should the bulb or power supply fail unnecessary delays and confusion can result. Umpires and scorers should not require reminding that, often, a series of signals may be made, all requiring separate acknowledgement. For example, No ball followed by the boundary 4 signal.

- **acknowledgement of signals for No ball, Wide and Dead ball** – when calling and signalling these the umpire's **first** call and signal is only for the benefit of the on-field participants. The scorers are **not** to acknowledge these signals but must wait until the signals are repeated. The umpires will not see any acknowledgement of the first signal because they will be concentrating on the action taking place on the field. The scorers must wait until the ball becomes dead before they can expect a repeat of the signal, which will be directed, specifically, at them.

- **location of scorers** – umpires need to know where the scorers are situated at all times and must not assume that they always sit in the scorebox. They may decide to sit outside in the sun and move around the boundary following the warmth. This practice is not recommended, but if followed, the umpires must be informed.

The two scorers must always sit together during the match and not separately as this practice makes signalling and acknowledging a potential nightmare. Also, the difficulty of communication between the two scorers comes into play as they attempt to perform the various checks and balances during the match.

• **any other relevant points** that will help them undertake their respective duties.

The principal purpose behind all these discussions with captains and scorers is to clarify all eventualities **before** play starts thus ensuring an incident-free match.

5. THE WICKETS, CREASES AND BOUNDARIES

Before the toss and during the match, the umpires shall satisfy themselves that

(i)   the wickets are properly pitched. See Law 8 (The wickets).

(ii) the creases are correctly marked. See Law 9 (The bowling, popping and return creases).

(iii) the boundary of the field of play complies with the requirements of Law 19.2 (Defining the boundary – boundary marking).

The checking of the crease markings and the wickets is usually attended to during the umpires' walking tour of the ground prior to the toss, any problems being sorted out before the toss. The importance of umpires arriving at the venue to give them ample time to check these matters cannot be overstated.

If it is found that the wickets are incorrectly pitched, the umpires should try to get the problem rectified. However, if the error is of a minor nature it may well be prudent to leave things as they are.

On occasions it may be found that there are errors in the crease markings and if this can be remedied then it should be done. If not, the captains must be informed. If they agree, it is in order to continue with the markings as painted.

If it is found that the boundary markings are inadequate, all attempts must be made to remedy the situation before the match starts. If this is not possible both captains must be advised of the matter and of the solutions.

6. CONDUCT OF THE GAME, IMPLEMENTS AND EQUIPMENT

Before the toss and during the match, the umpires shall satisfy themselves that

(a) the conduct of the game is strictly in accordance with the Laws.

(b) the implements of the game conform to the requirements of Laws 5 (The ball) and 6 (The bat), together with either Laws 8.2 (Size of stumps) and 8.3 (The bails) or, if appropriate, Law 8.4 (Junior cricket).

(c) (i) no player uses equipment other than that permitted. See Appendix D.

(ii) the wicket-keeper's gloves comply with the requirements of Law 40.2 (Gloves).

This clause details the umpires' obligations to ensure that all implements used in a match – from balls, bats, stumps and bails to the wicket-keeper's gloves – comply with the Laws. Some of these duties must be undertaken prior to the toss, however some events may require action during the progress of the match. No player may use any equipment that does not conform to the Laws.

7. FAIR AND UNFAIR PLAY

The umpires shall be the sole judges of fair and unfair play.

Note the plural: *both umpires* are the *sole judges of fair and unfair play*. To emphasise the importance of this clause, this statement is contained in the Preamble and repeated in Law 42.2.

In cases of unfair play the umpires are empowered to act independently of each other and it is not necessary for them to consult. However, consultation is always encouraged in borderline cases or where an umpire senses that trouble is brewing. Consultation, in such cases, often results in both umpires becoming aware of imminent problems and, because of this, they may be able to act early in order to stop them escalating into serious, uncontrollable ones.

8. FITNESS OF GROUND, WEATHER AND LIGHT

The umpires shall be the final judges of the fitness of the ground, weather and light for play. See 9 below and Law 7.2 (Fitness of the pitch for play).

The match situation may cause some players to attempt to pressurise umpires to make a decision that may not be fair to their opponents. This Law is clear. The umpires, not just one, but both acting together, are the final judges. Any decisions that the umpires make regarding ground, weather and light must be made together – one umpire cannot take it upon himself to make the judgement, he must involve his colleague.

9. SUSPENSION OF PLAY FOR ADVERSE CONDITIONS OF GROUND, WEATHER OR LIGHT

(a) (i) All references to ground include the pitch. See Law 7.1 (Area of pitch).
(ii) For the purpose of this Law and Law 15.9(b)(ii) (Intervals for drinks) only, the batsmen at the wicket may deputise for their captain at any appropriate time.
(b) If at any time the umpires together agree that the condition of the ground, weather or light is not suitable for play, they shall inform the captains and, unless
(i) in unsuitable ground or weather conditions both captains agree to continue, or to commence, or to restart play,

or (ii) in unsuitable light the batting side wishes to continue, or to commence, or to restart play,

they shall suspend play, or not allow play to commence or to restart.

(c) (i) After agreeing to play in unsuitable ground or weather conditions, either captain may appeal against the conditions to the umpires before the next call of Time. The umpires shall uphold the appeal only if, in their opinion, the factors taken into account when making their previous decision are the same or the conditions have further deteriorated.

(ii) After deciding to play in unsuitable light, the captain of the batting side may appeal against the light to the umpires before the next call of Time. The umpires shall uphold the appeal only if, in their opinion, the factors taken into account when making their previous decision are the same or the condition of the light has further deteriorated.

(d) If at any time the umpires together agree that the conditions of ground, weather or light are so bad that there is obvious and foreseeable risk to the safety of any player or umpire, so that it would be unreasonable or dangerous for play to take place, then notwithstanding the provisions of (b)(i) and (b)(ii) above, they shall immediately suspend play, or not allow play to commence or to restart. The decision as to whether conditions are so bad as to warrant such action is one for the umpires alone to make.

The fact that the grass and the ball are wet and slippery does not warrant the ground conditions being regarded as unreasonable or dangerous. If the umpires consider the ground is so wet or slippery as to deprive the bowler of a reasonable foothold, the fielders of the power of free movement, or the batsmen of the ability to play their strokes or to run between the wickets, then these conditions shall be regarded as so bad that it would be unreasonable for play to take place.

(e) When there is a suspension of play it is the responsibility of the umpires to monitor the conditions. They shall make inspections as often as appropriate, unaccompanied by any of the players or officials. Immediately the umpires together agree that conditions are suitable for play they shall call upon the players to resume the game.

(f) If play is in progress up to the start of an agreed interval then it will resume after the interval unless the umpires together agree that conditions are or have become unsuitable or dangerous. If they do so agree, then they shall implement the procedure in (b) or (d) above, as appropriate, whether or not there had been any decision by the captains to continue, or any appeal against the conditions by either captain, prior to the commencement of the interval.

The decision to suspend or to continue play is, on occasions, the cause of much controversy. It will often depend on the state of the game as to whether the players of both or just one side wish to come off the field. The umpires must remain totally neutral in the matter – the state of the game is of no consequence to them. Their decision as to whether play should continue or be suspended should be based purely on grounds of safety and, to a large extent, common sense.

When dealing with the question of adverse conditions of the ground (including the pitch), weather or light it is essential that the umpires understand the three distinct levels of fitness that the Law refers to.

SUITABLE (LEVEL 1)

This means that, in the umpires' opinion, conditions are perfectly acceptable and play **has** to take place.

UNSUITABLE (LEVEL 2)

This means that the umpires consider that conditions are not ideal for play but are not actually dangerous. The umpires are of the opinion that play should be suspended, or not restarted, but they will accede to any agreement that the captain(s) may come to with regards to play continuing, starting or restarting.

UNREASONABLE OR DANGEROUS (LEVEL 3)

This means that the umpires consider that the conditions are such that any reasonable person could foresee the likelihood of injury to those on the field of play. The umpires will, **in no circumstances**, allow play to take place.

Using these three levels of fitness the procedures appertaining to the various scenarios surrounding ground, weather and light can be explained.

GROUND CONDITIONS AND WEATHER CONDITIONS

GROUND CONDITIONS – GENERAL

- Play must not be suspended solely because the ball and grass have become wet and slippery.
- All decisions made by the umpires regarding whether play is possible or not are based on the premise that the players wear footwear and clothing suitable for the prevailing conditions. Whether the players are, in fact, wearing the correct attire is immaterial to any decision. Play should not be suspended, or a restart delayed, solely because the players lack suitable clothing or footwear.

GROUND CONDITIONS – FIELDING SIDE

- Umpires must ensure that the bowlers' run-ups, footholds and run-offs are safe. The prerequisite for safety is the ability of a bowler to deliver the ball without the risk of serious injury.

- The ground conditions must not be so wet and slippery as to deprive fielders of free movement when fielding, or attempting to field, the ball.
- There should be no puddles or water hazards anywhere on the playing area.

GROUND CONDITIONS – BATTING SIDE
- There must be secure footholds around the popping crease so that the batsmen can receive a delivery and play their shots without fear of slipping.
- The ground must be firm enough so that the batsmen can set off for a run without slipping.
- Batsmen must have freedom to run safely between the wickets and to turn for subsequent runs.

WEATHER CONDITIONS
Examples of adverse weather conditions could be rain or drizzle, either continuous or intermittent, snow or gale force winds.

Procedures the umpires must adopt when dealing with adverse ground and weather conditions
As conditions deteriorate the umpires must consult with each other.
As long as one or both consider the conditions to be **suitable** play will continue.
Only when both umpires consider that the conditions are **unsuitable** must they take the following action:
- tell the batsmen (who are acting for their team's captain while they are at the wicket) and fielding captain that the conditions are **unsuitable**
- if **both** wish to continue, play continues
- if **one of them** agrees with the umpires, play is suspended.
Consider it a matter of a simple vote: the fielding captain has one vote, the batsmen at the wicket have one vote, the umpires have one vote. The majority rules.
Having agreed to play in **unsuitable** conditions, **either** (fielding captain or batsmen at the wicket) may later appeal prior to the next call of Time. Umpires will uphold that appeal provided that the conditions and/or the factors previously considered are the same or have deteriorated since the original decision. If the conditions/factors have become **suitable** (i.e. level 1 has been reached), the appeal will not be upheld and play will continue.

LIGHT CONDITIONS

Light conditions may be any conditions that adversely affect the batsmen's ability to play the ball. Normally these procedures would be implemented because of poor light, however there have been cases when sunlight reflecting off buildings has caused problems for the batsmen.

PROCEDURES THE UMPIRES MUST ADOPT WHEN DEALING WITH
ADVERSE LIGHT CONDITIONS

As conditions deteriorate the umpires must consult with each other.

As long as one or both consider the light to be **suitable** play will continue.

Only when both umpires consider that the light is **unsuitable** must they take the following action:

- tell the batsmen that the light is **unsuitable**
- if the batsmen wish to continue, play continues
- if the batsmen agree with the umpires, play is suspended
- the fielding captain has no influence or input in this matter.

Although it is often acknowledged that poor light is as difficult for the fielding side as it is for the batting side the Law grants the fielding captain no voice in the decision-making process. The Law only permits the batting side the option of deciding whether or not to continue.

Having agreed to play in **unsuitable** light conditions any batsman may later appeal prior to the next call of Time. Umpires will uphold that appeal provided the light conditions and/or the factors previously considered are the same or have deteriorated since the original decision. If the conditions/factors have become **suitable** (i.e. level 1 has been reached), the appeal will not be upheld and play will continue.

Factors to be considered would include the comparison between the types of bowling at the time of the original offer and the subsequent appeal. It may be that when the umpires made the original offer there were slow bowlers operating. However, if the fielding captain decides to bring back his fast bowlers the umpires would have to consider whether or not the conditions/factors were the same or worse due to this change in the speed of bowling.

Having said that the batsmen at the wicket can make the decision to leave the field in adverse light conditions, what happens if the batting captain disagrees with them and wishes play to continue? In this circumstance the captain's wishes would be met and the players would have to return to the field and play would continue. The batsmen at the wicket can only make decisions on behalf of the captain while they are at the wicket – once off the field it is the captain who makes the decisions. However, the umpires would only allow play to recommence if the conditions were at level 1 or 2. If, by the time the captain made his request, level 3 had been reached the umpires would deny that request.

PROCEDURE UMPIRES SHOULD ADOPT WHEN NOT ON THE FIELD OF PLAY –
GROUND, WEATHER AND LIGHT CONDITIONS

- The criteria and procedures given above remain the same. However, instead of suspending play the captains must be told that the conditions are **unsuitable** for play to commence.

- In the case of ground and weather, both captains may agree to play (as they can when on the field) in which case play will restart.
- In the case of **unsuitable** light conditions, only the batting captain may make that decision to play.

UMPIRES FINAL OVERRIDING DECISION

Notwithstanding the captains' right to play in **unsuitable** conditions, if both umpires agree that the conditions are such that there is obvious and foreseeable risk to the safety to players and/or umpires, making it **unreasonable** or **dangerous** to play, they have the authority to, and must, **suspend play immediately**, until conditions improve.

If play is not taking place this clause permits the umpires to delay the start of play until conditions improve.

UMPIRES TO MONITOR CONDITIONS

When off the field the umpires have an overriding duty to monitor the conditions constantly. They must be aware of any improvements that cause the fitness of the ground, weather or light to change between the three levels previously mentioned. They should be proactive in ensuring that the captains are kept notified of when playing conditions have improved.

Improvement in the levels of fitness must be notified to the captains when the improvement goes from:

- **unreasonable and dangerous (level 3) to unsuitable (level 2).** In these cases the umpires must instigate the procedures laid down to see whether or not the captains wish to start, or recommence, play under such conditions.
- **unreasonable and dangerous (level 3)** or **unsuitable (level 2) to suitable (level 1).** In these cases the umpires must tell both captains that play **will** restart and give them a specific time for when this will happen.

Any inspection of the ground and the subsequent decision regarding its fitness must be made without influence from any player or club/match official. Umpires must not be pressurised by anyone – their decision to play or not must be made purely on the grounds of safety. However, it is desirable for umpires to consult groundstaff and seek their co-operation wherever necessary. Groundstaff will know the drying properties of their ground and will give sound advice that will help the umpires make their decision as to when play can restart. Having received that advice, umpires are not bound to accept it, though prudent umpires will.

As soon as it is practical to do so the umpires should instigate the **removal of the covers** and any **clearing up** that is necessary. These actions will be necessary in order for them to make their decision as to whether or not conditions have reached level 2 or level 1. Once they have decided that, at least, level 2 has been reached they will instigate the procedures laid out above.

The umpires must ensure the scorers are fully aware of any suspension of play and when play will resume.

10. EXCEPTIONAL CIRCUMSTANCES

The umpires shall have the discretion to implement the procedures of 9 above for reasons other than ground, weather or light if they consider that exceptional circumstances warrant it.

The umpires may, in exceptional circumstances, suspend play in response to events taking place either inside or outside the ground. There have been instances of bomb scares, riots, fires and the like which have caused the umpires to suspend play and the umpires have the authority to do this whenever they feel that it would be prudent to do so.

The umpires must ensure the scorers are fully aware of any suspension of play and when play will resume.

11. POSITION OF UMPIRES

The umpires shall stand where they can best see any act upon which their decision may be required.

Subject to this over-riding consideration the umpire at the bowler's end shall stand where he does not interfere with either the bowler's run up or the striker's view.

The umpire at the striker's end may elect to stand on the off side instead of the on side of the pitch, provided he informs the captain of the fielding side, the striker and the other umpire of his intention to do so.

The overriding requirement is that the umpires must be in a position from where they can give a decision about the action before them. This means that they will on occasions have to move very quickly to get into such a position.

With experience, umpires quickly learn to anticipate when decisions may be required and to get into the correct position early so that, when the decision has to be made, they are in the ideal position and **stationary.**

Notwithstanding the need to move quickly into a decision-making position, the needs of players must be considered. The umpires should always endeavour to get into the required position without interfering with the fielding side's attempts to field the ball or a batsman running. These techniques are not learned overnight and take time to develop.

AT THE BOWLER'S END

AT THE WICKET
As the bowler is running in to deliver the ball, the umpire must stand in a position that he finds comfortable to judge that delivery. As the bowler starts his run-up or

bowling action, the umpire should turn to face the striker. As he hears the bowler approaching, the umpire should fill his lungs, ready if necessary to call No ball for a foot fault – impossible to do if the lungs are empty.

The umpire must be able to see the placement of the bowler's feet in the delivery stride. If standing too far back, it is difficult to see the front foot; too far forward, it is difficult to see the back foot. He must also be able to pick up the flight of the ball without moving his head – impossible if standing too close. The umpire must position himself where he can do all these things without moving either his body or head. Crouching as the ball is delivered should be avoided – it is tiring and when picking up the flight of the ball, the head is likely to be moving.

In the following two examples the umpire is watching:

a the bowler's back foot – the eyes are lowered to watch where the back foot lands and as soon as possible the eyes should move to watch

b the bowler's front foot – the eyes moving just a little to facilitate this, with the lungs full of air, should it be necessary to call No ball

then, without dwelling too long on the front foot, the eyes should be raised in order

c to pick up the flight of the ball as it travels towards the striker.

In the **first picture** the umpire is too far back and would have difficulty in seeing both feet in the delivery stride, especially the front foot.

In the **second picture** the umpire is too close to the stumps and would have to keep moving his head in order to see both feet clearly, reducing his ability to pick up the flight of the ball. During the extra time it takes him to locate and focus on the ball it would have travelled further down the pitch and vital information regarding its flight will have been missed. Constant moving of the head during a day's play can also be very tiring, adding unnecessarily to the stress of the day.

Between these two extremes there is an optimum position for each umpire, governed partly by his stature, that allows him to see the feet and then pick up the flight of the ball, without movement of the head. Once satisfied with that position, many umpires mark it on the ground.

There are occasions when a bowler will ask the umpire to move either closer to or further from the stumps. If this request does not prevent the umpire fulfilling his duties, that request should be granted. However, if asked to stand too far back the umpire should explain to the bowler that by doing so he may be unable to detect bat/pad catches or fine snicks to the wicket-keeper; assess L.B.W. appeals confidently; or have time to move into a square-on position to judge run outs – all resulting in decisions in favour of the batsman. This will usually result in an amicable compromise.

On occasions a slow bowler, having delivered the ball, will stop in front of the umpire making it impossible to see what the ball does as it travels towards the striker and what happens once it reaches him. The umpire's best course of action is to explain to the bowler that if he cannot see the action he cannot give the batsman out.

WHEN THE BATSMEN ARE ATTEMPTING RUNS

In most cases. when the batsmen are attempting runs the umpire should run to the same side as the ball so that when the ball is thrown back in to his end he is more likely to have an unimpeded view of his wicket and any attempt to break it. If the umpire goes to the opposite side it is likely that a fielder will be blocking his view at the vital moment when the wicket is broken.

The illustration here shows where the umpire should run to when the ball is hit into the green area of the playing field. When this occurs, the umpire should **follow the ball** i.e. if the ball is hit to the off side he will go to the off side, if it is hit to the leg side he will follow it to that side. In this illustration the umpire has followed the ball and should be in a good position to see that the wicket is fairly broken when the ball is returned.

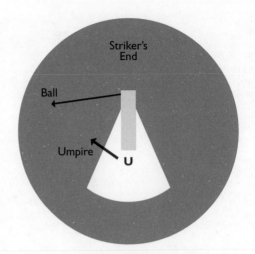

Problems arise when the ball is hit into the white area i.e. an area between mid on and mid off. If the umpire follows the ball, he is liable either to get in the way of a fielder running in to field the ball (which could cause serious injury to either parties or, at best, interference with the fielder trying to field the ball) or to be hit by the return throw. The umpire is therefore advised **not to follow the ball** but to go to the opposite side. By doing this he will be well out of the path of both fielder and ball.

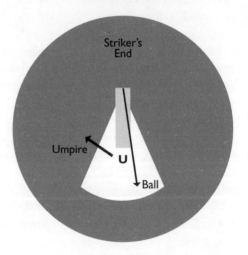

Worries about not being in a position to judge the legality of the wicket being broken can be allayed because in the majority of cases when the ball is fielded in this area any attempt to hit the wicket is more likely to be direct, since no fielder will have had the time to reach the stumps. Thus the umpire's view remains unobstructed.

In this illustration the umpire will neither impede the fielder nor be hit by the ball when it is returned to the wicket.

As the umpire moves to judge a run out, ideally he should move quickly to his position in line with the popping crease **without losing sight of the ball**. This may require him to run sideways or even backwards. While moving into position, he must also make regular glances to check the position of each batsman in order to be able to

confirm the completion of each run at his end. His prime objective is to be level with the popping crease and **stationary** when the ball is returned to his wicket and to gain a clear and unobstructed view of that occurrence.

A hard straight drive along the pitch may not give sufficient time for such movement. If necessary the umpire may have to remain close to his original position but he must always be stationary as the ball is coming towards him. This does not negate the requirement that the umpire must watch the ball, perhaps being deflected, in that split second, on to the non-striker's stumps by the bowler, and to note the position of the non-striker. It is far easier to judge the respective positions of the ball and players if the eyes are level and the head stationary at that precise moment of decision. Experience and practice hone these skills.

AT THE STRIKER'S END

Normally, the umpire would stand at square leg in line with the striker's popping crease at a distance of about 22–24 yards (20–24 m) from the wicket. This is about the same distance from the striker as he would be when at the bowler's end. By maintaining that distance, the eyes become used to the relative distance irrespective of the ends. He should not be so far back as to affect his ability to judge runs, run outs and stumpings, nor should he be so close as to impede a fielder or, worse still, to be hit by a ball. Sometimes, when a wicket-keeper is standing up to the wicket, the umpire may wish to stand a little closer in order to see clearly the wicket-keeper's actions.

Wherever the umpire stands he should always try to keep out of the way of nearby fielders, adjusting his position forward or back as necessary and, if required, moving slightly off line with the popping crease. If the ball is hit towards the striker's end umpire, it may be necessary to move out of the way of the travelling ball or away from a fielder, particularly if a catch is imminent.

There are occasions when it is preferable for the umpire to stand on the off side, such as when:

- a player is obstructing the umpire's view of the wicket and/or popping crease
- the umpire wishes to get a clearer/different view of a bowler's action
- the umpire needs a better view of the leg-side field behind the popping crease
- the sun is shining in the eyes of the umpire and/or obscures the popping crease marking
- the popping crease cannot be seen because of the slope of the ground
- there are reflections from obstacles outside the boundary
- there is a runner acting for a batsman (when this occurs it is **expected** of the umpire to move to the off side in order to keep the runner and non-striker in full view).

If the striker's end umpire decides to change sides he must inform his colleague and both the fielding captain and batsmen. Moving must only be done when the ball is dead.

RIGHT- AND LEFT-HANDED BATSMEN

When the batsmen change ends the umpire would normally move to remain at square leg. However, if this wastes time it is acceptable to remain on one side for the duration of the over.

The umpire should **never hold the game up** while he moves from one side to the other. He should be able to anticipate when a single or three runs are going to be scored, walking forward as the ball is returned and then moving quickly into his new position. If play is likely to be held up because the umpire is late with this movement, he should stay where he is and move at the next available opportunity.

12. UMPIRES CHANGING ENDS

The umpires shall change ends after each side has had one completed innings. See Law 14.2 (Forfeiture of an innings).

When a game is played as a single-innings match, the umpires stay at the same end for the duration of the match. When a game is a played as a two-innings match (i.e. when each team has the opportunity to bat twice) the umpires should change ends when the team batting second has concluded its first innings. If a team forfeits its first innings, that innings is deemed completed.

13. CONSULTATION BETWEEN UMPIRES

All disputes shall be determined by the umpires. The umpires shall consult with each other whenever necessary. See also Law 27.6 (Consultation by umpires).

Umpires must work as a team both on and off the field. This will at times involve consultation to resolve matters; indeed, several Laws require the umpires to consult. However, consultation does not necessarily mean that the umpires have to talk to each other. Very often they can communicate by means of discreet signals and provided these signals are clear and unambiguous it becomes an efficient and unobtrusive method of doing so. Observant players will notice this and gain confidence in their officials. Conversely, players will get frustrated if the umpires constantly stop the flow of the game in order to discuss matters that should be dealt with by signals.

The pre-match discussions between umpires should be the time when they decide on a series of signals for commonly occurring events. Such signals might include ones to:
- confirm the number of balls still to be delivered in the over
- indicate the height of a delivery for a bouncer or beamer
- indicate the last over of a session or when drinks are due
- indicate that the ball was caught cleanly
- indicate whether the batsmen had crossed when a catch was taken.

Signals should be agreed between umpires and scorers, for example:

- to indicate to the scorers there is a change of bowler
- for clarification when scorers need to be advised of the number of runs to be scored it may be necessary for the closest umpire to move towards them to give verbal confirmation. When overthrows occur, a signal for 5 runs or 7 runs may be necessary followed by a verbal confirmation.
- a 'pre-signal' signal. This is a low-key signal that the umpire gives while the ball is in play to indicate to the scorers that an official signal is going to be given once the ball is dead. This 'pre-signal' signal is not acknowledged by the scorers, who must wait for the official one. For example, this signal would be given as Leg byes are being attempted thus informing the scorers that the official Leg bye signal is going to follow as soon as the ball is dead. Scorers acknowledge the Leg bye signal.

If an umpire is required to leave his position to consult on a matter then he should only do so when the ball is dead. If the matter needs to be discussed before the ball becomes naturally dead the umpire must call and signal Dead ball before leaving his position. This is to prevent any on-field action while the umpire's back is turned.

Umpires will gain much greater satisfaction and enjoyment from standing with a colleague whom they consider offers them full support whenever requested. Players also come to acknowledge that co-operation and appreciate their competence.

14. SIGNALS

(a) The following code of signals shall be used by umpires.

    (i) Signals made while the ball is in play

      Dead ball – by crossing and re-crossing the wrists below the waist.

      No ball – by extending one arm horizontally.

      Out – by raising an index finger above the head. (If not out the umpire shall call Not out.)

      Wide – by extending both arms horizontally.

    (ii) When the ball is dead, the signals above, with the exception of the signal for Out, shall be repeated to the scorers. The signals listed below shall be made to the scorers only when the ball is dead.

      Boundary 4 – by waving an arm from side to side finishing with the arm across the chest.

      Boundary 6 – by raising both arms above the head.

      Bye – by raising an open hand above the head.

      Commencement of last hour – by pointing to a raised wrist with the other hand.

> Five penalty runs awarded to the batting side – by repeated tapping of one shoulder with the opposite hand.
>
> Five penalty runs awarded to the fielding side – by placing one hand on the opposite shoulder.
>
> Leg bye – by touching a raised knee with the hand.
>
> New ball – by holding the ball above the head.
>
> Revoke last signal – by touching both shoulders, each with the opposite hand.
>
> Short run – by bending one arm upwards and touching the nearer shoulder with the tips of the fingers.

(b) The umpire shall wait until each signal to the scorers has been separately acknowledged by a scorer before allowing play to proceed.

Signalling is a method of communication between the umpires and scorers. As with all communication it should be clear and free from ambiguity.

The Law defines the actions that the umpires need to undertake when they wish to communicate certain information to the scorers and it is incumbent upon them to use a clear and correct signal. Flamboyant signals, while they may appear to be entertaining, could confuse the scorers, with the result that incorrect information is entered into the scoring record.

In the following illustrations it is made clear not only how the signal should be given but also when.

In the cases of No ball, Wide ball, and Dead ball the umpire will call and signal while the ball is in play. These actions are for the benefit of the on-field participants and scorers should not attempt to acknowledge the signal. Once the ball is dead the umpire will turn to the scorers and repeat the signal – this is the one that the scorers will acknowledge.

All other signals (other than the one for Out) will be given when the ball is dead. These should be acknowledged by the scorers.

In cases where the striker's end umpire has to call and signal No ball or Dead ball, it is recommended that the bowler's end umpire assume responsibility for any repetition of the signal to the scorers.

Often an umpire will be required to make more than one signal for a delivery, in which case they should be made in the following order, ensuring each is acknowledged before making the next:

- Penalty runs
- Short runs (also indicating how many runs are to be scored)
- No balls or Wides
- Byes or Leg byes
- Boundary.

EXAMPLE 1

No ball is called and signalled and the ball is missed by the striker and wicket-keeper and travels to the boundary.

The sequence of signals is No ball, followed by Bye, followed by Boundary 4. The use of the Bye signal indicates to the scorers that the striker did not make contact with the ball and cannot be credited with the runs. They are not recorded as Byes but as No ball extras: 1 for the No ball, plus 4 for the boundary, total 5 – all No ball extras.

EXAMPLE 2

No ball is called and signalled and the ball is missed by striker and wicket-keeper and the batsmen run 3. When the ball is dead the striker's end umpire calls and signals Short run.

The bowler's end umpire assumes responsibility for all signals. The sequence of signals is Short run, followed by No ball, followed by Bye. In this example the use of the Bye signal indicates to the scorers that the striker did not make contact with the ball and only the 2 completed runs are scored in addition to the penalty for the No ball. They are not recorded as Byes but as No ball extras: 1 for the No ball, plus 2 for the completed runs, total 3 – all No ball extras.

EXAMPLE 3

The striker in attempting to hit the ball misses and it is deflected off his pads and reaches the boundary.

The sequence of signals is Leg bye, followed by Boundary 4. This indicates to the scorers that the striker's bat did not make contact with ball and the boundary is scored as leg byes.

Scorers are charged with the responsibility of acknowledging **each separate signal** given by umpires. Umpires must ensure that the scorers can see the signal clearly. This should involve turning side on for Leg bye, and may involve moving away from the wicket or players to ensure a clear line of sight.

UNOFFICIAL SIGNALS

There are a number of unofficial signals given by umpires that do not form part of the Laws. Some are used by the umpires to save moving position to confer, others being used to keep scorers informed. These should be agreed between umpires and scorers prior to the match, with additional ones being made up as and when required – see pages 70 and 71 for further details.

Additional signals

Special match regulations may contain additional signals to be used only in that competition. It would be prudent to confirm with the scorers the correct presentation of these signals and how such events should be scored or entered in the scoring record.

Dead ball

Crossing and re-crossing the wrists
  below the waist with a call Dead ball.
Made when the ball is in play and signal
  is repeated for the scorers.

Out

Index finger raised above the head.
(If not out the umpire shall call Not out.)
Made when the ball is in play or dead.
  The only signal scorers do not
  acknowledge.

No ball

One arm extended horizontally with a
  call of No ball.
Made immediately upon an
  infringement and repeated for the
  scorers when the ball is dead.

Wide

Both arms extended horizontally with a
  call of Wide ball.
Made when the ball passes the striker's
  wicket and repeated for the scorers
  when the ball is dead.

Boundary 4

Waving an arm from side to side,
   finishing with the arm across the chest.
Made when the ball is dead.

Boundary 6

Both arms raised above the head.
Made when the ball is dead.

Bye

An open hand held above the head.
Made when the ball is dead.

Leg bye

A raised knee touched with the hand.
Made when the ball is dead.
Best done side-on to the scorers.

Five penalty runs awarded to the batting side
Repeatedly tap one shoulder with
  the opposite hand.
An exaggerated signal made when the
  ball is dead.

Five penalty runs awarded to the fielding side
One hand placed on the
  opposite shoulder.
Made when the ball is dead.

Commencement of last hour
Pointing to a raised wrist with the other
  hand.
Made when the ball is dead.

New ball
The ball held above the head.
Made when the ball is dead.

Revoke last signal

Touching both shoulders, each with the opposite hand.

Made when the ball is dead.

To avoid any misunderstanding, the umpire should resignal all the correct signals for that delivery.

Short run

One arm bent upwards, touching the nearer shoulder with the tips of the fingers, and a call of Short run.

Made when the ball is dead.

15. CORRECTNESS OF SCORES

Consultation between umpires and scorers on doubtful points is essential. The umpires shall satisfy themselves as to the correctness of the number of runs scored, the wickets that have fallen and, where appropriate, the number of overs bowled. They shall agree these with the scorers at least at every interval, other than a drinks interval, and at the conclusion of the match. See Laws 4.2 (Correctness of scores), 21.8 (Correctness of result) and 21.10 (Result not to be changed).

At every interval when the players leave the field, umpires must check and agree the following with the scorers:

• runs scored

• number of wickets fallen

• number of overs bowled if relevant

• any other doubtful point which requires clarification.

As part of the third team in a match, umpires and scorers must have full confidence in each other and this can only be maintained by consultation and communication. Each must seek advice and clarification from the other whenever necessary.

While scorers traditionally keep records of each bowler and batsman and extras, the essential points for umpires are the cumulative tally and the wickets fallen in each innings (and, if appropriate, the overs bowled). Provided, the scorers' records agree on these points, it is sufficient for the match result to be declared.

In order to acquire this information and thus be in the position to check it accurately with the scorers, some umpires carry a run counter in their pockets on which they click up every run scored during the match. At the end of each over they record this information on their overs card.

When confirming the result, umpires should be available to offer assistance, if required.

Although it is not a requirement in Law, umpires may initial the scoresheet to confirm the result.

Law 4 The scorers

1. APPOINTMENT OF SCORERS

Two scorers shall be appointed to record all runs scored, all wickets taken and, where appropriate, number of overs bowled.

This clause requires two scorers to be appointed to a match. While not stated in Law, the umpires should ensure that this requirement is met before play commences. It is usual for each side to appoint its own scorer. The minimum duties of a scorer are to:

• record runs scored
• record number of wickets fallen
• record number of overs bowled if relevant.

In fact many scorers do very much more.

2. CORRECTNESS OF SCORES

The scorers shall frequently check to ensure that their records agree. They shall agree with the umpires, at least at every interval, other than a drinks interval, and at the conclusion of the match, the runs scored, the wickets that have fallen and, where appropriate, the number of overs bowled. See Law 3.15 (Correctness of scores).

Scorers should consult with each other frequently to ensure their records agree. In fact most scorers are constantly talking to each other to that end.

Whenever the players leave the field (drinks intervals are taken on the field and are excluded), scorers must check and agree the following with the umpires:

• runs scored
• wickets fallen
• overs bowled if relevant
• any other doubtful points which require clarification.

As part of the third team in a match, scorers and umpires need to have total confidence in each other and this can only be maintained by consultation and communication. Each should seek advice and clarification from the other whenever necessary.

Where there is only one scorer, the solo scorer should be particularly alert to what is happening on the field of play and take every opportunity to check that his record balances. Umpires should be aware of the extra demands placed on a scorer working on his own and should request that a member of the batting team be nearby to assist whenever necessary, particularly in the naming of players.

3. ACKNOWLEDGING SIGNALS

The scorers shall accept all instructions and signals given to them by the umpires. They shall immediately acknowledge each separate signal.

The scorers must accept all instructions and signals given by umpires. If they believe the umpires have made a mistake, it may be appropriate to raise the matter during the next consultation.

Scorers must acknowledge every signal made by the umpires. When the umpire gives a series of signals, each one should be acknowledged separately. It is not necessary for both scorers to do this.

When an umpire calls and signals No ball, Wide ball or Dead ball he will give the signal twice. The first call and signal is for the benefit of those on the field and the scorers are not to acknowledge this one – the umpire will be concentrating on what is happening in the game and will not be watching for an acknowledgement. When the ball becomes dead, the bowler's end umpire will turn to the scorers and repeat the signal. It is then that acknowledgement is made.

Before the start of play, scorers should confirm with the umpires how they are going to acknowledge the signals. It is very helpful if a white or fluorescent card is used since these can be clearly seen in any light conditions and from some distance away.

Many scorers are expected to maintain the scoreboard. This additional duty distracts from their principal task – to keep the scoring record. It is preferable for others to maintain the scoreboard, with the scorer ensuring that the operators display the correct information.

Section 3 of this edition contains information of direct importance to scorers as they fulfil their duties. It also contains relevant information for umpires who, according to the Laws, must satisfy themselves as to the correctness of the score and the match result. All umpires are recommended to take the time to study Section 3 in order to understand better the complexities of the duties of a scorer.

Law 5 The ball

1. WEIGHT AND SIZE

The ball, when new, shall weigh not less than 5½ oz/155.9 g, nor more than 5¾ oz/163 g, and shall measure not less than 8¹³⁄₁₆ in/22.4 cm, nor more than 9 in/22.9 cm in circumference.

This clause deals with the actual size and weight of balls when new. It does not take into account any wear and tear that the ball may suffer during the match. In order to ensure these measurements are correct there are ball gauges available to help the umpire. Such aids may be purchased but it is very rare to find a ball made by a recognised manufacturer that does not comply with this Law.

2. APPROVAL AND CONTROL OF BALLS

(a) All balls to be used in the match, having been approved by the umpires and captains, shall be in the possession of the umpires before the toss and shall remain under their control throughout the match.
(b) The umpire shall take possession of the ball in use at the fall of each wicket, at the start of any interval and at any interruption of play.

Prior to the toss, all the balls to be used in the match must be approved by the umpires and the two captains, and any problems resolved. In some competitions the ball may be supplied by the sponsor or competition organisers and as such cannot really be queried or 'approved' by the umpires or captains. The only form of query under these circumstances would be if the size or weight were incorrect. Once agreed upon, the balls – both new and used – remain under the control of the umpires for the duration of the match.

During the match, the umpires must take possession of the ball at:
- the start of each interval and interruption of play, and
- the fall of each wicket.

During such times, it is usual for the ball to be held by the bowler's end umpire. This avoids confusion over which end the next ball is to be delivered from.

3. NEW BALL

Unless an agreement to the contrary has been made before the match, either captain may demand a new ball at the start of each innings.

Before the toss the two captains are required to agree between themselves and inform the umpires how many new balls are to be used during the match. It may be that the competition regulations state how many balls are to be used, and when they are to be taken, in which case the need for any such agreement is negated. If there is no such regulation, the two captains must agree between themselves **prior to the toss** because, if they do not, the Law states that at the start of each innings either captain may demand a new ball.

Note that the clause states **either** captain – it is not the sole prerogative of the fielding captain to take the new ball at the start of an innings, either captain may do so provided that no prior agreement/regulation is in existence. It is important that umpires make this point in their pre-match discussions with the captains, otherwise they could have a disagreement that may be very difficult to sort out. By being proactive in this area, the umpires can prevent future problems.

The scorers must be informed of any agreement made prior to the toss.

4. NEW BALL IN MATCH OF MORE THAN ONE DAY'S DURATION

In a match of more than one day's duration, the captain of the fielding side may demand a new ball after the prescribed number of overs has been bowled with the old one. The Governing Body for cricket in the country concerned shall decide the number of overs applicable in that country, which shall not be less than 75 overs.

The umpires shall indicate to the batsmen and the scorers whenever a new ball is taken into play.

In a match of two days or more the fielding captain is allowed to demand a new ball after a prescribed number of overs have been bowled with the old one. (The 'prescribed number' will differ from country to country depending upon the decisions made by each country's Board of Control/Governing Body. However, this cannot be less than 75 overs.) There is no obligation for the fielding captain to take the option of a new ball and he can continue to use the 'old' ball for as long as he wishes.

The new ball may be taken at any time after the prescribed number has been reached, and may be taken during an over. If the new ball is taken during an over, for the purposes of calculating when the next new ball is due the ball is deemed to have been taken at the start of that over.

When the new ball is taken:

- The umpires must inform the batsmen at the crease and the scorers that the fielding captain has taken the new ball.
- After signalling this information to the scorers the umpires must await acknowledgement before permitting play to resume.
- The scorers must immediately acknowledge this signal and record the time and over in which the new ball was taken.

5. BALL LOST OR BECOMING UNFIT FOR PLAY

If, during play, the ball cannot be found or recovered or the umpires agree that it has become unfit for play through normal use, the umpires shall replace it with a ball which has had wear comparable with that which the previous ball had received before the need for its replacement. When the ball is replaced the umpires shall inform the batsmen and the fielding captain.

It is not uncommon for the ball to become lost, requiring it to be replaced. This may occur either within the field of play e.g. down a rabbit hole or goalpost hole, or outside the field of play e.g. a river, stream or dense trees or bushes.

It is also not uncommon for the ball to become damaged during play and this provision applies where such damage occurs through normal use. Any damage occurring outside normal use is dealt with under Law 42.3 The match ball – changing its condition.

So that play is not unduly delayed when a replacement ball is necessary, the umpires should always have available a selection of spares to choose from. It is usual practice for each umpire to carry a spare in his pocket so that no time is wasted finding a suitable replacement. Each umpire should carry a ball of differing wear and tear so that the condition of the replacement is as near to that of the 'old' ball as possible. It is good practice if umpires also leave a box of spares with the scorers, giving a wider choice if necessary.

In order to know what condition the ball was in before it was lost or damaged, the umpires are required to undertake frequent, though irregular, inspections of the match ball throughout the game. Such overt inspection of the ball will also deter fielders from tampering with it.

Before allowing the game to continue, the umpires must inform the fielding captain and the batsmen at the crease that the match ball has been changed. Note that they are not required to consult with the captains but only to advise them that a change has been made. Neither captain plays any part in the decision as to which ball shall be used as the replacement.

The replacement of the match ball because of loss or damage has no effect on the number of overs to be bowled before a new ball can be taken.

EXAMPLE 1

The match regulations state that a new ball can be claimed after 90 overs. If the original match ball is replaced after 60 overs because it has become unfit for use, the replacement, which would be of similar 'age', would only have to be used for the remaining 30 overs, after which the new ball could be taken.

In cases where the ball is lost outside the playing area and the umpires have replaced it, the question arises as to what to do if the original one is found. Is the original ball automatically brought back into play, or does the match continue with the replacement?

The answer is left to the discretion of the umpires. The length of time it took for the ball to be found and its condition on return in comparison to the replacement will play a large part in the decision. Obviously if the original ball is soaking wet because it has been lying in a river or pond for any length of time it may not be fit for use. Similarly if it has taken thirty overs to find the original ball it would be unfair to start using it again when the replacement has had thirty overs of extra wear and tear since it was brought into use. The umpires must decide on the evidence before them and their decision will take into account the Spirit of the Game as well as its Laws.

6. SPECIFICATIONS

The specifications as described in 1 above shall apply to men's cricket only. The following specifications will apply to

(i) **Women's cricket**
Weight: from 4^{15}/$_{16}$ oz/140 g to 5^{5}/$_{16}$ oz/151 g
Circumference: from 8^{1}/$_{4}$ in/21.0 cm to 8^{7}/$_{8}$ in/22.5 cm

(ii) **Junior cricket – under 13**
Weight: from 4^{11}/$_{16}$ oz/133 g to 5^{1}/$_{16}$ oz/144 g
Circumference: from 8^{1}/$_{16}$ in/20.5 cm to 8^{11}/$_{16}$ in/22.0 cm

Everything that applies to the balls for men's cricket applies to these grades, the only differences being the respective sizes and weights.

Law 6 The bat

1. WIDTH AND LENGTH

The bat overall shall not be more than 38 in/96.5 cm in length. The blade of the bat shall be made solely of wood and shall not exceed 4^{1}/$_{4}$ in/10.8 cm at the widest part.

2. COVERING THE BLADE

The blade may be covered with material for protection, strengthening or repair. Such material shall not exceed ^{1}/$_{16}$ in/1.56 mm in thickness, and shall not be likely to cause unacceptable damage to the ball.

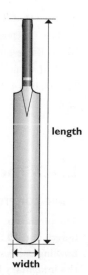

length

width

This Law details the specific measurements and composition of the bat. While umpires do not have to measure every bat used in a game, there are times when a bat may appear unusual or oversize causing umpires to suspect that it is illegal. Should this occur, umpires are required to check the bat's conformance to specification.

• There are no minimum measurements laid down, only maximum ones: overall **length** should not exceed 38 in (96.5 cm) while overall **width** should not exceed 4^{1}/$_{4}$ in (10.8 cm). The measurements are for the overall length of the bat, there being no stipulations as to the length of the handle or the blade.
• The Law permits the bat to be protected or repaired using a binding tape, plastics or similar but states that, where such material is used, it should not protrude from the surface more than ^{1}/$_{16}$ in (1.56 mm). Once repaired, the overall bat width may

be increased to a maximum of $4\frac{3}{8}$ in (11.11 cm). Such binding must not be of a type that could damage the ball.

• The Law also dictates that the blade of the bat must be made of wood.

• It should be noted that the Law stipulates no weight requirements, each batsman choosing the weight to suit his own needs.

Should an umpire suspect that a bat or covering fails to meet the above specifications, he should consult with his colleague and together they should examine the bat closely. If it does fail to meet the specifications, they must prohibit its use.

3. HAND OR GLOVE TO COUNT AS PART OF BAT

In these Laws,
(a) reference to the bat shall imply that the bat is held by the batsman.
(b) contact between the ball and
   either (i)   the striker's bat itself
   or   (ii) the striker's hand holding the bat
   or   (iii) any part of a glove worn on the striker's hand holding
   the bat shall be regarded as the ball striking or touching the bat, or
   being struck by the bat.

Provided that the striker's hand is holding the bat, that hand is deemed to be part of the bat. This point is of relevance in several other Laws, notably when dealing with a catch off the glove or hand that is holding the bat.

The Law covers any part of the glove being worn on the hand holding the bat. This includes the wristband of the glove irrespective of how far it extends up the arm.

Law 7 The pitch

I. AREA OF PITCH

The pitch is a rectangular area of the ground 22 yards/20.12 m in length and 10 ft/3.05 m in width. It is bounded at either end by the bowling creases and on either side by imaginary lines, one each side of the imaginary line joining the centres of the two middle stumps, each parallel to it and 5 ft/1.52 m from it. See Laws 8.1 (Width and pitching) and 9.2 (The bowling crease).

It should be noted that the Laws refer to the playing area as the **pitch**, not the wicket. Umpires and scorers should always use the correct terminology, thus avoiding any confusion. In doing so, they will encourage players and others to follow suit.

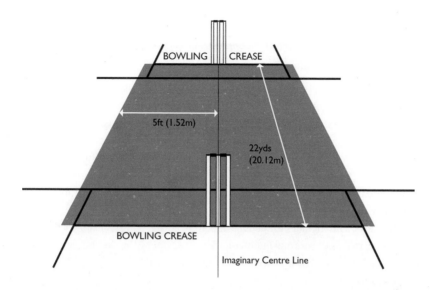

In the above diagram the green area represents the pitch, whose measurements are:

LENGTH   22 yards (20.12 m) between the two bowling creases

WIDTH   10 ft (3.05 m) i.e. 5 ft (1.52 m) either side of an imaginary line joining
the two middle stumps.

The pitch is usually mown closer than the rest of the square and outfield so it is fairly easy to distinguish. There are times, however, when the mown area is not always the correct width. The square may not be big enough to accommodate all the pitches that have to be used during the course of the season causing the groundsman, in an attempt to save space, to cut the pitch only as far as the return crease markings. This will mean that the prepared area is 8 in too narrow on each side. This does not mean that the pitch is now only 8 ft 8 in wide – it is still 10 ft wide even though it is not fully prepared as such. All Laws relating to the pitch are based on it always being 10 ft wide. If the umpires find that the pitch has not been prepared to its full width they must inform the captains who, it is hoped, will accept the situation and agree to play on the pitch so prepared.

By informing the groundsman and Ground Authority of such issues, umpires are more likely to ensure the pitch is properly prepared for future matches.

2. FITNESS OF THE PITCH FOR PLAY

**The umpires shall be the final judges of the fitness of the pitch for play.
See Laws 3.8 (Fitness of ground, weather and light) and 3.9 (Suspension
of play for adverse conditions of ground, weather or light).**

While the captains can agree to play in unsuitable conditions, the final arbiters of the fitness of the pitch for play rests with the umpires – both umpires. The criteria for umpires in deciding if the pitch is suitable for play are detailed in Law 3.

3. SELECTION AND PREPARATION

Before the match, the Ground Authority shall be responsible for the selection and preparation of the pitch. During the match, the umpires shall control its use and maintenance.

The decision of which pitch is to be used in a match is outside the jurisdiction of all participants in a match. It rests solely with the Ground Authority.

Any preparation of the pitch **before the game** is for the executive of the ground concerned and is of no concern to the umpires. The umpires, however, must, as part of their pre-match duties, ensure the pitch has been marked correctly. It is only **after the toss** that the pitch becomes solely the responsibility of the umpires who, from that moment on, are in charge of its use and maintenance for the duration of the game. The umpires must ensure that all maintenance is carried out in accordance with the Laws. This includes the actions of players during play (for example the use of sawdust) as well as the normal maintenance carried out by the Ground Authority. As supervisors, the umpires will need to liaise closely with the groundstaff who may seek guidance from them.

4. CHANGING THE PITCH

The pitch shall not be changed during the match unless the umpires decide that it is unreasonable or dangerous for play to continue on it and then only with the consent of both captains.

Once the match has commenced it is not permissible to change the pitch unless it becomes 'unreasonable or dangerous' for play to continue. The Law does not use the word 'unplayable'. There have been many occasions when a pitch has been unplayable, causing wickets to fall and the game to finish earlier than expected, but that does not necessarily mean that it was 'dangerous'. 'Unplayable' is not a reason to change the pitch and the umpires must be careful to distinguish between what is 'unplayable' and what is 'unreasonable or dangerous' – the criteria for 'unreasonable or dangerous' are given in Law 3.9 (d).

Having established that the pitch has become 'unreasonable or dangerous' and that it should be changed, the umpires must:
- inform both captains of their decision
- ask both captains if they wish to change pitches.

It requires the consent of **both** captains in order for this change to take place. If one or both decline the offer then the match is abandoned. If the captains agree, it is permissible to change from a turf pitch to a non-turf pitch or vice versa. If both captains wish they may delay such a decision and wait to see if the condition of the pitch improves. Should it do so, and the umpires consider that it is no longer dangerous, play can resume on the original pitch.

The scorers must be informed of any decisions and will make a margin note, particularly if the match is moved to a different pitch. If the game does not continue the result of the match shall be recorded as a Draw.

5. NON-TURF PITCHES

In the event of a non-turf pitch being used, the artificial surface shall conform to the following measurements:
Length – a minimum of 58 ft/17.68 m
Width – a minimum of 6 ft/1.83 m
See Law 10.8 (Non-turf pitches).

The construction of artificial pitches and any covering used is the sole responsibility of the Ground Authority.

Common sense dictates that Laws relating to rolling, mowing and repairing of footholds are not applicable but all other Laws relating to the pitch still apply.

It is essential that umpires standing in matches on non-turf pitches make themselves aware of any special regulations regarding the pitch and its surrounds. Matters that may require clarification and agreement at the pre-match meeting with the captains could include:

- the type of footwear allowed on the pitch. Some grounds will not permit spiked footwear as it can damage the surface
- the type of wickets used and how they are pitched. Holes may not be available, requiring the use of spring-loaded stumps
- what happens if the ball hits the base (as opposed to the actual stumps) of the spring-loaded stumps
- what happens if the bowler delivers a ball that pitches either on the edge of the pitch or off the pitch altogether.

Law 8 The wickets

1. WIDTH AND PITCHING

Two sets of wickets shall be pitched opposite and parallel to each other at a distance of 22 yards/20.12 m between the centres of the two middle stumps. Each set shall be 9 in/22.86 cm wide and shall consist of three wooden stumps with two wooden bails on top. See Appendix A.

2. SIZE OF STUMPS

The tops of the stumps shall be 28 in/71.10 cm above the playing surface and shall be dome shaped except for the bail grooves. The portion of a stump above the playing surface shall be cylindrical, apart from the domed top, with circular section of diameter not less than 1⅜ in/3.49cm nor more than 1½ in/3.81cm. See Appendix A.

3. THE BAILS

(a) The bails, when in position on the top of the stumps,
    (i) shall not project more than ½ in/1.27 cm above them.
    (ii) shall fit between the stumps without forcing them out
    of the vertical.
(b) Each bail shall conform to the following specifications.
    See Appendix A.

Overall length:	**4⁵/₁₆ in/10.95 cm**
Length of barrel:	**2⅛ in/5.40 cm**
Longer spigot:	**1⅜ in/3.49 cm**
Shorter spigot:	**¹³/₁₆ in/2.06 cm**

This Law deals with what constitutes a wicket by defining the component parts, their dimensions and the overall width of the wicket when properly pitched. If everything is in accordance with the Law, the ball will not pass between the stumps without disturbing them. The umpires may wish to use a ball to check that this is so.

If a problem is found, the appropriate remedial action will have to be taken. This might include replacing the stumps with ones that conform to the Law, or re-pitching the existing, legal, ones so that their position conforms to the Law.

Each wicket is made up of:

- **three stumps** which extend 28 in (71.10 cm) above the ground – that is to say that they are <u>not</u> 28 in in length, but when placed correctly in the ground will extend to a height of 28 in

- **two bails**, each made of wood, having the dimensions set out above. The bails should not protrude more than ½ in (1.27 cm) above the tops of the stumps and when in place should not force the stumps out of their vertical position.

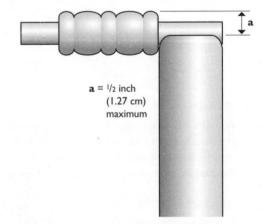

a = ½ inch
(1.27 cm)
maximum

The above dimensions mean that a correctly erected wicket is 28½ in (72.37 cm) maximum in height and 9 in (22.86 cm) wide.

The stumps:

- **must be made of wood** – it is no longer legal, nor is it safe, to have stumps with metal/plastic tips covering the pointed ends or rings fitted to the tops. While such tips may help to get the stumps into the ground they can become extremely dangerous when a stump is knocked out of the ground

- **should be cylindrical** and of the required diameter
- **should be dome shaped on the top and grooved** in order to house the two bails.

The umpires must check that each wicket is 9 in (22.86 cm) wide and the bails placed so that they do not force the stumps out of their vertical position. Ensuring that the wickets are correctly pitched will normally ensure that the ball will not pass between the stumps without dislodging the bails. This is particularly important when dealing with how and when the wicket is down.

Umpires, working together, will need to align the wickets at the start of the game and every time they are disturbed. In dry conditions it is often the case that the stumps, although secure at the start of the game, become loose following repeated disturbance. Umpires should ask the groundstaff to moisten the stump holes, whenever possible, sufficiently to reduce the risk of the stumps becoming loose.

4. JUNIOR CRICKET

In junior cricket, the same definitions of the wickets shall apply subject to the following measurements being used.

Width:	**8 in/20.32 cm**
Pitched for under 13:	**21 yards/19.20 m**
Pitched for under 11:	**20 yards/18.29 m**
Pitched for under 9:	**18 yards/16.46 m**
Height above playing surface:	**27 in/68.58 cm**

Each stump

Diameter: not less than 1 1/4 in/3.18 cm nor more than 1 3/8 in/3.49 cm

Each bail

Overall:	**3 13/16 in/9.68 cm**
Barrel:	**1 13/16 in/4.60 cm**
Longer Spigot:	**1 1/4 in/3.18 cm**
Shorter Spigot:	**3/4 in/1.91 cm**

These requirements apply only to the junior grades stated. Umpires officiating in these grades must ensure they are aware of these requirements.

5. DISPENSING WITH BAILS

The umpires may agree to dispense with the use of bails, if necessary. If they so agree then no bails shall be used at either end. The use of bails shall be resumed as soon as conditions permit. See Law 28.4 (Dispensing with bails).

Windy conditions can cause several difficulties, most commonly the bails being blown off the top of the stumps. This is not always because the wind is too strong: sometimes the bail grooves are not deep enough. If the constant blowing off of the bails becomes irritating, umpires can do one of two things:

- replace them with heavy bails, which are designed for this very purpose. They are made of a heavier wood that helps keep them in place but does not prevent their removal by the ball hitting the wicket. Experienced umpires take a set with them on to the field, finding them worthwhile and well worth the expense
- dispense with the bails altogether until the wind dies down.

Although the problem may be occurring at only one end, once the decision has been made to dispense with the bails they are removed from both wickets. Only the umpires can make this decision, not the captains. While playing without bails the conditions for the wicket being broken change and the umpire should study the requirements detailed in Law 28. Having agreed to dispense with the bails the umpires must constantly monitor the situation and restore both sets as soon as conditions permit.

LAW 9 The bowling, popping and return creases

1. THE CREASES

A bowling crease, a popping crease and two return creases shall be marked in white, as set out in 2, 3 and 4 below, at each end of the pitch. See Appendix B.

2. THE BOWLING CREASE

The bowling crease, which is the back edge of the crease marking, shall be the line through the centres of the three stumps at that end. It shall be 8ft 8 in/2.64 m in length, with the stumps in the centre.

3. THE POPPING CREASE

The popping crease, which is the back edge of the crease marking, shall be in front of and parallel to the bowling crease and shall be 4 ft/1.22 m from it. The popping crease shall be marked to a minimum of 6 ft/1.83 m on either side of the imaginary line joining the centres of the middle stumps and shall be considered to be unlimited in length.

4. THE RETURN CREASES

The return creases, which are the inside edges of the crease markings, shall be at right angles to the popping crease at a distance of 4 ft 4 in/1.32 m either side of the imaginary line joining the centres of the two middle stumps. Each return crease shall be marked from the popping crease to a minimum of 8 ft/2.44 m behind it and shall be considered to be unlimited in length.

This Law deals solely with the markings found at each end of the pitch. The origins of their respective names have little relevance to the modern game, but the terms and words used retain their importance. Umpires and scorers should ensure they always use the correct terminology, thus avoiding any confusion. In doing so they will encourage players and others to follow suit.

All creases must be marked in white at each end of the pitch and look like this:

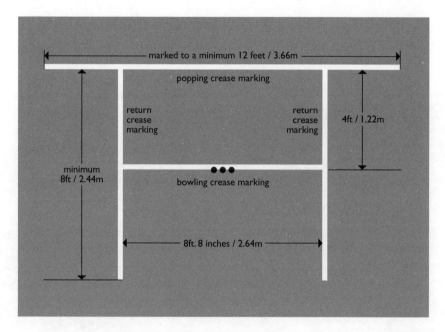

It is important to note that the popping creases and return creases are of unlimited length. They should be marked to the minimum required length, but in reality they extend all the way to the boundary. This is particularly important when dealing with run outs and bowler No ball foot faults.

Umpires must be fully aware of the difference between the **crease markings** and the actual **crease**. The crease markings are the white lines painted on the ground. They are there to show where the creases actually are. In practice these markings will differ in width from ground to ground, and may be as narrow as ¼ in (6 mm) or as wide as 2 in (50 mm). Their actual width is totally irrelevant because it is the back or inside edge of the marking that is the crease itself. It is vital that umpires and players know and fully understand this because, in many of the Laws, there is reference to the fact that someone/something must be behind the popping crease (Law 29) or within the return crease (Law 24). Note that the terminology, in these Laws, states 'crease' not 'crease marking'.

- The **bowling crease** is the back edge of the crease marking closest to where the umpire stands at that end

- The **popping crease** is the back edge of the crease marking closest to where the umpire stands at that end
- Each **return crease** is the inside edge of the crease marking closest to where the umpire stands at that end

The wickets should be pitched so that the centres of the stumps are on the bowling crease, i.e. the back edge of the marking, as shown here. The photograph below also shows an unofficial marking that may be painted on the bowling crease. This optional marking is to indicate the width of the protected area and is painted 1 ft (30.48 cm) from the centre of the middle stump. Full details of this are dealt with under Law 42.11.

MISTAKES IN CREASE MARKINGS

It is not uncommon for umpires to arrive at a match without groundstaff present and to find the pitch has not been mown to the correct width or the crease markings are incorrect. Although the umpires are required to ensure that the creases are correctly marked, with experience it should not be necessary to measure them as a trained eye will soon detect any error. If it is not possible to have an error corrected, or it is of a minor nature, the umpires must, before the toss, discuss the matter with the captains and seek their agreement to accept the situation.

Umpires may offer assistance to inexperienced groundsmen to ensure they are aware of the requirements of this Law.

Law 10 Preparation and maintenance of the playing area

1. ROLLING

The pitch shall not be rolled during the match except as permitted in (a) and (b) below.

(a) FREQUENCY AND DURATION OF ROLLING

During the match the pitch may be rolled at the request of the captain of the batting side, for a period of not more than 7 minutes, before the start of each innings, other than the first innings of the match, and before the start of each subsequent day's play. See (d) below.

(b) ROLLING AFTER A DELAYED START

In addition to the rolling permitted above, if, after the toss and before the first innings of the match, the start is delayed, the captain of the batting side may request to have the pitch rolled for not more than 7 minutes. However, if the umpires together agree that the delay has had no significant effect on the state of the pitch, they shall refuse the request for the rolling of the pitch.

(c) CHOICE OF ROLLERS

If there is more than one roller available the captain of the batting side shall have the choice.

(d) TIMING OF PERMITTED ROLLING

The rolling permitted (maximum 7 minutes) before play begins on any day shall be started not more than 30 minutes before the time scheduled or rescheduled for play to begin. The captain of the batting side may, however, delay the start of such rolling until not less than 10 minutes before the time scheduled or rescheduled for play to begin, should he so desire.

(e) INSUFFICIENT TIME TO COMPLETE ROLLING

If a captain declares an innings closed, or forfeits an innings, or enforces the follow-on, and the other captain is prevented thereby from exercising his option of the rolling permitted (maximum 7 minutes), or if he is so prevented for any other reason, the extra time required to complete the rolling shall be taken out of the normal playing time.

Law 7 The Pitch deals with the physical properties of the pitch, that is the size, and its fitness for play. This Law details the work that is allowed to be done to the pitch in preparation for, and during, the match. Whenever possible the umpires should ensure the groundstaff are aware of the provisions of this Law and give them guidance whenever they require it – there is a history of cooperation between umpires and groundsmen and umpires should ensure that this cooperation continues.

As stated in Law 7 **rolling prior to the toss** comes under the general preparation of the pitch and is required to be undertaken by the home Ground Authority. Therefore, prior to the toss, the umpires have no involvement. It is only rolling that takes place **after the toss** that the umpires are interested in, and have to supervise. Supervision can take place from a discreet distance and unless the Law is contravened the umpires should not interfere.

ROLLING AFTER THE TOSS

BEFORE THE FIRST INNINGS – AFTER THE TOSS AND BEFORE PLAY STARTS
As any preparation of the pitch will have taken place prior to the toss it is not permitted for the pitch to be re-rolled prior to play starting unless something unusual occurs.

Should the start of the first innings be delayed after the toss, for any reason, the captain of the batting side has the right to ask that the pitch be rolled again prior to the innings starting. The umpires will only uphold this request if they consider that the state of the pitch has been **significantly** altered as a result of the delay. It depends, therefore, on the nature of the delay and how long it lasted as to whether or not the umpires consider that a significant change in the state of the pitch has occurred. A short delay for bad light will have had no effect on the pitch, however a long delay brought about by rain or drizzle may well have changed the state of the pitch from when it was first rolled. Whatever the situation, the captain can only **request** that the pitch be rolled again; the umpires will decide whether to grant that request.

It is worth repeating that this clause applies only to a delay in starting the match after the toss and is only applicable prior to the start of the first innings. If there was any delay in starting play on subsequent days then this clause does not apply. Any rolling on these days would be dealt with as outlined below and any delay in starting play, on these days, would not be a reason for the captain to request the pitch to be re-rolled.

ON SUBSEQUENT DAYS
On any day other than the first – see above – the pitch may be rolled before play starts for that day but only at the request of the batting captain. This clause details strict time limits as to when rolling can take place and the umpires do need to ensure that they are strictly observed. Rolling cannot start any earlier than 30 minutes before the scheduled (or rescheduled) time for play to start, and can be delayed until, but not later than, 10 minutes before play is due to start.

EXAMPLE 1

If play is scheduled to start at 11.30 a.m, rolling cannot start before 11.00 a.m. but must have started by 11.20 a.m.

ROLLING DURING THE DAY ON ANY DAY OF THE MATCH
Once play has started for the day the only other rolling that is allowed during that day is when there is a change of innings. No other rolling is permitted.

GENERAL POINTS REGARDING ROLLING
- The maximum time allowed for any one period of rolling is 7 minutes – it is permissible to roll for less than 7 minutes, but not more. During this period the whole of the pitch must be rolled – it is not permissible to roll just one part of it. The rolling should be as evenly spread as possible over its full width and length.
- Any weight of roller can be used, and if there is a choice then the batting captain must be given that choice. If the captain asks for a heavy roller and only a light roller is available he cannot compensate by having the pitch rolled for a longer period – he must accept the roller that is available.
- Only the incoming batting captain has the choice of whether or not to have the pitch rolled – he may decide not to roll the pitch and that is perfectly in order. The fielding captain has no say in the matter.
- It is important that the batting captain be allowed time to have the pitch rolled, if required. This is not usually a problem, except when there is a late declaration during an interval.

EXAMPLE 2

Lunch is being taken between 1.30 p.m. and 2.10 p.m. At 2.00 p.m. the batting captain declares his innings closed. The groundstaff are not available when this happens and the incoming batting captain wishes to have the pitch rolled.

The incoming batting captain must be allowed to exercise his right to have the pitch rolled and play will not start until the rolling has been completed. If the rolling encroaches into the playing time that playing time is lost and is never made up.

2. SWEEPING

(a) If rolling is to take place the pitch shall first be swept to avoid any possible damage by rolling in debris. This sweeping shall be done so that the 7 minutes allowed for rolling is not affected.

(b) The pitch shall be cleared of any debris at all intervals for meals, between innings and at the beginning of each day, not earlier than 30 minutes nor later than 10 minutes before the time scheduled or rescheduled for play to begin. See Law 15.1 (An interval).

(c) Notwithstanding the provisions of (a) and (b) above, the umpires shall not allow sweeping to take place where they consider it may be detrimental to the surface of the pitch.

- It is unsatisfactory to have loose particles of soil and debris rolled into the pitch. This clause provides for the removal of such debris, **prior to rolling**, thus stopping potential damage to the pitch surface. The removal of any debris is not to be included in the 7 minutes allowed for pitch rolling.
- The pitch should be swept at any interval for meals and between innings. The umpires should ensure that any such sweeping does not have a detrimental effect on the pitch.
- The debris should be removed expediently to ensure there is no undue delay to the start of play. This is particularly important between innings.
- When done before the scheduled or rescheduled start of a day's play sweeping must be done no earlier than 30 minutes and no later than 10 minutes before the start of play. This is the same time frame as for rolling.

3. MOWING

(a) THE PITCH

The pitch shall be mown on each day of the match on which play is expected to take place, if ground and weather conditions allow.

(b) THE OUTFIELD

In order to ensure that conditions are as similar as possible for both sides, the outfield shall be mown on each day of the match on which play is expected to take place, if ground and weather conditions allow.

If, for reasons other than ground and weather conditions, complete mowing of the outfield is not possible, the Ground Authority shall notify the captains and umpires of the procedure to be adopted for such mowing during the match.

(c) RESPONSIBILITY FOR MOWING

All mowings which are carried out before the match shall be the responsibility of the Ground Authority.

All subsequent mowings shall be carried out under the supervision of the umpires.

(d) TIMING OF MOWING

(i) Mowing of the pitch on any day of the match shall be completed not later than 30 minutes before the time scheduled or rescheduled for play to begin on that day.

(ii) Mowing of the outfield on any day of the match shall be completed not later than 15 minutes before the time scheduled or rescheduled for play to begin on that day.

MOWING THE PITCH

Pre-match preparation of the pitch is the responsibility of the Ground Authority and, therefore, any mowing of the pitch, at that time, is of no concern to the umpires. On the second and each subsequent day of a match any mowing that takes place must be done under the supervision of the umpires. It is therefore important that the umpires and groundstaff come to an agreement as to when this will be done so that the umpires can carry out their supervisory role. Should inclement weather prevent the pitch from being mowed the groundstaff should inform the umpires.

As with rolling and sweeping there are time limits on mowing the pitch, which must be completed no later than **30 minutes** before the start of the day's play.

EXAMPLE 3

In a match scheduled to start at 11.00 a.m. the mowing of the pitch has to be completed by 10.30 a.m.

Having completed the mowing it is now possible to start any rolling that is required. The rolling can be started at any time between 10.30 a.m. and 10.50 a.m.

MOWING THE OUTFIELD

Pre-match preparation of the playing area is the responsibility of the Ground Authority and, therefore, any mowing of the outfield, at that time, is of no concern to the umpires.

On the second and each subsequent day of a match, whenever possible the out-field must be mowed before the start of play. The umpires should supervise such mowing. Should inclement weather prevent the outfield being mowed, the ground-staff should inform the umpires and both captains before the start of the day's play. The umpires may direct the groundstaff to mow only part of the field as they see fit.

As with the mowing of the pitch, there are time limits on the mowing of the outfield which should be completed no later than **15 minutes** before the start of the day's play.

EXAMPLE 4

For a match starting at 11.00 a.m. the mowing of the outfield has to be completed by 10.45 a.m.

4. WATERING

The pitch shall not be watered during the match.

This clause is clear and concise. The pitch may not be watered during a match. This includes overnight.

5. RE-MARKING CREASES

The creases shall be re-marked whenever either umpire considers it necessary.

At times the pitch markings can become obliterated causing problems to both umpires and players. Either umpire may call to have the creases re-marked whenever necessary. This would normally be carried out when players are off the field for an interval or interruption, but could be done while drinks are being taken.

6. MAINTENANCE OF FOOTHOLES

The umpires shall ensure that the holes made by the bowlers and batsmen are cleaned out and dried whenever necessary to facilitate play. In matches of more than one day's duration, the umpires shall allow, if necessary, the re-turfing of footholes made by the bowler in his delivery stride, or the use of quick-setting fillings for the same purpose.

The possibility of injury to players can never be entirely eliminated but every opportunity should be taken to reduce any potential accidents. When necessary, the umpires have authority to instruct groundstaff to clean out and dry the holes made by bowlers and batsmen, thus reducing the risk of injuries.

In a match of more than one day's duration, this clause also provides for the repair of the footholes made by the bowler in his delivery stride. These holes can either be re-turfed or, if that is not sufficient, repaired using quick-setting fillings.

7. SECURING OF FOOTHOLDS AND MAINTENANCE OF PITCH

During play, the umpires shall allow the players to secure their footholds by the use of sawdust provided that no damage to the pitch is caused and that Law 42 (Fair and unfair play) is not contravened.

This clause clarifies what the players are allowed to do to secure any footholds that need minor repairs. They are allowed to use sawdust to dry any area that may be causing a problem but cannot use this sawdust on areas that may cause damage to the pitch.

8. NON-TURF PITCHES

Wherever appropriate, the provisions set out in 1 to 7 above shall apply.

Where an artificial pitch is being used the umpires must ensure that the Law is applied wherever applicable.

Countdown to Play

The start of play on each day is 11.00 a.m

Time	First Day	Subsequent Days
Early as possible	Remove covers	Remove covers
	Umpires must be present at ground.	Umpires must be present at ground.
	Mowing of the pitch must be completed.	Mowing of the pitch must be completed.
	Earliest time at which toss can be made.	Earliest time at which rolling may commence.
	Practice on the square must cease.	Earliest time at which debris may be removed.
		Practice on the square must cease.
	Latest time at which toss can be made.	Mowing of the outfield must be completed.
	Mowing of the outfield must be completed.	
	Latest time at which decision to bat or field can be notified to opposing captain.	Latest time at which rolling may commence.
		Latest time at which debris may be removed.
		Latest time at which the time of drinks intervals may be agreed.
	Although not stipulated in Law the umpires usually take the field five minutes before the time for play to commence.	
	Bowler's end umpire calls Play.	Bowler's end umpire calls Play.

Full covering prior to match.

Part covering during match. Bowlers' run ups and 5 ft in front of popping crease.

Law 11 Covering the pitch

1. BEFORE THE MATCH

The use of covers before the match is the responsibility of the Ground Authority and may include full covering if required. However, the Ground Authority shall grant suitable facility to the captains to inspect the pitch before the nomination of their players and to the umpires to discharge their duties as laid down in Laws 3 (The umpires), 7 (The pitch), 8 (The wickets), 9 (The bowling, popping and return creases) and 10 (Preparation and maintenance of the playing area).

2. DURING THE MATCH

The pitch shall not be completely covered during the match unless provided otherwise by regulations or by agreement before the toss.

3. COVERING BOWLERS' RUN UPS

Whenever possible, the bowlers' run ups shall be covered in inclement weather, in order to keep them dry. Unless there is agreement for full covering under 2 above the covers so used shall not extend further than 5 ft/1.52 m in front of each popping crease.

Covering of the pitch during the match is subject to strict regulations:
- Under clause 2 the whole pitch cannot be fully covered during a match.
- The only areas allowed to be covered are the bowlers' run ups and the areas up to 5 ft (1.52 m) in front of the popping crease at each end, thus leaving the rest of the pitch open to the elements.
- However, in the event of rain or the threat of rain, the whole pitch, together with the bowlers' run ups, may be covered if competition regulations allow or if the captains have agreed to this in the pre-match conference. Without any such agreement or competition regulation, the pitch cannot be completely covered during the match.

4. REMOVAL OF COVERS

(a) If after the toss the pitch is covered overnight, the covers shall be removed in the morning at the earliest possible moment on each day that play is expected to take place.
(b) If covers are used during the day as protection from inclement weather, or if inclement weather delays the removal of overnight covers, they shall be removed promptly as soon as conditions allow.

When covers are in use, condensation can become a problem, particularly if their use is prolonged. The covers should therefore be removed as early as possible to allow condensation to evaporate and to enable any final preparation or maintenance on the pitch.

Before the toss on the first day of scheduled play, the Ground Authority has sole responsibility for directing the removal of the covers. After the toss, such responsibility is transferred to the umpires, who should make their decision without influence from any player or match official.

Law 12 Innings

1. NUMBER OF INNINGS

(a) A match shall be one or two innings of each side according to agreement reached before the match.

(b) It may be agreed to limit any innings to a number of overs or by a period of time. If such an agreement is made then

(i) in a one innings match it shall apply to both innings.

(ii) in a two innings match it shall apply to

either the first innings of each side

or   the second innings of each side

or   both innings of each side.

2. ALTERNATE INNINGS

In a two innings match each side shall take their innings alternately except in the cases provided for in Law 13 (The follow-on) or Law 14.2 (Forfeiture of an innings).

In a match not governed by special regulations, conditions of play should be established before the toss.

- A match can be of **one** or **two** innings for each side, to be agreed by the captains and umpires prior to the toss.
- It is possible to limit either the number of **overs** in any innings or the **time** allowed for an innings, provided that these limitations apply equally to both sides.
- The scorers must be informed of the final decision.
- If it is agreed that a two innings match is played then each innings will be taken alternately unless there is a follow-on or forfeiture of an innings.

3. COMPLETED INNINGS

A side's innings is to be considered as completed if

(a) the side is all out

or (b) at the fall of a wicket, further balls remain to be bowled, but no further batsman is available to come in

or (c) the captain declares the innings closed

or (d) the captain forfeits the innings

or (e) in the case of an agreement under 1(b) above,

either (i) the prescribed number of overs has been bowled

or   (ii) the prescribed time has expired.

This clause clearly defines when an innings has ended and covers all eventualities that may arise due to injured or absent batsmen. An innings is deemed to be completed if:

- all batsmen have been dismissed
- at the fall of a wicket or retirement of a batsman, further balls remain to be bowled but no further batsman is available to come in
- the batting captain declares his innings closed
- the incoming captain forfeits his next innings
- in an innings limited by overs, the agreed number of overs have been bowled
- in an innings limited by time, time has been reached.

EXAMPLE 1

Close of play is at 6.30 p.m. An injured batsman is away from the ground when the 9th wicket falls at 6.15 p.m.

Since he is not available to bat and there are further balls to be bowled, his side's innings is complete. If this were the last innings of the match, any result would be based on the fact that the batting side had completed its innings.

EXAMPLE 2

Close of play is at 6.30p.m. An injured batsman is away from the ground when the 9th wicket falls on the last ball of the day.

Although the injured batsman is not available, since no further balls remain in the day he would not be able to bat even if he were at the ground. His side's innings is not closed and if play were to start again the next day the innings would continue, provided the injured batsman was ready to take the field. If this were the last day of the match, any result would be based on the fact that they had lost only nine wickets.

4. THE TOSS

The captains shall toss for the choice of innings on the field of play not earlier than 30 minutes, nor later than 15 minutes, before the scheduled or any rescheduled time for the match to start. Note, however, the provisions of Law 1.3 (Captain).

5. DECISION TO BE NOTIFIED

The captain of the side winning the toss shall notify the opposing captain of his decision to bat or to field, not later than 10 minutes before the scheduled or any rescheduled time for the match to start. Once notified the decision may not be altered.

The importance of the toss cannot be stressed enough since many Laws carry the phrases 'before the toss' or 'after the toss'. There are certain regulations regarding the toss:

- it must take place on the field of play, not in the privacy of the pavilion
- the captain must make the toss (though in his absence anyone else may do so – it

need not be a nominated member of the team)

• the toss must take place no earlier than 30 minutes and no later than 15 minutes prior to the scheduled start of the match or, if the start of play is delayed, the revised start time.

EXAMPLE 3

In a match scheduled to start at 2.00 p.m. the toss can only take place between 1.30 p.m. and 1.45 p.m.

If the toss has not been made within this time frame the umpires must insist that it is done immediately. Any excuse, such as the captain not being available, is not acceptable. Anyone associated with the team can and must perform this duty. However, while anyone associated with the team can make the toss, any decision arising from it can only be made by a **nominated** member of the team.

The winner of the toss can elect to bat or field first and must notify his intentions to the opposing captain and the umpires no later than **10 minutes** before the start of the game. In the example above the decision can be delayed until 1.50 p.m. If the actual start time is delayed, the captain may wait until 10 minutes before the rescheduled start time to announce his decision. This allows him to take into consideration any changes to the ground or pitch conditions.

Once notified to the opposing captain, the decision cannot be changed, even if the start of play is unexpectedly delayed.

As most scoring records provide for recording which team won the toss and their decision to bat or field, the scorers should be notified as soon as possible to allow them to record the information before the start of the match.

Law 13 The follow-on

1. LEAD ON FIRST INNINGS

(a) In a two innings match of 5 days or more, the side which bats first and leads by at least 200 runs shall have the option of requiring the other side to follow their innings.

(b) The same option shall be available in two innings matches of shorter duration with the minimum required leads as follows:
(i) 150 runs in a match of 3 or 4 days;
(ii) 100 runs in a 2-day match;
(iii) 75 runs in a 1-day match.

2. NOTIFICATION

A captain shall notify the opposing captain and the umpires of his intention to take up this option. Law 10.1(e) (Insufficient time to complete rolling) shall apply.

3. FIRST DAY'S PLAY LOST

If no play takes place on the first day of a match of more than one day's duration, I above shall apply in accordance with the number of days remaining from the actual start of the match. The day on which play first commences shall count as a whole day for this purpose, irrespective of the time at which play starts.

Play will have taken place as soon as, after the call of Play, the first over has started. See Law 22.2 (Start of an over).

This Law applies in games where there are two innings per side. Under normal circumstances the four innings would be taken alternately i.e. Side A, Side B, Side A, Side B. If the requirements of this Law are met, Side A has the right to ask Side B to take their two innings consecutively, leaving themselves to bat last if necessary. The order then becomes Side A, Side B, Side B, Side A.

The follow-on is not automatic. It is the choice of the captain whose side should bat as to whether he requests the other team to bat again. He is not obliged to do so.

In order to exercise this option Side A has to have a first innings lead in excess of a 'specified figure'. Since two-innings matches can be of differing lengths – ranging from one day to five day Test matches – the specified figure depends on the actual duration of the game:

1 day game	the follow-on figure	=	75 runs or more
2 day game	the follow-on figure	=	100 runs or more
3 or 4 day game	the follow-on figure	=	150 runs or more
5 days or more	the follow-on figure	=	200 runs or more

This means that Side A must be at least this number of runs in front in order to enforce the follow-on.

EXAMPLE 1
In a 2 day game, Side A scores 135 and Side B scores 35.
Side A leads by 100 runs so can enforce the follow-on.

EXAMPLE 2
In a 2 day game, Side A scores 135 and Side B scores 36.
Side A leads by only 99 runs so cannot enforce the follow-on.

EXAMPLE 3
In a 3 day game, Side A scores 220 and Side B scores 71.
Side A leads by only 149 runs so cannot enforce the follow-on.

On the face of it, the above examples seem quite straightforward but there has to be a provision for when a match is affected by stoppages and is therefore shortened:
- The above figures apply from the first day when play takes place. Once the match has started, for the purposes of this Law only, it remains a game of that duration, irrespective of the number of days subsequently lost due to the weather conditions.

Should there be no play on the first day of a match, the duration of the match is reduced by one day. Similarly, if there is no play at all on the first two days of a match, the duration of the match is reduced by two days. Play has to actually start for this clause to apply.

- The call of Play on the first day is not enough for it to be deemed that play has taken place on that day. The opening bowler must also have commenced his run up or, if he does not have a run up, his bowling action.
- Once play takes place, any subsequent loss of a day or more's play is ignored.

EXAMPLE 4

In a 3 day match, day 1 is so wet that the players are unable to take the field at all. Play begins on day 2 – the game becomes a 2 day game.

The follow-on figure is reduced from 150 runs (the 3 day figure) to 100 runs (the 2 day figure).

EXAMPLE 5

In a 4 day match, days 1 and 2 are completely washed out and the game begins on day 3 – the game becomes a 2 day game.

The follow-on figure is reduced to 100 from the original 150.

EXAMPLE 6

In a 5 day match, days 2 and 3 are lost completely, but since play actually started on day 1 it remains a 5 day match.

The follow-on figure remains 200 runs.

EXAMPLE 7

In a 5 day match, days 1 and 4 are completely lost. The game is now a 4 day one, because only day 1 is deducted from the original match length.

The subsequent loss of day 4 is ignored and the follow-on figure therefore becomes 150 runs.

SAVING THE FOLLOW-ON

When calculating how many runs are required to save the follow-on, take the score in the first innings, subtract the follow-on figure and add 1. It is easy to forget to add the 1!

EXAMPLE 8

Side A scores 200 batting first in a 3 day match. The follow-on figure is 150.

Side B has to score 200 – 150 + 1 = 51 in order to save being asked to follow-on.

EXAMPLE 9

Side A scores 472 in a 5 day match. The follow-on figure is 200.

Side B has to score 472 – 200 + 1 = 273 in order to save being asked to follow-on.

It is very important that the batting captain is allowed time to have the pitch rolled during the 10-minute interval between innings. Therefore it is important that any decision to enforce the follow-on be made almost immediately the previous innings closes. This will give the groundstaff time to roll the pitch, if requested. Should there be insufficient time to undertake this work, the time taken to accomplish it will be taken out of playing time and will not be added back at any stage. This follows the procedures detailed in Law 10.1 regarding rolling entitlements.

In the event of a follow-on the umpires and opposing captain must be informed. It follows, therefore, that the scorers should also be promptly informed as such decisions affect their duties.

Law 14 Declaration and forfeiture

1. TIME OF DECLARATION

The captain of the batting side may declare an innings closed, when the ball is dead, at any time during a match.

2. FORFEITURE OF AN INNINGS

A captain may forfeit either of his side's innings. A forfeited innings shall be considered as a completed innings.

3. NOTIFICATION

A captain shall notify the opposing captain and the umpires of his decision to declare or to forfeit an innings. Law 10.1(e) (Insufficient time to complete rolling) shall apply.

A captain may declare his innings closed at any time provided the ball is not in play. An innings has to have started in order for it to be terminated by a declaration. If an innings has not started, an early termination is a forfeiture. A captain is permitted to forfeit either innings. Ideally, a forfeiture should be made almost immediately the previous innings closes.

Having made a decision to forfeit or declare an innings closed, the umpires and the opposing captain must be told immediately. This decision must also be conveyed to the scorers as soon as possible.

The incoming batting captain must be allowed time to have the pitch swept, rolled and re-marked during the 10-minute interval between innings. Therefore it is important that any decision to forfeit an innings or declare an innings closed be made so that there is ample time for the pitch preparation to take place before the next innings is due to start. Should there not be sufficient time in which to undertake this work then any time needed to complete it will be taken out of the playing time and will not be added back at any stage.

Both a forfeited innings and one ended by a declaration are deemed to be completed ones and any result is based on the fact that the innings in question are complete. A forfeited innings is recorded as Innings forfeited. A declared innings is recorded as Declared (for example 112 for 1 declared).

Some match regulations may prevent a captain from forfeiting an innings or declaring an innings closed. These usually apply in limited-overs matches. If such restrictions apply, it may be necessary for the umpires to make sure that both captains are aware of them.

Law 15 Intervals

1. AN INTERVAL

The following shall be classed as intervals.

(i) The period between close of play on one day and the start of the next day's play.

(ii) Intervals between innings.

(iii) Intervals for meals.

(iv) Intervals for drinks.

(v) Any other agreed interval.

All these intervals shall be considered as scheduled breaks for the purposes of Law 2.5 (Fielder absent or leaving the field).

All the above are referred to as 'scheduled intervals', that is they are specified and agreed before the toss, or provided for in match regulations. Whenever a Law specifies any of the above it means that there is an agreed break in play which everyone is entitled to. They are never counted as playing time and any calculations regarding playing matters do not take these periods of inactivity into account.

While most of the intervals listed are self-evident, the last one does require a little explanation. There may be occasions when the captains/managers request that a special interval take place – for example, a visit by a local or national dignitary. Any such interval will be counted as a scheduled one, even though it may only apply to that particular match.

2. AGREEMENT OF INTERVALS

(a) Before the toss:

(i) the hours of play shall be established;

(ii) except as in (b) below, the timing and duration of intervals for meals shall be agreed;

(iii) the timing and duration of any other interval under 1(v) above shall be agreed.

(b) In a one-day match no specific time need be agreed for the tea interval. It may be agreed instead to take this interval between the innings.

(c) Intervals for drinks may not be taken during the last hour of the match, as defined in Law 16.6 (Last hour of match – number of

overs). Subject to this limitation the captains and umpires shall agree the times for such intervals, if any, before the toss and on each subsequent day not later than 10 minutes before play is scheduled to start. See also Law 3.3 (Agreement with captains).

Unless provided for in the match regulations, prior to the toss the two captains and umpires must agree upon several issues regarding the match. Those relating to intervals are:

- the hours of play
- the timing and duration of all intervals for meals. It may not always be feasible to arrange an actual time for tea or for lunch in a one-day game as this may be taken between innings. The 'agreement' here, is that it will be taken between innings and will last for the agreed length of time.
- the timing of any other intervals
- the timing of the drinks interval. It should be noted that this clause prohibits the taking of drinks during the last hour. In order to comply with this umpires may need to advise the captains that any drinks taken must be completed before the last hour begins. If the game is of two or more days' duration, the decision whether or not to have drinks and any relevant timings are agreed before the toss on the first day and at least 10 minutes before the start of play on subsequent days.

If any or all of the above are provided for in match regulations, there may be no need to discuss them at all (although confirmation with the captains of the competition regulations on these points is often worthwhile).

3. DURATION OF INTERVALS

(a) An interval for lunch or for tea shall be of the duration agreed under 2(a) above, taken from the call of Time before the interval until the call of Play on resumption after the interval.

(b) An interval between innings shall be 10 minutes from the close of an innings to the call of Play for the start of the next innings, except as in 4, 6 and 7 below.

4. NO ALLOWANCE FOR INTERVAL BETWEEN INNINGS

In addition to the provisions of 6 and 7 below,

(a) if an innings ends when 10 minutes or less remain before the time agreed for close of play on any day, there will be no further play on that day. No change will be made to the time for the start of play on the following day on account of the 10 minutes between innings.

(b) if a captain declares an innings closed during an interruption in play of more than 10 minutes duration, no adjustment shall be made to the time for resumption of play on account of the 10 minutes between innings, which shall be considered as included in the interruption. Law 10.1(e) (Insufficient time to complete rolling) shall apply.

(c) if a captain declares an innings closed during any interval other than an interval for drinks, the interval shall be of the agreed duration and shall be considered to include the 10 minutes between innings. Law 10.1(e) (Insufficient time to complete rolling) shall apply.

These clauses deal with the duration of intervals, when they start and the provisions for the 'between innings' interval.

The lunch and tea intervals will start as soon as the umpire calls Time at the end of the session and will then be of the duration agreed prior to the toss. This means that even if the interval commences later than scheduled, the interval will still last for the agreed duration.

EXAMPLE 1
Lunch is scheduled to start at 1.30 p.m. and last until 2.10 p.m. (40 minutes). The over in progress finishes and the umpire calls Time at 1.34 p.m.
The interval of 40 minutes is then taken in full, meaning that the match restarts at 2.14 p.m.

The duration of the 'between innings' interval is provided in Law to be 10 minutes – this being the only interval to have a fixed duration. If there is a change of innings during an interval (other than a drinks interval) the 10 minutes is not added on to the interval time, but is included in that interval, with the match restarting, as normal, at the conclusion of that interval.

Drinks intervals are excluded from this provision as they are less than 10 minutes in duration. If the captain declares his innings closed during the drinks interval then the 10 minutes 'between innings' interval is taken in full.

The provisions of Law 10.1(e) should be noted here, in that no matter what time the declaration comes during an interval, the new batting captain must be allowed his right to have the pitch rolled for a maximum of 7 minutes. This is a statutory right that must not be denied him purely because the declaration has been delayed.

EXAMPLE 2
Lunch of 40 minutes is taken between 1.30 p.m and 2.10 p.m. The captain of the team batting at lunch decides, at 2.00 p.m, to declare his innings closed. The groundstaff are unavailable when the incoming batting captain asks to have the pitch rolled.
He must be permitted to exercise his right of 7 minutes' rolling. Should this mean that the resumption of play is delayed then so be it. Play will not start until the captain has had any rolling to which he is entitled. Time lost, due to this rolling, is lost to the game and is never added on to the hours of play.

5. CHANGING AGREED TIMES FOR INTERVALS

If for adverse conditions of ground, weather or light, or for any other reason, playing time is lost, the umpires and captains together may

alter the time of the lunch interval or of the tea interval. See also 6, 7 and 9(c) below.

Should adverse conditions cause a loss of play it may be desirable to change the scheduled time for an interval. Either the umpires or the captains may initiate a discussion on this and all parties must agree if the timing of an interval is to be changed. The purpose of changing the time of an interval is to ensure there is as much play as possible – everyone must be prepared to be flexible to enable the game to be played. Any changes must be conveyed to the scorers.

6. CHANGING AGREED TIME FOR LUNCH INTERVAL

(a) If an innings ends when 10 minutes or less remain before the agreed time for lunch, the interval shall be taken immediately. It shall be of the agreed length and shall be considered to include the 10 minutes between innings.

(b) If, because of adverse conditions of ground, weather or light, or in exceptional circumstances, a stoppage occurs when 10 minutes or less remain before the agreed time for lunch then, notwithstanding 5 above, the interval shall be taken immediately. It shall be of the agreed length. Play shall resume at the end of this interval or as soon after as conditions permit.

(c) If the players have occasion to leave the field for any reason when more than 10 minutes remain before the agreed time for lunch then, unless the umpires and captains together agree to alter it, lunch will be taken at the agreed time.

This clause permits an alteration in the timing of the lunch interval due to unforeseen events. It provides for occasions when the players have cause to leave the field before the scheduled time for lunch. This may occur because an innings concludes or there is an interruption of play for any reason.

If the players have cause to leave the field when 10 minutes, or less, remain before the scheduled time for the lunch interval, lunch must be taken immediately. It will last for the agreed length of time – no extra time is added on. Play will resume at the end of the interval or as soon after as conditions permit.

EXAMPLE 3

Lunch is scheduled for 1.30 p.m. to 2.10 p.m. (40 minutes). Play is suspended due to rain at 1.23 p.m.

Lunch must be taken immediately and will last for the agreed 40 minutes. Play will therefore restart at 2.03 p.m., provided that conditions allow.

If the players have cause to leave the field earlier than 10 minutes prior to the lunch interval, lunch will not, automatically, be taken immediately. In practice, of course, it would depend on how long before lunch this occurred and the captains and umpires would normally discuss the matter before making any final decisions.

EXAMPLE 4

Lunch is scheduled for 1.30 p.m to 2.10 p.m (40 minutes) and the players leave the field at
12.45 p.m. because of a light shower.

As it is feasible that play could resume fairly quickly, there would be no need to take
an early lunch. If, however, there was then a torrential downpour at 1.00 p.m., it
would be highly unlikely that play would be able to restart before the time for lunch
arrived. Under such circumstances the captains and umpires may well agree to take
an early lunch and resume play at 1.40 p.m. if conditions permit. (Umpires would be
well advised to seek the cooperation of the caterers before making any rash suggestions
since any rescheduling of lunch will depend largely on the caterers' ability to bring
forward their preparations.)

The guiding principle must be to make the best of the situation and get in as much
play as possible. Umpires and captains should at all times be flexible (within the confines of the Laws) in order to achieve this aim.

7. CHANGING AGREED TIME FOR TEA INTERVAL

(a) (i) If an innings ends when 30 minutes or less remain before the
agreed time for tea, then the interval shall be taken immediately. It
shall be of the agreed length and shall be considered to include the
10 minutes between innings.
(ii) If, when 30 minutes remain before the agreed time for tea, an
interval between innings is already in progress, play will resume at
the end of the 10 minute interval.

(b) (i) If, because of adverse conditions of ground, weather or light, or
in exceptional circumstances, a stoppage occurs when 30 minutes
or less remain before the agreed time for tea, then unless

either   there is an agreement to change the time for tea, as
permitted in 5 above

or   the captains agree to forgo the tea interval, as permitted in
10 below

the interval shall be taken immediately. The interval shall be of the
agreed length. Play shall resume at the end of this interval or as
soon after as conditions permit.
(ii) If a stoppage is already in progress when 30 minutes remain
before the time agreed for tea, 5 above will apply.

8. TEA INTERVAL – 9 WICKETS DOWN

If either 9 wickets are already down when 2 minutes remain to the
agreed time for tea

or   the 9th wicket falls within these 2 minutes or at any later
time up to and including the final ball of the over in progress
at the agreed time for tea

then notwithstanding the provisions of Law 16.5(b) (Completion of an

over) tea will not be taken until the end of the over in progress 30 minutes after the originally agreed time for tea, unless the players have cause to leave the field of play or the innings is completed earlier.

The tea interval is the most common interval in a game. Although the time for it may have been agreed prior to the toss, there are occasions when the interval will be taken at a different time:

- if an innings ends when there are 30 minutes or less remaining before the scheduled time for the tea interval then tea is taken immediately
- if there is a stoppage for any other reason and there are 30 minutes or less remaining before the scheduled time for the tea interval then either the time for tea can be changed by mutual agreement between the two captains or, in the absence of such an agreement, tea is taken immediately.

If the umpires consider that an early tea may be required they should alert the catering staff. If it is possible to bring tea forward under these circumstances then umpires must do so. For example, umpires should try to avoid waiting around while it rains, then having five minutes' play and then going off again for tea – having tea while it is raining is always the better option. If tea is taken under these circumstances, the interval remains the same length as agreed prior to the toss.

EXAMPLE 5

Tea is scheduled for 4.30 p.m. to 4.50 p.m. (20 minutes). Play is suspended at 4.10p.m.
Tea is taken immediately and lasts for the agreed 20 minutes. Play will resume at 4.30 p.m. if conditions permit.

If a 'between innings' interval is already in progress 30 minutes before the scheduled tea interval then the 10 minute interval will be completed and the new innings will start immediately. Tea must be taken at the originally agreed time.

EXAMPLE 6

Tea is scheduled for 4.30 p.m. The innings ends at 3.55 p.m. The 10 minutes change of innings takes place and the new innings must start at 4.05 p.m.
Tea will be taken as scheduled at 4.30 p.m.

If, having reached the time for the tea interval, the state of the game is such that 9 wickets are down, play will continue until one of the following happens:

- the last wicket falls
- players have to leave the field for any reason
- the over in progress 30 minutes after the original time for tea is completed.

If the 9th wicket falls when less than 2 minutes remain to the scheduled time for tea, the provisions of Law 16.5 (b) are set aside and play continues as described above.

EXAMPLE 7

Tea is scheduled for 4.30 p.m. At 4.30 p.m. there are 9 wickets down. At the end of the over

in progress at 5.00 p.m. the last pair of batsmen are still at the wicket.
Tea is taken at this point.

EXAMPLE 8

Tea is scheduled for 4.30 p.m. At 4.29 p.m. the 9th wicket falls with 2 balls of that over left to be bowled.
The new batsman must take the crease. Play must continue until either the last wicket falls, or the over in progress at 5.00 p.m. is completed, or the players have cause to leave the field.

EXAMPLE 9

Tea is scheduled for 4.30 p.m. At 4.31 p.m. the 9th wicket falls off the last ball of the over.
The new batsman must take the crease. Play must continue until either the last wicket falls, or the over in progress at 5.00 p.m. is completed, or the players have cause to leave the field.

The tea interval can be **cancelled** provided that both captains agree. This is usually done where the game has been badly affected by interruptions and more time has been spent in the pavilion than on the field. It therefore makes sense that if the weather is fine, when the time arrives for tea, that tea is cancelled and play continues. But remember: **both** captains have to agree to this in order for it to happen. The umpires have no say in this matter and, while this may not meet with their approval, the captains' wishes, so long as they do not breach the Law, take precedence.

9. INTERVALS FOR DRINKS

(a) If on any day the captains agree that there shall be intervals for drinks, the option to take such intervals shall be available to either side. Each interval shall be kept as short as possible and in any case shall not exceed 5 minutes.

(b) (i) Unless both captains agree to forgo any drinks interval, it shall be taken at the end of the over in progress when the agreed time is reached. If, however, a wicket falls within 5 minutes of the agreed time then drinks shall be taken immediately. No other variation in the timing of drinks intervals shall be permitted except as provided for in (c) below.
(ii) For the purpose of (i) above and Law 3.9(a)(ii) (Suspension of play for adverse conditions of ground, weather or light) only, the batsmen at the wicket may deputise for their captain.

(c) If an innings ends or the players have to leave the field of play for any other reason within 30 minutes of the agreed time for a drinks interval, the umpires and captains together may rearrange the timing of drinks intervals in that session.

Drinks intervals are optional intervals and are arranged at the request of **both** captains. If only one captain wishes to have drinks then there will be no drinks interval.

Any drinks interval in a one-day match, or on the first day of a match lasting two or more days, has to be arranged prior to the toss, and the timing must be conveyed to the scorers. If the game is of two or more days duration it is neither necessary nor prudent to arrange drinks for the entire match prior to the toss on the first day. Weather conditions will vary as the match progresses and the Law allows for drinks intervals to be arranged prior to each day's play – provided such agreements are completed at least 10 minutes before the start of play.

Drinks intervals should always be as short as possible and never exceed 5 minutes. Umpires should ensure that they finish their drinks as soon as possible and get the game restarted promptly.

Drinks should never be arranged so that they take place within the last hour. Any drinks interval arranged during the last session of the match should be timed to finish before the last hour is scheduled to start.

If a wicket falls within 5 minutes of the agreed time for the drinks interval, the interval should be taken immediately. To do otherwise is time-wasting – as soon as the wicket falls, the umpires should call for drinks and take them while the incoming batsman takes his place.

If an innings ends or there is a stoppage for any reason, thus causing the players to leave the field during the 30 minutes prior to the agreed time for a drinks interval, the captains and umpires can agree to rearrange or cancel the drinks interval.

In limited-overs matches, drinks are often arranged so that they are taken at the end of a particular over and therefore no specific time can be laid down. In these circumstances it would be the umpires' decision as to when drinks are taken should a wicket fall during the designated over. No hard and fast rule can be applied here but umpires should be aware that time should be used to its best advantage and that drinks should not unnecessarily delay play.

UNSCHEDULED DRINKS FOR INDIVIDUAL PLAYERS
It is often asked whether individual players should be allowed to have additional drinks during play. The answer, as far as the fielding side is concerned, is yes and no! Play should not be stopped to allow fielders to take extra drinks. However, it is perfectly acceptable for fielders to take drinks placed for them just beyond the boundary so long as play is not held up.

While it is appreciated that batsmen, too, may require an unscheduled drink during a session, especially a batsman who has been batting for a long time, it is undesirable for the game to be interrupted too often. However, medical needs should be borne in mind and the umpires should explain that they can have drinks provided that they do so quickly and do not waste time. Umpires should request that a member of their team bring the drink out at the end of the over, or at the fall of a wicket, and should ensure play is not held up for longer than is necessary. This 'common sense' approach is always best and it is rare for umpires to find anyone abusing the privilege. Although not strictly within the Law, it helps to keep the game flowing with no one becoming ill through dehydration.

If the umpires agree that these privileges are being abused, they have authority to put a stop to them.

10. AGREEMENT TO FORGO INTERVALS

At any time during the match, the captains may agree to forgo the tea interval or any of the drinks intervals. The umpires shall be informed of the decision.

Both captains can agree to forgo the tea interval or any drinks intervals during the day. One captain cannot decide to arbitrarily force this decision on his opponent. Once the decision is made, the umpires must be informed and, as soon as possible, this information must be conveyed to the scorers.

11. SCORERS TO BE INFORMED

The umpires shall ensure that the scorers are informed of all agreements about hours of play and intervals, and of any changes made thereto as permitted under this Law.

Umpires are reminded that they are under an obligation to ensure that the scorers are kept fully aware of all aspects that affect their role in the game. If there are any changes, and play continues, they should endeavour to get a message to the scorers telling them of the on-field decisions.

UMPIRES' OBLIGATIONS AND DUTIES AT INTERVALS

GENERAL POINTS ABOUT ALL INTERVALS
- umpires should make sure that they adhere to the agreed times
- they should always ensure that they are on time for each session of play
- a session of play should never start late because of some act or omission by the umpires
- players always take their lead from the umpires: if they are punctual the players will follow suit
- umpires should always let the players know when they are ready to take the field to start or restart play – this should occur 5 minutes before play begins. If there is a bell one umpire should ring it as he and his colleague leave the pavilion. If there is no bell, then the umpires should knock on the dressing-room doors and tell the players that they are going out on to the field. Alternatively, the umpires should tell each captain. The players will then have no excuse for late arrival on the field. By being proactive the umpires set a positive example and ensure play starts on time

- at the drinks interval umpires should not stand around chatting – they should finish their drinks promptly, return to their respective positions, and get play restarted with the minimum amount of delay

INTERVAL DUTIES

When an interval is taken:

- the bowler's end umpire must call Time
- the umpires must ensure the bails are removed from each wicket
- the umpire at whose end play is to resume should take possession of the match ball. This is a good practice to adopt as both umpires will then know where the ball is and at which end play is to restart.

Just because an interval has been reached it does not mean that the umpires' responsibilities are over. Even though it may be lunch, or tea, they are always 'on duty' and still have a little work to do before they can settle down with their refreshments.

Each umpire must write down:

- the time when the call of Time was made – this is essential for two reasons: i) this is the starting point for the timing of the interval; ii) any playing time lost is calculated from this moment for an unscheduled interruption
- the number of balls left in the over – this only applies when Time is called during the over in progress
- if the second point applies, the name of the bowler bowling that over and also the name of the bowler who bowled the previous over. This will ensure that, if the current bowler is unable to complete the over when play is resumed, the bowler who bowled the previous over does not bowl consecutive overs
- if the over has been completed it is only necessary to record the name of the bowler who bowled the last delivery as he is the only member of the side who cannot bowl the next over
- which end play is to restart – if the appropriate umpire has the ball this may be obvious nevertheless it does pay to make a note of it
- the identity of the batsmen and at which end they are to resume. It is not unheard of for the batsmen to resume at the wrong ends after a break but by writing it down the umpires should be in a position to ensure that it does not happen in their game.

Each individual will have their own system of recording this information. The important point is that the umpire has a written record of the above information. He should never rely upon memory – if it rains during an interval it may be some time before play resumes, and an interval may last overnight, or several days.

At all intervals when the players leave the field the umpires must:

- check/confirm with the scorers:
    the score
    the number of wickets fallen

the number of overs bowled if relevant

any awards for penalty runs

sort out any unresolved issues they may have, for example any dismissals that were not clearly understood

- advise the batting captain of any cautions/final warnings/penalty runs that have been issued either for or against his side
- supervise any sweeping, rolling and re-marking that is required. This does not mean that they have to stand over the person undertaking this work – supervision can be done from the pavilion, while the umpires are having their break. Supervision means keeping an eye on the timing of the work and the evenness of any rolling undertaken – umpires only need to get directly involved if the requirements are breached
- be ready themselves to ensure that play resumes on time. Often, when completing their duties, umpires will find they have insufficient time to enjoy refreshments without rushing – this is unfortunate but has to be accepted as part of the job. Depending on where they are officiating, umpires discover that a quiet word with catering staff will result in them being served before the players thus helping them to overcome this problem. Scorers may also find themselves subject to the same problems, and should follow this example.

UPON RESUMPTION OF PLAY

Using the information previously noted, when play resumes the umpires should be able to ensure that:

- play resumes at the correct end
- if completing an over which was interrupted prior to the interval, the correct bowler completes the over and the correct number of balls are bowled
- if a new over is due to start, a bowler who did not bowl the previous over before the interval restarts play
- the batsmen are the correct ones and
- that they are at the correct ends.

Law 16 Start of play; cessation of play

1. CALL OF PLAY

The umpire at the bowler's end shall call Play at the start of the match and on the resumption of play after any interval or interruption.

2. CALL OF TIME

The umpire at the bowler's end shall call Time on the cessation of play before any interval or interruption of play and at the conclusion of the match. See Law 27 (Appeals).

3. REMOVAL OF BAILS

After the call of Time, the bails shall be removed from both wickets.

The call of Play signifies that play is about to start or to restart. This call should be loud and clear so that all the players, and the striker's end umpire, can hear. The bowler's end umpire makes this call after he has completed all the duties laid out below.

The call of Time signifies that play has officially ended, for whatever reason, and should be made in a loud, clear voice so that it can be heard by the players and the striker's end umpire. The bowler's end umpire makes this call:

- when a session of play ends
- at the beginning of any interval (including drinks)
- when an innings ends
- when the players have cause to leave the field for any reason.

It is especially important that the striker's end umpire knows the instant that Time is called as the Law regarding appeals asserts that an appeal made after the call of Time is invalid. After that call runs cannot be scored and wickets cannot be taken. When Time has been called the bails are removed to show that play has concluded.

DUTIES OF UMPIRES LEADING TO PLAY BEING CALLED

The most important points to be made here are those which deal with the duties/actions undertaken by the umpires before Play is called, whether at the start of the match, the resumption after an interval, or the resumption after an interruption.

- 5 minutes before play the umpires will inform both teams that play is about to start. This may be done by either word of mouth or by ringing the pavilion bell.

Before play can start each umpire must:

- fit the bails in place on the stumps at his end
- ensure that his own wicket is correctly pitched
- help his colleague align his wicket. It is often easier to see from a distance whether or not a wicket is vertical and each umpire should look down the pitch at his colleague's wicket and give assistance to get that wicket vertical.

When the players arrive, the bowler's end umpire should:

- give the bowler a bowling marker
- give him the ball, if it has not already been given to another member of the fielding side. It is not unusual to give the match ball to the fielding side as soon as they come on to the field if they ask for it
- collect any items of clothing from the bowler
- at the same time enquire as to his intended delivery action
- inform the striker of the bowler's action
- give the striker his guard

- anticipate the required position of the sightscreen and ensure that any adjustments are made. The umpire may assist the screen adjustment by raising an arm into the position it would be at the point of delivery. (It would be prudent at this point for the striker's end umpire to help with the adjustment of the sightscreen at his end. This will save time at the beginning of the next over.)
- count the fielders to ensure that there are no more than eleven present – these should conform to the nominated list. The umpire is not required to conduct a roll call, confirmation should have been received from the captain prior to taking the field that his eleven nominated players are present. If there are fewer than eleven on the field, the umpire must enquire the reason and whereabouts of the absent player(s) and inform both batsmen and colleague of the situation
- ensure that the fielders are ready
- ensure that the batsmen are ready
- ensure the striker's end umpire is ready
- ensure that the correct start time has been reached
- receive acknowledgment from the scorers that they are ready – the game must not start until they are in position and ready
- call Play in a loud and clear voice.

While all this is being done and before the call of Play the striker's end umpire should be undertaking the following duties:
- if requested, give the bowler, at that end, the bowler's marker so that he can mark out his run-up
- get the sightscreen aligned (see above)
- count the number of fielders – as confirmation for his colleague
- ensure that the correct time for the start of play has been reached – as confirmation for his colleague
- be aware that his colleague will be requiring confirmation of number of players and time and be ready to signal this confirmation when requested.

DUTIES OF SCORERS

During the period up to and including the call of Play, the scorers should:
- complete all pre-match entries in the scorebooks as the players move on to the field
- when requested by the bowler's end umpire, promptly acknowledge they are ready for the game to start
- record the time at the call of Play – not the scheduled time – as the time play started. This is the time that is entered in the scoring record as the time when the opening batsmen started their innings.

4. STARTING A NEW OVER

Another over shall always be started at any time during the match, unless an interval is to be taken in the circumstances set out in 5

below, if the umpire, after walking at his normal pace, has arrived at his position behind the stumps at the bowler's end before the time agreed for the next interval, or for the close of play, has been reached.

5. COMPLETION OF AN OVER

Other than at the end of the match,

(a) if the agreed time for an interval is reached during an over, the over shall be completed before the interval is taken except as provided for in (b) below.

(b) when less than 2 minutes remain before the time agreed for the next interval, the interval will be taken immediately if

either (i) a batsman is out or retires

or (ii) the players have occasion to leave the field

whether this occurs during an over or at the end of an over. Except at the end of an innings, if an over is thus interrupted it shall be completed on resumption of play.

When the game is nearing the end of a session the fielding side often decide that if they are quick getting into their positions there will be time for another over before the interval. While admirable, this is irrelevant to whether or not another over is bowled. It is the umpire who is going to be at the bowler's end for the next over who decides this. If, **by walking at his normal pace**, he reaches his new position before time is reached then another over must be started in that session. Unless a wicket falls, the over will be completed before the interval is taken.

EXAMPLE 1

Lunch is scheduled for 1.30 p.m. The over immediately before lunch commences at 1.29 p.m. and concludes at 1.34 p.m.

Lunch will be taken at 1.34 p.m. and the timing for the duration of the interval begins at 1.34 p.m.

If he reaches his position at or after the scheduled time for that interval, Time must be called and the interval is then taken. The umpire should not hurry to his position, nor should he dawdle. He must walk in at the same pace that he has been employing throughout the session – no quicker and no slower.

If, during the last over of a session, a wicket falls or a batsman retires and less than **2 minutes** remain before the agreed time for the interval, Time will be called and the interval will begin. The incoming batsman is not required to take his place on the field of play until after the interval. Any balls remaining in the over will be bowled by the same bowler when play resumes.

EXAMPLE 2

Lunch of 40 minutes is scheduled for 1.30 p.m. A batsman is dismissed at 1.29 p.m. off the 4th ball of the over.

Lunch must be taken immediately as less than 2 minutes are available before the scheduled time of the interval – and the interval is timed from 1.29 p.m. The remaining 2 balls will be bowled by the same bowler when play resumes at 2.09 p.m.

However, if the interval in question is the tea interval then the '2 minute rule' above may not apply. If the 9th wicket falls with 2 minutes or less remaining of the session then play will continue as described under Law 15.8. Tea will not be taken until either the last wicket falls, or the over in progress 30 minutes after the scheduled time is completed, or the players have cause to leave the field whichever comes soonest.

If, during this last over of a session, the players have cause to leave the field for any reason, usually weather or bad light, then the interval is taken immediately with any remaining balls in the over being bowled by the same bowler when play resumes.

These examples apply only to the last over before an interval – provisions applicable to the last over of a match are detailed in clause 10 below.

6. LAST HOUR OF MATCH – NUMBER OF OVERS

When one hour of playing time of the match remains, according to the agreed hours of play, the over in progress shall be completed. The next over shall be the first of a minimum of 20 overs which must be bowled, provided that a result is not reached earlier and provided that there is no interval or interruption in play.

The umpire at the bowler's end shall indicate the commencement of this 20 overs to the players and the scorers. The period of play thereafter shall be referred to as the last hour, whatever its actual duration.

In any timed game the Law requires that there must be a **minimum** of 20 overs bowled in the last hour of the match. This is to prevent either side from slowing the game down and affecting how many overs can be achieved in one hour's play. By stipulating that there has to be a minimum of 20 bowled, any such delaying tactics are ineffective. In a game of two or more days, this part of the Law applies only to the last day's play, not to any other day.

Play must continue until either the required 20 overs are completed, or until the scheduled time for the close of play, whichever is the later. If more than 20 overs can be completed within the statutory hour, play continues.

When the time for the last hour is reached it may well be in the middle of an over. The umpire does not stop the game at this point to signal to the scorers, he waits until the end of the over before doing so. It is the start of the next over that signifies the start of this minimum of 20. The fact that this may well be two to three minutes after the agreed time is immaterial.

EXAMPLE 3

It has been agreed, before the toss, that the last hour will begin at 5.30 p.m. At 5.30 pm. an over is still in progress. The over ends at 5.35 p.m.

The umpire having walked in from his position at striker's end now signals 'last hour' which means that the next over signifies the first of a minimum of 20. There will now have to be at least 20 overs bowled unless a result is achieved. If the 20 overs are completed before 6.30 p.m., say 6.25 p.m., play continues until 6.30 p.m. If the 20 overs are not completed by 6.30 p.m., play must continue until they have been completed.

Scorers should ensure the scoreboard displays the overs bowled during the last hour. If they are shown counting from 1 upwards, and more than 20 are bowled, then the count can continue. If they are shown from 20 downwards then the count should stop at 0 when the minimum number have been bowled.

7. LAST HOUR OF MATCH – INTERRUPTIONS OF PLAY

If there is an interruption in play during the last hour of the match, the minimum number of overs to be bowled shall be reduced from 20 as follows.

(a) The time lost for an interruption is counted from the call of Time until the time for resumption of play as decided by the umpires.

(b) One over shall be deducted for every complete 3 minutes of time lost.

(c) In the case of more than one such interruption, the minutes lost shall not be aggregated; the calculation shall be made for each interruption separately.

(d) If, when one hour of playing time remains, an interruption is already in progress,

(i) only the time lost after this moment shall be counted in the calculation;

(ii) the over in progress at the start of the interruption shall be completed on resumption of play and shall not count as one of the minimum number of overs to be bowled.

(e) If, after the start of the last hour, an interruption occurs during an over, the over shall be completed on resumption of play. The two part-overs shall between them count as one over of the minimum number to be bowled.

Having established that a minimum of 20 overs must be bowled in the last hour, this clause details what must happen if time is lost should players be required to leave the field for an interruption. It does not matter how the time is lost during the last hour since the Law caters for all eventualities, including time lost through adverse weather conditions such as rain and bad light (dealt with in this clause) and time lost because of a change of innings (dealt with in clause 8).

If 20 overs are to be bowled in 1 hour then the average time taken to bowl an over is 3 minutes. All calculations are therefore based on this figure.

PROCEDURE WHEN ANY INTERRUPTION OCCURS

When time is lost the calculation for any time lost is based on the formula: 1 over for every **full** 3 minutes lost. Therefore:

10 minutes lost = 3 overs (the odd minute is ignored)

14 minutes lost = 4 overs (the odd 2 minutes are ignored).

When a stoppage occurs the umpires must:

• note the time

• agree the time when play will resume and calculate the number of overs lost, based on the formula above

• inform captains and scorers of the minimum number of overs that must be bowled when play resumes.

Time lost is calculated from the moment Time is called to the time that the umpires designate for play to resume. This means that even if play starts a little earlier, or later, than the designated time, the calculations remain unchanged.

EXAMPLE 4

Last hour starts at 6.30 p.m. Play is suspended at 6.50 p.m. The umpires decide that play will restart at 7.05 p.m. and inform the captains and scorers. Play actually starts at 7.08 p.m.

The minimum number of overs to be bowled remain as stated for the restart time of 7.05 p.m. – they are not adjusted to cater for the slight delay in actually getting play restarted.

The best way to explain how to deal with any stoppage for adverse conditions is to run through a few examples. Once the principles are understood all calculations should become routine. In the examples below, and wherever a part over is described, a point is used to describe that part over. It refers to the number of balls that have been bowled up to that moment, and should not be confused with a decimal. Therefore 4.5 overs means 4 overs and 5 balls NOT 4½ overs.

EXAMPLE 5

Last hour commences at 6.30 p.m. At 6.45 p.m. Time is called, because of rain, after 4 overs have been bowled. The umpires decide that play will restart at 7.00 p.m.

Overs left to bowl   20 less 4 (already bowled)   = 16

Stoppage   15 minutes   = 5 overs deducted

(deduct 1 over for every full 3 minutes lost)

Minimum number of overs left to bowl   = 11

EXAMPLE 6

Last hour commences at 6.30 p.m. At 6.45 p.m. Time is called, because of rain, after 4.4 overs have been bowled. The umpires decide that play will restart at 7.10 p.m.

Overs left to bowl   20 less 4.4 (already bowled) = 15.2

Stoppage   25 minutes   = 8 overs deducted

(deduct 1 over for every full 3 minutes lost)

Minimum number of overs left to bowl   = 7.2

In practice this will mean that when play resumes at 7.10 p.m. the over that was in progress before the interruption must be completed (2 balls) and then a further 7 overs will be bowled.

PROCEDURE WHEN SEVERAL INTERRUPTIONS OCCUR

If there are several interruptions in play then the principle behind the calculations remains the same. However, each interruption is treated as a separate entity and multiple interruptions should never be added together. The starting point for subsequent calculations is not 20 overs but the number of overs that remained in the match when play resumed after the previous interruption.

EXAMPLE 7

Last hour commences at 6.30 p.m. At 6.45 p.m. Time is called, because of rain, after 4 overs have been bowled. The umpires decide that play will restart at 7.00 p.m.

Overs left to bowl	20 less 4 (already bowled)	=	16
Stoppage	15 minutes	=	5 overs deducted
(deduct 1 over for every full 3 minutes lost)			
Minimum number of overs left to bowl		=	11

At 7.17 p.m. Time is called, because of bad light, after a further 5 overs have been bowled. The umpires decide that play will restart at 7.26 p.m.

Overs left to bowl	11 less 5 (already bowled)	=	6
Stoppage	9 minutes	=	3 overs deducted
(deduct 1 over for every full 3 minutes lost)			
Minimum number of overs left to bowl		=	3

PROCEDURE WHEN AN INTERRUPTION IS ALREADY IN PROGRESS WHEN LAST HOUR IS CALLED

If an interruption is already in progress when the last hour is due to start only the time lost within that last hour applies in any calculation.

The two examples below show what happens when the over in progress at the time of the interruption was completed (example 8) and not completed (example 9). In these circumstances the procedure that the umpires will follow is:

• inform the captains and scorers that the last hour has been reached and that overs will be deducted as from that time
• when the resumption time is established by the umpires, calculate the number of overs lost, based on the formula above
• inform captains and scorers of the minimum number of overs that must be bowled in the remainder of the match.

EXAMPLE 8

Last hour commences at 6.30 p.m. At 6.15 p.m. Time is called, because of rain, at the end of the over in progress. The umpires decide that play will restart at 7.10 p.m.

Overs left to bowl at 6:30 p.m.	20 less 0 (already bowled)	=	20
Time lost within the last hour	40 minutes	=	13 overs deducted
Minimum number of overs left to bowl		=	7

EXAMPLE 9

Last hour commences at 6.30 p.m. At 6.10 p.m. Time is called, because of bad light, after 2 balls of the over have been bowled.* The umpires decide that play will restart at 7.15 p.m.

Overs left to bowl at 6.30 p.m.   20 less 0 (already bowled) = 20

Time lost within the last hour   45 minutes   = 15 overs deducted

(deduct 1 over for every full 3 minutes lost)

Minimum number of overs left to bowl   = 5

*Because the 4 balls of the unfinished over were outside the last hour these 4 balls must be bowled when play resumes followed by the 5 overs arrived at from the calculation.

8. LAST HOUR OF MATCH – INTERVALS BETWEEN INNINGS

If an innings ends so that a new innings is to be started during the last hour of the match, the interval starts with the end of the innings and is to end 10 minutes later.

(a) If this interval is already in progress at the start of the last hour, then to determine the number of overs to be bowled in the new innings, calculations are to be made as set out in 7 above.

(b) If the innings ends after the last hour has started, two calculations are to be made, as set out in (c) and (d) below. The greater of the numbers yielded by these two calculations is to be the minimum number of overs to be bowled in the new innings.

(c) Calculation based on overs remaining.

(i) At the conclusion of the innings, the number of overs that remain to be bowled, of the minimum in the last hour, to be noted.

(ii) If this is not a whole number it is to be rounded up to the next whole number.

(iii) Three overs to be deducted from the result for the interval.

(d) Calculation based on time remaining.

(i) At the conclusion of the innings, the time remaining until the agreed time for close of play to be noted.

(ii) Ten minutes to be deducted from this time, for the interval, to determine the playing time remaining.

(iii) A calculation to be made of one over for every complete 3 minutes of the playing time remaining, plus one more over for any further part of 3 minutes remaining.

This clause deals with what happens when there is a change of innings during the last hour and how to calculate the minimum number of overs to be bowled in the next innings. The calculations necessary follow the requirements of clause 7 above with an extra calculation to be undertaken.

PROCEDURE WHEN AN INNINGS ENDS WITHIN THE LAST HOUR

When time is lost because of a change of innings, two calculations are necessary:

- one based on the number of **overs** that have already been bowled (referred to as Calculation A)
- the other based on the amount of playing **time** remaining (referred to as Calculation B)

Very often these two calculations arrive at different answers. The one producing the greater number of overs is used, the aim being to ensure the maximum amount of cricket being played. The calculations are as follows:

CALCULATION A
- note the time that the innings closed
- note the number of completed overs that have been bowled (ignore any part overs e.g. 4.4 overs becomes 4 overs)
- deduct that number from 20
- deduct 3 overs for the 10 minute interval between innings, to give you the minimum number of overs that must be bowled in the match

CALCULATION B
- note the time that the innings closed
- establish the time when play should restart
- divide the remaining playing time by 3 to work out how many overs should be bowled by using the formula **1 over = 3 minutes or part thereof** (e.g. 16 minutes = 5 overs + 1 minute = 6 overs). Umpires must always remember to add on one over for any odd minutes that remain – if they don't they will, in effect, be finishing the game early

Having done both calculations always take the higher answer of calculations A and B to be the minimum required to be bowled in the time remaining.

EXAMPLE 10
Last hour commences at 6.30 p.m. At 7.05 p.m.
Time is called when a side declares its innings closed. 13 overs have been bowled.
CALCULATION A

Overs left to bowl	20 less 13 (already bowled) =	7
10 minute interval between innings	=	3 overs deducted
Minimum number of overs left to bowl	=	4

CALCULATION B

Time remaining in last hour from close of innings	25 minutes
Interval between innings	10 minutes deducted
Remaining playing time	15 minutes
Minimum number of overs left to bowl (15 divided by 3) =	5

Calculation B gives the higher number of overs to bowl, so that is used. Therefore, in this example, a minimum of 5 overs must be bowled in the remainder of the match.

EXAMPLE 11

Last hour commences at 6.30 p.m. At 7.01 p.m. the side batting is bowled out after 9.4 overs.

CALCULATION A

Overs left to bowl	20 less 9 completed overs	= 11

(the 4 balls of the incomplete over are ignored – deduct completed overs only)

10 minute interval between innings	= 3 overs deducted
Minimum number of overs left to bowl	= 8

CALCULATION B

Time remaining in last hour from close of innings	29 minutes
Interval between innings	10 minutes deducted
Remaining playing time	19 minutes
Minimum number of overs left to bowl	
(19 divided by 3 = 6 overs plus 1 minute)	= 7

Calculation A gives the higher number of overs to be bowled, so that is used. Therefore, in this example, a minimum of 8 overs must be bowled in the remainder of the match.

EXAMPLE 12

Last hour commences at 6.30 p.m. At 6.25 p.m. the batting side declares.

In this case the time lost in the last hour, through this declaration, is only 5 minutes. Here the umpires need only make one calculation (both calculations will always arrive at the same answer.

Overs left to bowl	20 less 0 (already bowled)	= 20
Time lost in last hour	5 minutes	= 1 over deducted

(deduct 1 over for every full 3 minutes lost)

Minimum number of overs left to bowl	= 19

Demonstrating that Calculation B arrives at the same answer:

Time remaining from close of innings	65 minutes
Interval between innings	10 minutes deducted
Remaining playing time	55 minutes
Minimum number of overs left to bowl	
(55 divided by 3 = 18 overs plus 1 minute)	= 19

Whenever this particular rare scenario occurs the two calculations will always arrive at the same answer.

9. CONCLUSION OF MATCH

The match is concluded

(a) as soon as a result, as defined in sections 1, 2, 3 or 4 of Law 21 (The result), is reached.

(b) as soon as both

(i) the minimum number of overs for the last hour are completed and (ii) the agreed time for close of play is reached unless a result has been reached earlier.

(c) if, without the match being concluded either as in (a) or in (b) above, the players leave the field, either for adverse conditions of ground, weather or light, or in exceptional circumstances, and no further play is possible thereafter.

The wording of the Law is self-explanatory and needs no expansion.

10. COMPLETION OF LAST OVER OF MATCH

The over in progress at the close of play on the final day shall be completed unless

either (i) a result has been reached

or (ii) the players have occasion to leave the field. In this case there shall be no resumption of play, except in the circumstances of Law 21.9 (Mistakes in scoring), and the match shall be at an end.

This clause clarifies the situations that may arise during the over in progress at the close of play on the last day, not on any other day.

11. BOWLER UNABLE TO COMPLETE AN OVER DURING LAST HOUR OF MATCH

If, for any reason, a bowler is unable to complete an over during the last hour, Law 22.8 (Bowler incapacitated or suspended during an over) shall apply.

If a bowler is unable to complete any over during the last hour of a match, the umpires must instruct the fielding captain to assign another bowler to replace him. The replacement bowler must be a player who did not bowl in the previous over as bowlers are not, of course, permitted to bowl in consecutive overs.

Law 17 Practice on the field

1. PRACTICE ON THE FIELD

(a) There shall be no bowling or batting practice on the pitch, or on the area parallel and immediately adjacent to the pitch, at any time on any day of the match.

(b) There shall be no bowling or batting practice on any other part of the square on any day of the match, except before the start of play or after the close of play on that day. Practice before the start of play

(i) must not continue later than 30 minutes before the scheduled time or any rescheduled time for play to start on that day.

(ii) shall not be allowed if the umpires consider that, in the prevailing conditions of ground and weather, it will be detrimental to the surface of the square.

129

(c) There shall be no practice on the field of play between the call of Play and the call of Time, if the umpire considers that it could result in a waste of time. See Law 42.9 (Time wasting by the fielding side).

(d) If a player contravenes (a) or (b) above he shall not be allowed to bowl until

either   at least one hour later than the contravention

or   there has been at least 30 minutes of playing time since the contravention

whichever is sooner. If an over is in progress at the contravention, he shall not be allowed to complete that over.

The purpose of this Law is twofold: to prevent a player gaining an unfair advantage by evaluating the playing conditions of the pitch and its surrounds and to prevent time-wasting. This Law is best split into three parts in order to explain its requirements.

PRACTICE ON THE PITCH

There will be no practice on the pitch, neither batting nor bowling, at any time on any day of the match. This ban extends to the areas parallel and immediately adjacent to it. Umpires must use their judgement, but the green lines in the picture below illustrate a suitable area.

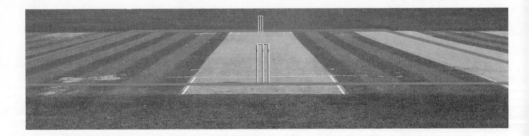

PRACTICE ON OTHER PARTS OF THE SQUARE

On all match days practice is allowed on other parts of the square but only until 30 minutes before play starts. If play is scheduled to start at 11.00 a.m., all practice on the square must cease at 10.30 a.m. Once play has started no practice is allowed on the square for the duration of that day's play, but practice can be resumed after play has ceased for the day.

Should the umpires decide that any practice is likely to be detrimental to the condition of any part of the square they must ban it completely.

CONTRAVENTION OF PRACTISING ON THE PITCH AND/OR
OTHER PARTS OF THE SQUARE

In all cases of illegal practice on the pitch itself or on parts of the square the penalty is severe. If a fielder contravenes either of the above then he is not allowed to bowl for:

- either 60 minutes after the offence has taken place
- or a period of 30 minutes' actual playing time

whichever is the sooner. The length of his suspension will be governed by whether or not play is taking place.

EXAMPLE 1

The match is due to start at 11.00 a.m. and practice should have ended at 10.30 a.m. At 10.45 a.m. the umpires notice that a player is practising on the square.

That player will not be allowed to bowl until either 11.30 a.m. (30 minutes' playing time will have elapsed) or 11.45 a.m. (one hour after the offence). If the match starts on time and there are no interruptions the player will be allowed to bowl at 11.30 a.m. If any delays or stoppages in play occur during this time, the umpires will have to recalculate the time when he can start bowling, but whatever happens he will be allowed to bowl at 11.45 a.m.

EXAMPLE 2

The match is in progress and after the first ball of the over the bowler bowls a practice delivery on the pitch adjacent to the match pitch. The time is 3.00 p.m.

The umpire will direct the captain to take the bowler off immediately. The over will be completed by another bowler, subject to the restrictions of Law 22.8. The suspended bowler will not be allowed to bowl again until either 3.30 p.m. (30 minutes' playing will have elapsed) or 4.00 p.m. (one hour after the offence). If the innings continues uninterrupted then he will be allowed to bowl at 3.30 p.m. If the innings is interrupted for any reason, the umpires will recalculate the time when he can resume bowling. However, this will not be later than 4.00 p.m.

PRACTICE ON THE REST OF THE FIELD

The umpires must also monitor any practice that takes place during the game on areas of the field other than the pitch and square. If they consider that any such practice constitutes time-wasting they are required to implement the time-wasting procedures detailed in Laws 42.9 and 42.10.

The most common form of practice occurs when a change bowler wishes to warm up by bowling a few practice deliveries to a teammate. Should he choose to practice alongside the pitch to the wicket-keeper, he is contravening the provisions of this Law and the umpire must act – he is not empowered to give consent to this form of practice. However, should any warm-up bowling be done to, say, mid-on or mid-off, this does not contravene the first two parts of this Law, practice on the pitch or square. It could, however, be regarded as time-wasting, though the umpire would be wise not to rush in and start implementing time-wasting procedures too quickly. If the captain is still setting the field or fielders are still moving into their new positions clearly no time is being wasted.

The downside of allowing the bowler a warm up is if the fielder misfields the ball and it runs towards the boundary. Even though this might waste time, if it was a mistake it would be excessive of the umpire to start issuing cautions. A prudent umpire will politely but firmly – and even perhaps with a bit of humour – inform the offenders that everyone is ready for play to continue.

The umpires must never be heavy handed nor should they act officiously. If they have cause for concern they should have a quiet word with the captain and/or players concerned requesting them to stop practising on the square, perhaps to explain the requirements of the Law and the penalties involved. By taking a pro-active approach, it is less likely that players will offend in this or in future matches.

Similarly, if such practice takes place on the square during the game a prudent umpire does not rush in and immediately start banning players. A quiet but firm word to the captain explaining what is wrong and asking him to see that it is stopped is far better than being over zealous and officious. If this informal approach is ineffective, the umpires have no option but to invoke the provisions the Law provides.

2. TRIAL RUN UP

No bowler shall have a trial run up between the call of Play and the call of Time unless the umpire is satisfied that it will not cause any waste of time.

This clause clearly states when it is permissible for a bowler to have a trial run up. It does not ban the practice altogether – all it does is to make the clear provision that no time must be wasted while the bowler is doing it.

If the batsmen and fielding side are ready to play, a trial run up should not be allowed, however, if the batsmen are not ready for play to continue then such practice may not be deemed to be time-wasting. It is for the umpires to make this distinction. If they decide that time is being wasted then they should invoke the time-wasting procedures as laid down in Law 42. Otherwise they should not intervene and allow the bowler his rights.

Law 18 Scoring runs

1. A RUN

The score shall be reckoned by runs. A run is scored
(a) so often as the batsmen, at any time while the ball is in play, have crossed and made good their ground from end to end.
(b) when a boundary is scored. See Law 19 (Boundaries).
(c) when penalty runs are awarded. See 6 below.
(d) when Lost ball is called. See Law 20 (Lost ball).

This Law deals specifically with the fundamentals of scoring runs. It is important to distinguish between runs that are scored by the batting side and runs that are awarded to either side for an offence.

Runs **scored** by the batting side are those obtained by either physically running or when the ball reaches the boundary. Runs are **awarded** for misdemeanours perpetrated by one side, causing runs to be credited to the other side, and for acts outside the control of the batting side. These would include penalty runs for No ball, Wide and 5 penalty runs and the rare occurrence of Lost ball being called.

RUNS SCORED – BY PHYSICALLY RUNNING

A run is scored when the ball is in play and the batsmen cross and make good their ground from end to end. Runs cannot be scored, by running, if the ball is not in play. The definition of when a ball comes into play is 'when the bowler starts his run up or, if he has no run up, his bowling action' – only then may runs be scored.

The phrase 'make good their ground' is detailed fully in Law 29 and states that in order for a batsman to comply with this he must have some part of his person or bat in hand grounded behind the popping crease. If it is not possible to have part of their person grounded, then the bat in hand will suffice, provided that it is grounded behind the popping crease.

RUNS SCORED – FROM A BOUNDARY

See Law 19 for further details.

RUNS AWARDED

These are instances where the batting side accrue runs due to No balls, Wides or penalty runs; or the fielding side accrue penalty runs due to the batting side transgressing the Laws. The receiving side has no control over these transgressions, they simply gain the benefit of any such runs. See clause 6 below for a summary of such penalties.

2. RUNS DISALLOWED

Notwithstanding 1 above, or any other provisions elsewhere in the Laws, the scoring of runs or awarding of penalties will be subject to any disallowance of runs provided for within the Laws that may be applicable.

This section deals with the disallowance of runs – i.e. where a run has been correctly completed, as described in clause 1 of this Law, but is not allowed by the umpire because of an infringement of another of the Laws. Runs are also not scored in some cases and the difference between these two phrases needs to be clearly understood by the umpires.

Runs are **disallowed** when:

- the injured striker, with a runner, runs himself out (Law 2.8 and Law 38.4)
- deliberate short runs occur (Law 18.5)
- Leg byes that are not legal are run (Law 26.3)

- runs are completed following a legitimate attempt to hit the ball twice without an overthrow occurring (Law 34)
- either batsman, having received the required warnings, causes damage to the pitch (Law 42.14).

  Runs are **not scored** when:
- unintentional short runs occur (Law 18.4)
- the striker is out Caught (Law 32.5)
- the striker is dismissed because he or the non-striker obstructed a catch (Law 37.3).

When runs are **disallowed** the batsmen must be returned to their original ends. When runs are **not scored** the batsmen stay at whichever end they are at when the ball becomes dead.

3. SHORT RUNS

(a) A run is short if a batsman fails to make good his ground on turning for a further run.

(b) Although a short run shortens the succeeding one, the latter if completed shall not be regarded as short. A striker taking stance in front of his popping crease may run from that point also without penalty.

When batsmen are running, each umpire must ensure that he observes each run being completed, at his end, before the next one is started.

If the batsman turns for, and attempts, a further run but has not grounded his person, or bat in hand, behind the popping crease before he sets off for that next run the original run is deemed to be incomplete. However, if he goes on to complete the subsequent run that run will count, even though it was not started from behind the popping crease.

If the striker takes guard outside the popping crease, he is permitted to start his first run from where he was receiving the delivery and that first run is not deemed short.

It is the failure to **complete** a run and the turning for a further attempt that makes it short, not the position from where it was started.

4. UNINTENTIONAL SHORT RUNS

Except in the circumstances of 5 below,

(a) if either batsman runs a short run, unless a boundary is scored the umpire concerned shall call and signal Short run as soon as the ball becomes dead and that run shall not be scored.

(b) if, after either or both batsmen run short, a boundary is scored, the umpire concerned shall disregard the short running and shall not call or signal Short run.

(c) if both batsmen run short in one and the same run, this shall be regarded as only one short run.

(d) if more than one run is short then, subject to (b) and (c) above, all runs so called shall not be scored.
If there has been more than one short run the umpire shall inform the scorers as to the number of runs scored.

In cases where the run is not correctly completed the umpire must wait until the ball is dead, then call and signal Short run. The call is for the players' benefit and the signal is to the scorers. When that signal is acknowledged, play may resume. The umpire may choose to inform the batsmen which run was short.

If both umpires call Short run, they are required to consult with each other and confirm which run(s) were short. If both umpires confirm the same run as short, only one run will be deducted from the score. If, however, they are calling different runs as short, each run that was short will be deducted. The bowler's end umpire then assumes responsibility for confirming the signal and runs scored to the scorers.

EXAMPLE 1
The batsmen run 3 and one umpire decides that the first one was short at his end. His colleague also considers that the first one was short at this end.
Deduct 1 run – 2 runs are scored.

EXAMPLE 2
The batsmen run 3 and one umpire decides that the first one was short at his end. His colleague decides that the second one was short at his end.
Deduct 2 runs – 1 run is scored.

In cases where runs have been deducted for accidental short running, the batsmen remain at the ends at which they had finished. So in Example 1, although only 2 runs have been added to the score it is the non-striker who is at the wicket-keeper's end because the batsmen had 'run' 3.

If the ball reaches the boundary then no action is taken, by the umpires, with regard to any accidental short running – the boundary allowance is scored in full.

Scorers must exercise additional care when short runs are signalled. If they have any doubt as to the number of runs to be scored or disallowed, they must seek clarification from the umpires when the players next leave the field. If, as a result of a short run, the batsmen are at the 'wrong end' of the pitch as suggested by the score, scorers may underline all entries for that delivery. When the scoring record is examined later the underlining confirms that the batsmen were at 'the wrong ends' for the number of runs scored. Margin notes may also be added.

5. DELIBERATE SHORT RUNS

(a) Notwithstanding 4 above, if either umpire considers that either or both batsmen deliberately run short at his end, the following procedure shall be adopted.

(i)   The umpire concerned shall, when the ball is dead, warn the batsmen that the practice is unfair, indicate that this is a first and final warning and inform the other umpire of what has occurred. This warning shall continue to apply throughout the innings. The umpire shall so inform each incoming batsman.

(ii)   The batsmen shall return to their original ends.

(iii) Whether a batsman is dismissed or not, the umpire at the bowler's end shall disallow all runs to the batting side from that delivery other than the penalty for a No ball or Wide, or penalties under Laws 42.5 (Deliberate distraction or obstruction of batsman) and 42.13 (Fielders damaging the pitch), if applicable.

(iv) The umpire at the bowler's end shall inform the scorers as to the number of runs scored.

(b) If there is any further instance of deliberate short running by any batsman in that innings, when the ball is dead the umpire concerned shall inform the other umpire of what has occurred and the procedure set out in (a)(ii) and (iii) above shall be repeated. Additionally, the umpire at the bowler's end shall

(i)   award 5 penalty runs to the fielding side. See Law 42.17 (Penalty runs).

(ii)   inform the scorers as to the number of runs scored.

(iii) inform the batsmen, the captain of the fielding side and, as soon as practicable, the captain of the batting side of the reason for this action.

(iv) report the occurrence, with the other umpire, to the Executive of the batting side and any Governing Body responsible for the match, who shall take such action as is considered appropriate against the captain and player or players concerned.

This part of the Law is to prevent the batsmen from unfairly manipulating who may face the next delivery from either end. Batsmen cannot benefit from **deliberately** running short in order to gain such an advantage.

If an umpire decides that any run is deliberately run short, irrespective of the reason, when the ball is dead the actions outlined in table 1 must take place. Any second or subsequent offence occurring in the same innings, by **any** member of the batting side, will attract the sanctions outlined in table 2.

It must be noted that any case(s) of deliberate short running are team offences and as such any warnings issued by the umpires are given to the whole team. It is therefore of paramount importance that each incoming batsman is appraised of the situation, and that the batting captain is informed at the next interval.

In cases of deliberate short runs, should the ball reach the boundary the requirements above prevail and the boundary is not scored. The offence of deliberately running short is not acceptable and is unfair and as such is punished even though the short run would not have altered the actual score because the ball had reached the boundary.

1. Deliberate short runs – first occurrence

As soon as the ball is dead the umpire will:

Action	Inform
• Warn **both** batsmen.	• Colleague.
• This is their **first** and **final** warning.	• Fielding captain.
• This is a team offence and applies to whole team.	• Each incoming batsman.
• **Disallow all the runs scored** by the batsmen from that delivery.	*During the next interval when players leave the field:*
• Allow the runs awarded for No ball, Wide and penalty runs.	• Batting captain.
• Ensure scorers know how many runs to record.	
• Return batsmen to their original ends.	

2. Deliberate short runs – any further occurrence in the same innings

As soon as the ball is dead the umpire will:

Action	Inform
• **Disallow all the runs scored** by the batsmen from that delivery.	• Colleague.
• Allow the runs awarded for No ball, Wide and penalty runs.	• Fielding captain.
• Award 5 penalty runs to the fielding side.	• Both batsmen at the crease.
• Ensure the scorers know how many runs to record.	• Each incoming batsman.
• Return batsmen to their original ends.	*During the next interval when players leave the field:*
	• Batting captain.
	As soon as possible, report the incident to:
	• The Executive of the fielding side.
	• The Governing body responsible for the match.

EXAMPLE 3

In a run chase at the end of the game, a team's 'star' batsman is going well but is accompanied by a less able one. The 'star' hits the last ball of the over and expects to get 3 runs, thus retaining the strike at the beginning of the next over. However, the run is tighter than he thought and so, in order to ensure that he is at the striker's end to take next delivery, he deliberately grounds his bat well short of the popping crease on the second run and races back to the other end. He is willing to concede a short run in order to reach the other end and take the first ball of the new over.

This act is unfair. When the ball is dead the umpire must follow the procedure detailed above. The batsmen fail to score the runs they completed, and the 'star' fails to gain his chosen end.

6. RUNS SCORED FOR PENALTIES

Runs shall be scored for penalties under 5 above and Laws 2.6 (Player returning without permission), 24 (No ball), 25 (Wide ball), 41.2 (Fielding the ball), 41.3 (Protective helmets belonging to the fielding side) and 42 (Fair and unfair play).

In clause 1 it states that runs are awarded for penalties. This clause summarises those Laws in breach of which penalties are awarded:

- Fielder returning to field without permission and fields the ball in play (Law 2.6)
- No ball (Law 24)
- Wide ball (Law 25)
- Illegal fielding (Law 41)
- Fielder unfairly changing the condition of the ball (Law 42.3)
- Deliberate attempt to distract striker (Law 42.4)
- Deliberate distraction or obstruction of batsman (Law 42.5)
- Time wasting by fielding side (Law 42.9)
- Batsmen wasting time (Law 42.10)
- Fielder damaging the pitch (Law 42.13)
- Batsman damaging the pitch (Law 42.14)
- Batsmen stealing a run (Law 42.16)

7. RUNS SCORED FOR BOUNDARIES

Runs shall be scored for boundary allowances under Law 19 (Boundaries).

The number of runs scored for boundaries must be confirmed prior to the toss when captains and umpires confer. In the absence of any such agreement:

- 6 runs are scored if the ball, having been struck by the bat, touches the boundary or is grounded beyond it without having pitched inside the field of play
- 4 runs are scored if the ball touches the boundary or is grounded beyond it, having first pitched within the field of play.

If an agreement for some other allowance has been made, that applies to all innings in the match. When agreed, this information must be conveyed to the scorers.

8. RUNS SCORED FOR LOST BALL

Runs shall be scored when Lost ball is called under Law 20 (Lost ball).

This is a rare event in the modern game as the ball must be lost within the pre-agreed boundaries as detailed in Law 20.

It must be noted that runs scored for Lost ball are not termed penalty runs – i.e. they are not scored in addition to any runs already scored by the batsmen. They are runs scored in lieu of runs being attempted, which cannot be completed because the fielding side cannot retrieve the ball.

The runs scored off that delivery are credited either to the striker, if hit by his bat, or to the appropriate extras.

9. BATSMAN DISMISSED

When either batsman is dismissed

(a) any penalties to either side that may be applicable shall stand but no other runs shall be scored, except as stated in 10 below.

(b) 12(a) below will apply if the method of dismissal is Caught, Handled the ball or Obstructing the field. 12(a) will also apply if a batsman is Run out, except in the circumstances of Law 2.8 (Transgression of the Laws by a batsman who has a runner) where 12(b) below will apply.

(c) the not out batsman shall return to his original end except as stated in (b) above.

10. RUNS SCORED WHEN A BATSMAN IS DISMISSED

In addition to any penalties to either side that may be applicable, if a batsman is

(a) dismissed Handled the ball, the batting side shall score the runs completed before the offence.

(b) dismissed Obstructing the field, the batting side shall score the runs completed before the offence.
If, however, the obstruction prevents a catch from being made, no runs other than penalties shall be scored.

(c) dismissed Run out, the batting side shall score the runs completed before the dismissal.
If, however, a striker with a runner is himself dismissed Run out, no runs other than penalties shall be scored. See Law 2.8 (Transgression of the Laws by a batsman who has a runner).

11. RUNS SCORED WHEN BALL BECOMES DEAD

(a) When the ball becomes dead on the fall of a wicket, runs shall be scored as laid down in 9 and 10 above.

(b) When the ball becomes dead for any reason other than the fall of a wicket, or is called dead by an umpire, unless there is specific provision otherwise in the Laws, the batting side shall be credited with

    (i)   all runs completed by the batsmen before the incident or call

and (ii) the run in progress if the batsmen have crossed at the instant of the incident or call. Note specifically, however, the provisions of Laws 34.4(c) (Runs permitted from ball lawfully struck more than once) and 42.5(b)(iv) (Deliberate distraction or obstruction of batsman).

and (iii) any penalties that are applicable.

12. BATSMAN RETURNING TO WICKET HE HAS LEFT

(a) If, while the ball is in play, the batsmen have crossed in running, neither shall return to the wicket he has left, except as in (b) below.

(b) The batsmen shall return to the wickets they originally left in the cases of, and only in the cases of

    (i)   a boundary;

    (ii) disallowance of runs for any reason;

    (iii) the dismissal of a batsman, except as in 9(b) above.

Even though a batsman may be dismissed from a No ball or Wide, the one-run penalty for bowling it will still be recorded.

The above four clauses summarise certain dismissals that occur where runs can also be scored in addition to the dismissal.

LAW 38 RUN OUT

Only the run in progress will not be scored when a batsman is run out. All **completed** runs are scored. When a batsman is run out, the last run was not completed so cannot be counted.

The only exception to this is where the batsman, who has a runner acting for him, **runs himself out** at the wicket-keeper's end. In this instance, no runs are scored, even though legitimate runs may have been completed between the runner and the non-striker.

LAW 37 OBSTRUCTING THE FIELD

Any **completed** run(s) scored before the actual obstruction are counted. It is only the run in progress at the time of the obstruction that is not scored. However, if a **deliberate** obstruction prevents a catch from being taken, the striker is dismissed, even though he may not have caused the obstruction, and no runs are scored.

LAW 32 CAUGHT

No runs at all will be scored if the striker is dismissed Caught, even though the two batsmen may have crossed and made good their ground from end to end before the catch was completed.

There are occasions when, having crossed, the batsmen **must** return to their original ends:

- when a boundary is scored
- when runs are disallowed (see clause 2 for a full list of these incidents)
- when deliberate short running occurs
- when the injured striker, with a runner, runs himself out.

There are occasions when the batsmen are **not** required to return to the end they have left:

- when the striker and non-striker cross before a catch is completed
- accidental short runs.

In all cases, when the batsmen are running each umpire must watch the actual position of the batsmen. This is so that, at any given moment, they know exactly where the batsmen are and whether or not they have crossed. This is particularly important when illegal fielding or overthrows occurs or a catch is imminent. (If the batsmen are level, they have not crossed (Law 29.2)).

In a catch situation, the bowler's end umpire must watch the fielder to ensure that the catch is correctly taken. At the same time, he must try to keep an eye on the position of the two batsmen. The striker's end umpire will, primarily, be watching the batsmen so that, once the catch has been completed, he can advise the not out batsman which end to go to.

In other cases, both umpires must know exactly where the batsmen are at the precise moment any event takes place. The runs scored and the information conveyed to the scorers are dependent on the actual position of the batsmen at that relevant moment and umpires are expected to be able to direct batsmen to the correct ends and ensure the correct number of runs is recorded.

Law 19 Boundaries

1. THE BOUNDARY OF THE FIELD OF PLAY

(a) Before the toss, the umpires shall agree the boundary of the field of play with both captains. The boundary shall if possible be marked along its whole length.
(b) The boundary shall be agreed so that no part of any sight-screen is within the field of play.
(c) An obstacle or person within the field of play shall not be regarded as a boundary unless so decided by the umpires before the toss. See Law 3.4(ii) (To inform captains and scorers).

2. DEFINING THE BOUNDARY – BOUNDARY MARKING

(a) Wherever practicable the boundary shall be marked by means of a white line or a rope laid along the ground.
(b) If the boundary is marked by a white line,
(i) the inside edge of the line shall be the boundary edge.
(ii) a flag, post or board used merely to highlight the position of a line marked on the ground must be placed outside the boundary edge and is not itself to be regarded as defining or marking the boundary. Note, however, the provisions of (c) below.
(c) If a solid object is used to mark the boundary, it must have an edge or a line to constitute the boundary edge.
(i) For a rope, which includes any similar object of curved cross

section lying on the ground, the boundary edge will be the line formed by the innermost points of the rope along its length.

(ii) For a fence, which includes any similar object in contact with the ground, but with a flat surface projecting above the ground, the boundary edge will be the base line of the fence.

(d) If the boundary edge is not defined as in (b) or (c) above, the umpires and captains must agree, before the toss, what line will be the boundary edge. Where there is no physical marker for a section of boundary, the boundary edge shall be the imaginary straight line joining the two nearest marked points of the boundary edge.

(e) If a solid object used to mark the boundary is disturbed for any reason during play, then if possible it shall be restored to its original position as soon as the ball is dead. If this is not possible, then

(i) if some part of the fence or other marker has come within the field of play, that portion is to be removed from the field of play as soon as the ball is dead.

(ii) the line where the base of the fence or marker originally stood shall define the boundary edge.

3. SCORING A BOUNDARY

(a) A boundary shall be scored and signalled by the umpire at the bowler's end whenever, while the ball is in play, in his opinion

      (i) the ball touches the boundary, or is grounded beyond the boundary.

      (ii) a fielder, with some part of his person in contact with the ball, touches the boundary or has some part of his person grounded beyond the boundary.

(b) The phrases 'touches the boundary' and 'touching the boundary' shall mean contact with

either (i) the boundary edge as defined in 2 above

or   (ii) any person or obstacle within the field of play which has been designated a boundary by the umpires before the toss.

(c) The phrase 'grounded beyond the boundary' shall mean contact with

either (i) any part of a line or a solid object marking the boundary, except its boundary edge

or   (ii) the ground outside the boundary edge

or   (iii)any object in contact with the ground outside the boundary edge.

4. RUNS ALLOWED FOR BOUNDARIES

(a) Before the toss, the umpires shall agree with both captains the runs to be allowed for boundaries. In deciding the allowances, the umpires and captains shall be guided by the prevailing custom of the ground.

(b) Unless agreed differently under (a) above, the allowances for boundaries shall be 6 runs if the ball having been struck by the bat pitches beyond the boundary, but otherwise 4 runs. These allowances shall still apply even though the ball has previously touched a fielder. See also (c) below.

(c) The ball shall be regarded as pitching beyond the boundary and 6 runs shall be scored if a fielder

(i) has any part of his person touching the boundary or grounded beyond the boundary when he catches the ball.

(ii) catches the ball and subsequently touches the boundary or grounds some part of his person beyond the boundary while carrying the ball but before completing the catch. See Law 32 (Caught).

5. RUNS SCORED

When a boundary is scored,

(a) the penalty for a No ball or a Wide, if applicable, shall stand, together with any penalties under either of Laws 18.5(b) (Deliberate short runs) or 42 (Fair and unfair play) that apply before the boundary is scored.

(b) the batting side, except in the circumstances of 6 below, shall additionally be awarded whichever is the greater of

(i) the allowance for the boundary.

(ii) the runs completed by the batsmen, together with the run in progress if they have crossed at the instant the boundary is scored.

(c) When the runs in (b)(ii) above exceed the boundary allowance, they shall replace the boundary for the purposes of Law 18.12 (Batsman returning to wicket he has left).

It is part of the umpires' pre-match duties to walk the boundary to learn how it is marked. The boundary may be marked in a variety of ways, from painted lines, ropes, fences and advertising hoardings to simple boundary boards, flags or cones. Where there is no visible line between boundary markers any line joining them is an imaginary straight one.

BOUNDARY ALLOWANCES

It is a prerequisite for the umpires to confirm the provisions of boundary allowances with the captains before the toss. In most cases the allowances are the standard 4 runs for a ball reaching the boundary (having first touched the ground or rolled along it) and 6 runs for a ball pitching on or over the boundary marking (without touching the ground before it does so).

It is worth noting here that a boundary 6 can only be scored if the ball is hit by the striker's bat and subsequently touches the boundary or is grounded beyond it without having pitched inside the field of play. If the ball is deflected off a fielder or umpire and goes over the boundary, without it making contact with the ground within the boundary, a boundary 6 is scored. It is not possible to get a boundary 6 from a Wide,

Leg bye or Bye even though the ball may reach the boundary full pitch from such a delivery. The ball must have hit the bat before a boundary 6 can be given.

OBSTACLES WITHIN THE FIELD OF PLAY

Before the toss, the umpires are required to inspect any obstacles within the boundary and decide how these are to be treated. Obstacles may range from rollers, seats and trees growing inside the boundary to spectators running on to the ground and fielding the ball – all must be dealt with and a decision made as to whether or not they are to constitute a boundary. Although it might be preferable to treat all such obstacles as boundaries, local customs should be clarified before doing so. The umpires should inform both captains of their decision.

OVERHANGING TREES

Where a tree overhangs the boundary or low-lying shrubbery encroaches on to the playing area a boundary will be scored as soon as the ball touches any part of that tree/shrubbery. The fact that it is rooted beyond the boundary means that as soon as the ball touches any part of it, it has touched an object that is beyond the boundary. The only local custom that is applicable under these circumstances is the allowance for boundaries.

Boundaries and their allowances are best explained by considering different examples.

FENCES, WALL AND ADVERTISING BOARDS

These are, essentially, items that stand upright from the ground, as opposed to lines and ropes that are laid on it. In the case of a fence, for example, the actual boundary is the point at which the fence comes into contact with the ground – shown, in the **photograph** below, by the green line. As soon as the ball touches any part of the fence a boundary is scored.

If a fielder touches the fence he is in contact with the boundary so if he is also in contact with the ball at that moment – as shown in the photograph on the left – he will have conceded a boundary. This will either be a boundary 4 or whatever allowance has been previously agreed.

In the lower photograph. the fielder is leaning against the fence. Should he catch or touch the ball he will concede 6 runs and a catch would not be allowed. Any previously agreed boundary allowance will not apply.

The allowance for the boundary depends on whether the ball has touched the ground before it reaches the boundary (4) or whether it hit the boundary on the full (6). If the ball went through the fence, on the full, and landed on the ground beyond the boundary that would also constitute a boundary 6

PAINTED LINES AND ROPES

The boundary is the **part of the line or rope that is closest to the umpires**. As soon as the ball touches any part of it a boundary is scored. The actual boundary is the inner edge of that line or rope. The width of the line or size of the rope is of no relevance.

The boundary allowance of 4 or 6 depends on whether the ball touches the ground before reaching the boundary (4) or lands on or over the boundary (6).

BOUNDARY FLAGS OR MARKERS WITH NO PAINTED LINES OR ROPE

Here, the boundary is not clearly defined by any markings so the umpires must assess where the boundary would be. In these cases, the boundary is the imaginary straight line joining the boundary markers (as indicated right). The allowances are the same as for painted lines and ropes.

SIGHTSCREENS

It is important that the umpires note where the sightscreens are in relation to the field of play. If the sightscreens are within, or partly within, the marked playing area, the umpires must ensure that the boundary at this point is re-marked so that the screens are **outside** the playing area. **Under no circumstances can the screens be inside the boundary.** The boundary must be marked so that it goes around the front of the screens thus ensuring that they are not within the boundary. When the boundary is re-marked, under these circumstances, the umpires must ensure that allowance is made for any movement of the screen(s) during the course of the match as the boundary cannot be changed during the match.

RUNS EXCEEDING BOUNDARY ALLOWANCE

It is possible, on a large field, for two batsmen to run 5 (or more) runs before the ball reaches the boundary. This is permissible, and the runs completed are scored including the run in progress provided the batsmen cross before the ball reaches the boundary. When this occurs the bowlers end umpire must:

- inform the scorers how many runs are to be recorded
- ensure the batsmen resume at the correct ends.

EXAMPLE 1

The striker hits the 2nd ball of the over along the ground and the batsmen run. Just before the ball reaches the boundary the batsmen cross on their 5th run.

The striker scores 5 runs (4 completed ones plus run in progress).
The non-striker faces next delivery.

EXAMPLE 2

The striker hits the 2nd ball of the over along the ground and the batsmen run. As the ball reaches the boundary the batsmen are on their 5th run but have not yet crossed.

The striker scores 4 runs (the 5th is not scored because they had not crossed).
The striker faces the next delivery.

6. OVERTHROW OR WILFUL ACT OF FIELDER

If the boundary results either from an overthrow or from the wilful act of a fielder the runs scored shall be

    (i) the penalty for a No ball or a Wide, if applicable, together with any penalties under either of Laws 18.5(b) (Deliberate short runs) or 42 (Fair and unfair play) that are applicable before the boundary is scored

and (ii) the allowance for the boundary

and (iii) the runs completed by the batsmen, together with the run in progress if they have crossed at the instant of the throw or act.

OVERTHROWS

Overthrows are where the fielding side, having fielded the ball, and by virtue of an inaccurate return, enable the batting side time to complete extra runs. These extra runs are scored either by the batsmen running or the ball reaching the boundary. It is only when the ball reaches the boundary that the umpires need to be in a position to calculate the number of runs to be added to the score.

BOUNDARY OVERTHROWS

The number of runs scored will be:

- the boundary **4** (for the overthrow) *plus*
- any **completed runs** that the two batsmen have made *plus*
- the **run in progress** provided that the batsmen cross before the act of the overthrow takes place, i.e. when the fielder actually throws the ball. The runs are not calculated from when the ball crosses the boundary, but from the moment the fielder releases the ball that subsequently reaches the boundary.

EXAMPLE 3

On the 5th ball of the over, the batsmen cross on their 3rd run when the fielder throws the
ball to the wicket-keeper who misses it, and the ball goes on to reach the boundary.
RUNS SCORED: 4 (boundary) + 2 (completed runs) + 1 (run in progress when the
fielder released the ball) = 7.
The non-striker faces the next delivery.

EXAMPLE 4

On the 4th ball of the over, the batsmen turn for the 3rd run when the fielder throws the ball
to the wicket-keeper who misses it and the ball goes on to reach the boundary.
RUNS SCORED: 4 (boundary) + 2 (completed runs) = 6.
The run in progress does not count because the batsmen had not crossed when the
fielder released the ball.
The striker faces the next delivery.

Note that if the batsmen are level at the instant of the throw then they are deemed
not to have crossed.

The umpires must ensure that the correct batsman faces the next delivery. It is more
than likely that, by the time the ball reaches the boundary, the batsmen will have
completed any runs they were attempting. The umpires must be aware of who was
where when the overthrow took place and direct the batsmen to the correct ends
when play resumes.

A suitable method for remembering this is for the umpire to repeat to himself something that will remind him of the position of the batsmen when the overthrow occurred.

EXAMPLE 5

The batsmen with a cap is at the bowler's end when the overthrow occurs. As soon as this
happens the umpire at that end says to himself 'cap my end' and repeats it to himself while
the ball travels to the boundary and the batsmen continue running. Once the ball is over the
boundary he will still be saying to himself 'cap my end' and will, easily, be able to ensure that
the batsmen are redirected to their correct ends i.e. batsman with cap at the bowler's end.

Umpires must always be alert to the possibility of overthrows and react accordingly –
it could happen at anytime when a fielder fields the ball; there is no warning. The
umpire must get into the habit of watching the batsmen and fielder every time there is a
run. If the umpire makes it part of his technique then he will be ready on the occasions
when it does happen.

DELIBERATE ACT OF A FIELDER

On rare occasions a fielder may deliberately kick or throw the ball over the boundary,
for some reason. It could be that he thinks, by doing this, he can reduce the number
of runs being scored by the batsmen. He cannot be further from the truth. While he
is allowed to let the ball run to the boundary under its own volition (he is under no
obligation to attempt to stop it from doing so), he must suffer the consequences of the

Law if he deliberately assists it to do so. Although this practice is not considered an act of illegal fielding invoking the provision of awarding 5 penalty runs, it is an act that attracts the awarding of:

- a boundary 4 *plus*
- any completed runs *plus*
- the run in progress if the batsmen cross before the deliberate act takes place (the same principle as overthrows).

The respective ends each batsman must assume after this act, follows the criteria for overthrows.

EXAMPLE 6

The striker hits the 2nd ball of the over towards the boundary. The batsmen cross on their 3rd run when a fielder deliberately kicks the ball over the boundary.

RUNS SCORED: 4 (boundary) + 2 (completed runs) + 1 (run in progress) = 7.

The non-striker faces the next delivery.

When an overthrow or a deliberate act occurs it may be necessary, and advisable, for the umpires to check with each other to agree on what happened and how many runs are to be recorded. Once they have agreed they must:

- inform the scorers how many runs have been scored (this may entail the closest umpire informing them verbally or by a suitable gesture)
- ensure the batsmen are at the correct ends.

Law 20 (Lost ball)

I. FIELDER TO CALL LOST BALL

If a ball in play cannot be found or recovered, any fielder may call Lost ball. The ball shall then become dead. See Law 23.1 (Ball is dead). Law 18.12(a) (Batsman returning to wicket he has left) shall apply as from the instant of the call.

2. BALL TO BE REPLACED

The umpires shall replace the ball with one which has had wear comparable with that which the previous ball had received before it was lost or became irrecoverable. See Law 5.5 (Ball lost or becoming unfit for play).

3. RUNS SCORED

(a)   The penalty for a No ball or a Wide, if applicable, shall stand, together with any penalties under either of Laws 18.5(b) (Deliberate short runs) or 42 (Fair and unfair play) that are applicable before the call of Lost ball.

(b)   The batting side shall additionally be awarded

either (i) the runs completed by the batsmen, together with the run in
progress if they have crossed at the instant of the call,

or (ii) 6 runs,

whichever is the greater.

4. HOW SCORED

If there is a one run penalty for a No ball or for a Wide, it shall be
scored as a No ball extra or as a Wide as appropriate. See Laws 24.13
(Runs resulting from a No ball – how scored) and 25.6 (Runs resulting
from a Wide – how scored). If any other penalties have been awarded
to either side, they shall be scored as penalty extras. See Law 42.17
(Penalty runs).

Runs to the batting side in 3(b) above shall be credited to the striker if
the ball has been struck by the bat, but otherwise to the total of Byes,
Leg byes, No balls or Wides as the case may be.

The term 'Lost ball' refers to the ball being lost or **irretrievable within the field of play**. A
ball which is lost outside the field of play, in undergrowth or in a neighbouring garden, is
not 'lost' under this Law, even though it cannot be retrieved. It may be that the ball is
stuck down a rabbit hole, or cannot be retrieved from a goalpost hole in the outfield.
These would constitute occasions where the call of Lost ball would be appropriate.

Only the fielding side can make the call of Lost ball. It is not for the umpires to
make any such call or even suggest that it be made. Until the call is made the ball is
still in play and the batting side can score runs. Once Lost ball is called, the ball
becomes dead and the batsmen can no longer score runs or be dismissed.

The runs scored when Lost ball has been called are calculated at the moment of
the call. The minimum to be scored is 6 runs. However, if the batsmen have run more
than 6 before Lost ball is called they will score the runs completed plus the run in
progress provided they have crossed before the call.

EXAMPLE 1

*The striker hits the ball and the batsmen complete 4 runs and turn for their 5th when Lost
ball is called.*

RUNS SCORED: 6 (the minimum).

EXAMPLE 2

*The striker hits the ball and the batsmen cross on their 7th run after which Lost ball is
called.*

RUNS SCORED: 6 (completed runs) + 1 (run in progress because they had crossed
before the call was made) = 7.

EXAMPLE 3

*The ball is missed by the striker and goes down a rabbit hole. The batsmen run 6 and are
running their 7th when Lost ball is called. They have not crossed.*

RUNS SCORED: 6 (the 7th is not counted because they had not crossed).

EXAMPLE 4

Wide ball is called and the ball goes down a goalpost hole. Lost ball is called after the batsmen have crossed on their 7th run.

RUNS SCORED: 1 (for the Wide) + 6 (completed runs) + 1 (run in progress because they had crossed before the call was made) = 8.

The runs scored are in addition to any penalty runs that may be awarded for No balls, Wides, or penalty runs. Therefore the runs in Example 4 are recorded as Wides and include the runs made by the batsmen (7) plus the 1 run penalty for the Wide delivery.

Runs are credited to the striker provided that he has hit the ball with his bat. Otherwise they are recorded under the appropriate extras. So in Examples 1 and 2 above the runs are credited to the striker as he has hit the ball. In Example 3 the runs are recorded as Byes and in Example 4 as Wides. If a No ball is called the 1 run penalty for the No ball is recorded as a No ball extra, while the runs scored are credited to the striker if he has hit the ball, or to No ball extras if he has not.

On resumption of play the batsmen resume at the ends they were nearest to when the call was made. Therefore in the above examples the striker would face the next delivery in Example 1 and 3; the non-striker would do so in Examples 2 and 4.

As with any change of ball, the replacement ball would be chosen by the umpires and would be one of comparable wear to the one which was lost. The umpires must inform the batsmen and fielding captain of their choice and neither side has any influence over this decision. It therefore follows that the umpires must make frequent inspections of the ball, thus enabling them to better choose the replacement.

If the scorers have any doubts as to how many runs are to be recorded they should not unduly delay their acknowledgements, however they should make notes and consult with the umpires when the players next leave the field. If the batsmen are at the wrong end according to the score, the scorer may underline all entries for that delivery. It is advisable for the scorers to make margin notes of the event.

Law 21 The Result

I. A WIN – TWO INNINGS MATCH

The side which has scored a total of runs in excess of that scored in the two completed innings of the opposing side shall win the match. Note also 6 below.
A forfeited innings is to count as a completed innings. See Law 14 (Declaration and forfeiture).

2. A WIN – ONE INNINGS MATCH

The side which has scored in its one innings a total of runs in excess of that scored by the opposing side in its one completed innings shall win the match. Note also 6 below.

3. UMPIRES AWARDING A MATCH

(a) A match shall be lost by a side which
either (i) concedes defeat
or   (ii) in the opinion of the umpires refuses to play
and the umpires shall award the match to the other side.

(b) If an umpire considers that an action by any player or players might constitute a refusal by either side to play then the umpires together shall ascertain the cause of the action. If they then decide together that this action does constitute a refusal to play by one side, they shall so inform the captain of that side. If the captain persists in the action the umpires shall award the match in accordance with (a)(ii) above.

(c) If action as in (b) above takes place after play has started and does not constitute a refusal to play
(i) playing time lost shall be counted from the start of the action until play recommences, subject to Law 15.5 (Changing agreed times for intervals).
(ii) the time for close of play on that day shall be extended by this length of time, subject to Law 3.9 (Suspension of play for adverse conditions of ground, weather or light).
(iii) if applicable, no overs shall be deducted during the last hour of the match solely on account of this time.

4. A TIE

The result of a match shall be a Tie when the scores are equal at the conclusion of play, but only if the side batting last has completed its innings.

5. A DRAW

A match which is concluded, as defined in Law 16.9 (Conclusion of match), without being determined in any of the ways stated in 1, 2, 3 or 4 above, shall count as a Draw.

In a **timed** match (one not limited by overs) there are six ways of expressing the result.

I) WIN FOR THE SIDE BATTING FIRST

This is where the side batting last has completed its final (or only) innings and therefore does not have the opportunity to add to its score. The result will be expressed as **a win by xxx runs** with xxx being the difference between the two sides' totals at the end of the match.

EXAMPLE 1	EXAMPLE 2
One innings match	*Two innings match*
Side A scored 160	Side A scored 150 and 300 (total 450)
Side B scored 140	Side B scored 160 and 170 (total 330)
RESULT: Side A won by 20 runs	RESULT: Side A won by 120 runs

II) WIN FOR THE SIDE BATTING LAST

This will be expressed as **a win by xx wickets** with xx being the number of wickets the side batting last have left at the time they pass the other side's total.

EXAMPLE 3	EXAMPLE 4
One innings match	*Two innings match*
Side A scored 176	Side A scored 200 and 150 for 4 declared (total 350 – see note below*)
Side B scored 178 for 3 wickets	Side B scored 225 and 127 for 7 wickets (total 352)
RESULT: Side B won by 7 wickets	RESULT: Side B won by 3 wickets

III) DRAW

This is where the side batting last does not score enough runs to exceed the total of the side batting first, but they do have some wickets in hand – that is they are not all out. In other words they have simply not had enough time to score the runs needed, nor has the bowling side had enough time to take all their wickets. The game is therefore a stalemate with neither side winning.

EXAMPLE 5	EXAMPLE 6
One innings match	*Two innings match*
Side A scored 128	Side A scored 230 for 6 declared and 130 for 2 declared (total 360 – see note below*)
Side B scored 116 for 4 wickets	Side B scored 245 and 95 for 1 (total 340)
RESULT: Match drawn	RESULT: Match drawn

IV) TIE

This is where both sides have scored exactly the same number of runs but the side batting last is all out.

EXAMPLE 7	EXAMPLE 8
One innings match	*Two innings match*
Side A scored 267	Side A scored 150 and 156 for 4 declared (total 306 – see note below*)
Side B scored 267 all out	Side B scored 175 and 131 all out (total 306)
RESULT: Tie	RESULT: Tie

*Note that for the purposes of deciding the result any declarations or forfeitures during the game have no bearing whatsoever on how the result is arrived at nor how it is recorded. A declaration simply means that the batting captain wishes, voluntarily, to bring his innings to a close, and a forfeiture that he wishes to, voluntarily, forgo taking one of his innings.

When playing a **limited-overs match** the result will generally be either i) or ii) above as the principal purpose of a limited-overs game is to produce a winner and eliminate draws. However, the method of determining the result, in the case where the scores are level at the end of the allotted overs, will depend on the competition regulations and umpires need to be aware of how the result will be determined in such a situation.

As the Laws do not deal specifically with limited overs it is not necessary to detail these various methods. Suffice to say that umpires must make themselves aware of any such regulations before the game begins.

V) UMPIRES AWARDING A MATCH

WHEN A SIDE CONCEDES DEFEAT

A captain can concede defeat at any time he wishes. The match will be awarded to the other side – no appeal is necessary.

WHEN A SIDE REFUSES TO PLAY

Here, the umpires must ensure that the captain of the side refusing to play is aware of the ramifications of his decision and that he is liable to have the match awarded against him. Careful consideration must be made before a match is awarded to the other side and before any such award is made the umpires must investigate the reasons/causes behind the incident.

If they decide that the incident amounts to a refusal to play:

- the umpires must inform the captain of the offending side and ask him to take the appropriate action to resume play
- if the incident continues – that is, he refuses to take action or his action is ineffective – then the umpires are required to award the match to the other side
- no appeal from the other side is necessary.

If, however, the umpires decide that the reason for the incident does not amount to a refusal to play:

- the umpires must calculate the time lost in the match due to the investigation (the time lost will be from the start of the incident until play is restarted)
- the time will be added to the end of the day's play and the close of play for that day only will be extended to cater for this time so added
- the time of the last hour (if applicable) will be adjusted to take into account the extension of the playing hours.

EXAMPLE 9

Last hour is scheduled to start at 5.30 p.m. During the day 5 minutes need to be added to the end of the day's play because of an incident involving a possible refusal to play.
The last hour is rescheduled to start at 5.35 p.m.

If an incident occurs during the last hour, resulting in time being lost, the time for the close of play will still be adjusted but no overs will be deducted due to the delay.

EXAMPLE 10

Last hour starts at 5.30 p.m. At 6.00 p.m., when 9 overs have been bowled, there is an incident that takes 7 minutes to clarify.
The scheduled closing time would be adjusted to 6.37 p.m. When play resumed at 6.07 p.m. there would still be a minimum of 11 overs left to bowl – no overs would be deducted for the 7 minutes that were taken up investigating the incident.

If a team declines to play or concedes the match the result is recorded in the scoring record as either 'Match conceded by' or 'Match awarded to', as applicable. In such circumstances, though not required by Law, umpires should sign the scoring record.

VI) WIN BY PENALTY RUNS

This is a very rare occasion and will only apply when the side batting last is all out.

The clause allows for the fact that during the course of the delivery in which the last wicket falls, penalty runs may need to be awarded to the batting side for something that the fielding does in contravention of a Law. In this case, the last wicket falls and the batting side is all out, but the 5 penalty runs are still awarded. If this results in the batting side overtaking the fielding side's total, they will have won the match – despite having lost all their wickets.

Since the side batting last has now won the game the result would normally be expressed as a win by xx wickets, but in this case they have no wickets left. The result is therefore expressed as a Win – by penalty runs.

EXAMPLE 11

Side A score 120. Side B is dismissed for 118, but during the delivery when the final wicket is taken the fielding side is guilty of deliberately damaging the pitch for the second time during the innings.

The 5 penalty runs for this offence are added to the batting side's total. The batting side thus scores 123 all out. The result is a win for Side B by penalty runs.

6. WINNING HIT OR EXTRAS

(a) **As soon as a result is reached, as defined in 1, 2, 3 or 4 above, the match is at an end. Nothing that happens thereafter, except as in Law 42.17(b), shall be regarded as part of it. Note also 9 below.**

(b) **The side batting last will have scored enough runs to win only if its total of runs is sufficient without including any runs completed before the dismissal of the striker by the completion of a catch or by the obstruction of a catch.**

(c) **If a boundary is scored before the batsmen have completed sufficient runs to win the match, then the whole of the boundary allowance shall be credited to the side's total and, in the case of a hit by the bat, to the striker's score.**

As soon as a result has been achieved, the match is over and no further action is relevant. This means that the umpires have to be very careful in deciding exactly when the winning run is scored.

EXAMPLE 12

2 runs are needed to win and the striker hits the ball towards the boundary.

If the batsmen complete the 2 runs before the ball reaches the boundary, the match is over and the boundary will not count. Remember that a run is not scored until it has been completed by both batsmen. If, however, the ball reaches the boundary before the batsmen complete the 2nd run, the boundary will count and the game will be over at the time the ball reaches the boundary.

EXAMPLE 13

The scores are equal and No ball or Wide ball is called.

The 1 run penalty for the No ball or Wide wins the match and the game is over. The umpire then calls Time and no further action is relevant.

EXAMPLE 14

The scores are equal and Wide ball is called. The wicket-keeper stumps the striker.

The game is over at the call of Wide ball as the 1 run penalty for bowling it is sufficient for the batting side to have won. The stumping comes after the match has been won and is irrelevant and does not count.

Should the side batting last score more runs than the fielding side then they will have won. The only proviso here is if there is a catch: even though the 'winning run' might be scored before the catch is actually taken, the catch will stand and the runs will not be scored. This is detailed in Law 32 which states that, when a catch is taken, no runs shall be scored. The same logic applies to the obstruction of a catch where the striker is dismissed.

7. STATEMENT OF RESULT

If the side batting last wins the match without losing all its wickets, the result shall be stated as a win by the number of wickets still then to fall.

If the side batting last has lost all its wickets but, as the result of an award of 5 penalty runs at the end of the match, has scored a total of runs in excess of the total scored by the opposing side, the result shall be stated as a win to that side by Penalty runs.

If the side fielding last wins the match, the result shall be stated as a win by runs.

If the match is decided by one side conceding defeat or refusing to play, the result shall be stated as Match Conceded or Match Awarded as the case may be.

This is covered under clauses 1–5 above.

8. CORRECTNESS OF RESULT

Any decision as to the correctness of the scores shall be the responsibility of the umpires. See Law 3.15 (Correctness of scores).

9. MISTAKES IN SCORING

If, after the umpires and players have left the field in the belief that the match has been concluded, the umpires discover that a mistake in scoring has occurred which affects the result, then, subject to 10 below, they shall adopt the following procedure.
(a) If, when the players leave the field, the side batting last has not completed its innings, and
either (i) the number of overs to be bowled in the last hour has not been completed,
or (ii) the agreed finishing time has not been reached,
then unless one side concedes defeat the umpires shall order play to resume.
If conditions permit, play will then continue until the prescribed number of overs has been completed and the time remaining has elapsed, unless a result is reached earlier. The number of overs

and/or the time remaining shall be taken as they were when the players left the field; no account shall be taken of the time between that moment and the resumption of play.

(b) If, when the players leave the field, the overs have been completed and time has been reached, or if the side batting last has completed its innings, the umpires shall immediately inform both captains of the necessary corrections to the scores and to the result.

While it is the scorer's duty to record the score it is the umpires' duty to satisfy themselves that the score is correct. This does not mean that the umpires have to check every entry in the scoring record, only that they must satisfy themselves that the final score is an accurate one. This is why Law 3 insists that the umpires check with the scorers at every interval to ensure that they all agree on the total score at that time. By doing this it is unlikely that a discrepancy in the score will be found at the end of the match. All discrepancies can be dealt with at the appropriate interval.

Umpires can help themselves by constantly checking the score while on the field of play. If they record the runs scored on their tally counter, any discrepancy in the score can be identified almost immediately it happens and can either be rectified there and then or a note made to check that particular event at the next interval.

It is the scorers' responsibility to record the events and the umpires must not usurp their position or, so long as the score is correct, interfere with the scoring process. Assisting the scorers whenever requested should ensure there are no problems with the result.

However, errors do occur and it is possible that, having left the field under the impression that a result has been achieved, an error is found which means that the game is not yet concluded. Should this happen there are two scenarios that come into play, both revolving around the state of the match when Time is originally called.

i) If, when Time was called, the batting side has not completed its innings and:
- the requisite number of overs have **not** been bowled or
- the scheduled time for the end of the match has **not** been reached

the umpires will advise the captains and tell them that play will resume. The players will return to the field and play will restart at the point when Time was originally called.

EXAMPLE 15

The scheduled close of play is 6 p.m. and at 5.20 p.m. a result is reached with 40 minutes' playing time left. At 5.35 p.m. an error is found in the scoring record and the umpires call upon the players to resume at 5.45 p.m.

When play resumes there are still 40 minutes' playing time left and play could continue until 6.25 p.m.

If conditions do not allow play to resume, both captains must be notified of the corrected (amended) result and that corrected result stands. The corrected result cannot subsequently be changed.

If it is possible to resume play, then unless one side concedes defeat, play will continue until either:

- a result is reached, or
- time is reached, or
- the requisite number of overs have been completed, or
- play is suspended due to ground, weather or light conditions.

Time is not deducted for the time lost while the players were off the field while the scoring record was being checked. This was an error which does not come under the interpretation and meaning of Law 16 (Last hour) and therefore no time or overs are deducted.

If either captain refuses to continue to play, the match must be awarded to the other side – as detailed above.

ii) If, when Time is called, the batting side has not completed its innings and:

- the requisite number of overs have been bowled or
- the scheduled time for the end of the match has been reached

then both captains must be notified of the corrected (amended) result and that corrected result stands. The corrected result cannot be subsequently changed.

10. RESULT NOT TO BE CHANGED

Once the umpires have agreed with the scorers the correctness of the scores at the conclusion of the match – see Laws 3.15 (Correctness of scores) and 4.2 (Correctness of scores) – the result cannot thereafter be changed.

Once the match is over and the umpires have satisfied themselves that the scores are correct, the result, as agreed by the umpires, cannot later be changed. Even if, at a later time, the scoring record is found to be inaccurate, the result has to remain as agreed by the umpires at the end of the match.

Match Authorities may decide, due to some irregularity or incident of unfair play, to award the match to the losing team, but this is different to changing a result as reported by the umpires.

While it is not a requirement of the Law it is desirable that the umpires sign the scoring record as confirmation of the result.

Law 22 The over

1. NUMBER OF BALLS

The ball shall be bowled from each wicket alternately in overs of 6 balls.

2. START OF AN OVER

An over has started when the bowler starts his run up or, if he has no run up, his delivery action for the first delivery of that over.

3. CALL OF OVER

When 6 balls have been bowled other than those which are not to count in the over and as the ball becomes dead – see Law 23 (Dead ball) – the umpire shall call Over before leaving the wicket.

4. BALLS NOT TO COUNT IN THE OVER

(a) A ball shall not count as one of the 6 balls of the over unless it is delivered, even though a batsman may be dismissed or some other incident occurs before the ball is delivered.

(b) A ball which is delivered by the bowler shall not count as one of the 6 balls of the over

(i) if it is called dead, or is to be considered dead, before the striker has had an opportunity to play it. See Law 23 (Dead ball).

(ii) if it is a No ball. See Law 24 (No ball).

(iii) if it is a Wide. See Law 25 (Wide ball).

(iv) if it is called dead in the circumstances of Law 23.3(b)(vi) (Umpire calling and signalling Dead ball).

(v) when 5 penalty runs are awarded to the batting side under any of Laws 2.6 (Player returning without permission), 41.2 (Fielding the ball), 42.4 (Deliberate attempt to distract striker) or 42.5 (Deliberate distraction or obstruction of batsman).

5. UMPIRE MISCOUNTING

If an umpire miscounts the number of balls, the over as counted by the umpire shall stand.

This Law deals, concisely, with what constitutes an over.

The over consists of 6 fair deliveries. This is now a standard throughout the world.

Overs must be bowled alternately from each wicket. Umpires must remember this when an innings spans an interval or interruption and ensure that play resumes from the correct end.

The over starts when the bowler begins his run up (or where he does not have a run up, his delivery action) for the first delivery of that over.

The umpire at the bowler's end is required to count the number of deliveries in the over and call Over when 6 fair deliveries have been bowled and he deems that the ball has become dead. The call of Over must be made loud enough for all participants to know that the ball is dead and the over completed. This is especially pertinent for the striker's end umpire who, if he does not hear the call, may well give a decision for something that happened after the call of Over.

In order for a delivery to be counted as one of the 6 balls in the over it must be delivered. However, even though a ball has been delivered it will not count as one in the over if:

- it is a No ball or a Wide
- there is an offence under any of Laws 2.6, 41.2, 42.4 and 42.5
- it becomes dead before the striker has had the opportunity to play it.

In the unfortunate event that the umpire miscounts the number of deliveries in the over, the over stands as counted. Any decision or event resulting from a seventh or subsequent delivery will stand including any runs scored or wickets taken. If Over is called before the sixth fair delivery the over is deemed complete, there being no opportunity for the additional delivery(ies) to be bowled later.

The best way to lessen the possibility of 5 or 7 ball overs is for the umpires to agree to exchange low-key signals after, say, 4 or 5 legal deliveries have been bowled.

Scorers must record the actual number of balls bowled; they must not add additional dots to make up a 6 ball over nor must they miss out dots if more than 6 balls are bowled. When adding up the number of balls bowled and received the scorer should remember to record the actual number not the number there should have been.

6. BOWLER CHANGING ENDS

A bowler shall be allowed to change ends as often as desired, provided that he does not bowl two overs, or parts thereof, consecutively in the same innings.

7. FINISHING AN OVER

(a) Other than at the end of an innings, a bowler shall finish an over in progress unless he is incapacitated, or he is suspended under any of the Laws.

(b) If for any reason, other than the end of an innings, an over is left uncompleted at the start of an interval or interruption of play, it shall be completed on resumption of play.

8. BOWLER INCAPACITATED OR SUSPENDED DURING AN OVER

If for any reason a bowler is incapacitated while running up to bowl the first ball of an over, or is incapacitated or suspended during an over, the umpire shall call and signal Dead ball. Another bowler shall complete the over from the same end, provided that he does not bowl two overs, or parts thereof, consecutively in one innings.

A bowler may bowl from whichever end his captain likes, and may change ends as many times as he wishes during the course of the innings, however, he cannot bowl two overs, or part overs, consecutively in the same innings.

Once the bowler has started an over he must complete it unless:

• he is suspended during the over for an offence under Law 42 or Law 17, or
• he is incapacitated (i.e. he is injured or becomes ill), or
• the innings concludes, or
• the match concludes.

In the case of the first two events, the over must be completed by another bowler. Any member of the fielding side may do this, provided that he did not bowl the previous over. Of course he is not permitted to bowl the next.

Although not part of the Law, it is worth noting that in **limited-overs matches** where bowlers are restricted to a predetermined number of overs, any part over bowled by a particular bowler is considered a complete one as far as his allocation for the match is concerned.

EXAMPLE 1

A bowler is injured after bowling 5 deliveries of his 5th over and another bowler who has already bowled 3 overs completes it.

The injured bowler is deemed to have bowled 5 overs, and his replacement 4. Even though in reality the replacement has only bowled 3 overs and 1 ball, the 1 ball counts as a complete over of his allocation.

This is logical because if, for example, the allocation was 9 overs per bowler, and the one ball did not count as a complete over, then our replacement bowler could go on and bowl the rest of his allocation. At the end of the innings he would have bowled 9.1 overs, which is more than the allocation allows.

If an over is left unfinished at the commencement of an interval or interruption, when play is resumed it must be completed if the same innings is being continued after the break in play. If a new innings is started after the break, the unfinished over remains unfinished and is recorded as such.

An unfinished over is recorded as the number of overs, followed by a point, followed by the number of balls. For example:

1 fair delivery bowled in the 9th over as 8.1
2 fair deliveries bowled in the 10th over as 9.2
3 fair deliveries bowled in the 27th over as 26.3
4 fair deliveries bowled in the 33rd over as 32.4
5 fair deliveries bowled in the 41st over as 40.5

It must be remembered that:

• this entry is not a true decimal
• a bowling extra No ball or Wide is not a fair delivery, therefore it is not a ball in the over
• a Wide is a ball bowled but not a delivery faced by the striker.

When a bowler is unable to complete an over for any reason, the uncompleted over must be ruled off vertically to show the end of his spell. The balls bowled to complete the over are recorded in the analysis of the player completing the over. The scorer should also record details of the event in the margin, the time it occurred and any time lost etc.

If the bowler is suspended for the rest of the innings, scorers should, in addition to the vertical line, rule a horizontal line through the remaining overs in that bowler's analysis – scorers should also record the time of the event on that line.

Law 23 Dead ball

I. BALL IS DEAD

(a) The ball becomes dead when
  (i)   it is finally settled in the hands of the wicket-keeper or the bowler.
  (ii)   a boundary is scored. See Law 19.3 (Scoring a boundary).
  (iii) a batsman is dismissed.
  (iv)   whether played or not it becomes trapped between the bat and person of a batsman or between items of his clothing or equipment.
  (v)   whether played or not it lodges in the clothing or equipment of a batsman or the clothing of an umpire.
  (vi)   it lodges in a protective helmet worn by a member of the fielding side.
  (vii) there is a contravention of either of Laws 41.2 (Fielding the ball) or 41.3 (Protective helmets belonging to the fielding side).
  (viii) there is an award of penalty runs under Law 2.6 (Player returning without permission).
  (ix)   Lost ball is called. See Law 20 (Lost ball).
  (x)   the umpire calls Over or Time.
(b) The ball shall be considered to be dead when it is clear to the umpire at the bowler's end that the fielding side and both batsmen at the wicket have ceased to regard it as in play.

2. BALL FINALLY SETTLED

Whether the ball is finally settled or not is a matter for the umpire alone to decide.

What does the term Dead ball actually mean? In cricket there are periods of the game when the ball is in play, when the action takes place – batsmen can score runs and the fielding side can take wickets. The reverse of this is when the ball is not in play, when the batsmen cannot score runs nor the fielding side take wickets – this is referred to as the ball being Dead. The sequence of events for every delivery in the match therefore becomes:

• ball comes into play

- action takes place
- ball becomes dead.

Players, umpires and scorers should know how and when the ball becomes dead during a match and to be able to distinguish between:

- when the ball becomes dead **automatically** i.e. the umpire does not have to take any action in order for it to be dead and
- when it is not dead until the umpire **calls and signals** it so.

Once the ball is dead any action that has occurred during that delivery ceases and from that moment onwards the batting side cannot score runs and the fielding side cannot take wickets.

This Law simply lists the occasions when the ball becomes automatically dead and when an umpire has to call it so. Although some incidents are fairly straightforward, others require explanation.

The ball is **automatically** dead when:

I) IT IS FINALLY SETTLED IN THE HANDS OF THE WICKET-KEEPER OR BOWLER

This is probably the only clause where there is no consistent defining moment when the ball actually becomes dead. Whether or not the ball has 'finally settled' is a subjective decision made by the umpire and will differ according to circumstances.

EXAMPLE 1

The ball is thrown in to the wicket-keeper with the batsmen safely in their ground, showing no interest in the ball or attempting to run.

Here the umpire's decision is relatively simple: soon after the ball has been safely gathered by the wicket-keeper the umpire will deem it to be dead.

EXAMPLE 2

The wicket-keeper is standing back to a fast bowler and the striker is taking guard outside his crease. The striker misses the ball and it goes through to the wicket-keeper and the striker stays out of his ground.

Until the striker moves back to the safety of his ground, or until the wicket-keeper disposes of the ball, the ball remains in play. Here, the ball is still in play, even though nothing seems to be happening, for a second or two. The umpire must wait to see what happens before he deems the ball to be dead.

These examples only deal with the wicket-keeper but the same principle applies when the ball is returned to the bowler.

II) THE UMPIRE AND BOTH SIDES HAVE CEASED TO REGARD IT AS IN PLAY

There are occasions when both sides cease to regard the ball as in play. This often happens when the ball is fielded, say, in the covers. It is not returned to the wicket-keeper but is passed round the field on its way back to the bowler. Once the umpire judges that **both** sides have considered that no further action will be attempted from that delivery the ball will be dead. Should one of the fielders miss the ball thrown to him the batsmen cannot run for the mis-field. If the batsmen attempt a run, since the ball is already dead, no runs can be scored nor wickets taken and the batsmen will be returned to their original ends.

III) A BOUNDARY IS SCORED

When the ball reaches the boundary no further action is possible.

IV) A BATSMAN IS DISMISSED, i.e. A WICKET FALLS

From any one delivery the fielding side can dismiss only one batsman.

EXAMPLE 3

The fielding side cannot run out a batsman at one end and then throw the ball down to the other end and run out the other batsman. As soon as the wicket has fallen the ball is dead and no further action from that delivery is possible.

V) IT IS TRAPPED BETWEEN THE BAT AND PERSON OF THE BATSMAN OR BETWEEN ITEMS OF HIS CLOTHING OR EQUIPMENT

See vi) below.

VI) IT LODGES IN A BATSMAN'S CLOTHING/EQUIPMENT OR THE CLOTHING OF AN UMPIRE

Trapped/lodges – batsman

These two situations are very similar and relate to the ball being trapped or lodged somewhere about the batsman's person or equipment, such as when the ball:

- drops into the top of the batsman's pad
- gets trapped between his gloves and pads
- lodges in his helmet.

The ball is dead as soon as it becomes lodged and there is no need for the batsman to take any action to release it. Should he wish to pick the ball out of his equipment and give it to the fielding side then he may do so and will not be penalised. Similarly, if the ball is trapped between his equipment and person it will be dead as soon as the entrapment occurs. This may be for only a moment but once the umpire considers that it has been trapped the ball is no longer in play. (If the ball is deflected off a batsman, his equipment or helmet, the deflection does not, in itself, make the ball dead. It is still in play at that moment but may later become dead through some other action.)

Lodges – umpire

Note the word 'lodge'. The ball must actually lodge in the clothing of an umpire in order for it to become dead. If the ball merely hits an umpire, without causing serious injury, the ball remains in play – it is not dead.

*VII) IT **LODGES** IN THE FIELDER'S HELMET (WHILE BEING WORN)*

The ball must actually lodge in the helmet worn by a fielder. It may only last a moment but that is sufficient for the ball to become automatically dead. (If the ball is deflected off a helmet being worn by the fielder it remains in play. However, the striker cannot be out Caught from the delivery. Neither can he be Run out should the ball rebound directly on to the wicket. These two points are dealt with fully under Laws 32 and 38 respectively.)

VIII) ANY FORM OF ILLEGAL FIELDING TAKES PLACE

Should the ball be illegally fielded it becomes automatically dead. Although not required to do so in Law, a prudent umpire may also call and signal Dead ball as soon as the offence occurs. This ensures the players know that the ball is dead and, as such, all action ceases.

IX) PENALTY RUNS ARE AWARDED FOR A PLAYER RETURNING TO THE FIELD, WITHOUT PERMISSION, AND FIELDING A BALL IN PLAY

This is dealt with more comprehensively under Law 2. Suffice to say, at this point, that once he comes into contact with the ball in play it becomes dead.

X) LOST BALL IS CALLED

If Lost ball is called the ball becomes automatically dead. This rare provision is detailed in Law 20.

XI) THE UMPIRE CALLS OVER OR TIME

It is essential that all participants hear the calls of Over and Time. When either of these calls is made the ball becomes automatically dead.

3. UMPIRE CALLING AND SIGNALLING DEAD BALL

(a) When the ball has become dead under I above, the bowler's end umpire may call Dead ball, if it is necessary to inform the players.

(b) Either umpire shall call and signal Dead ball when

(i) he intervenes in a case of unfair play.

(ii) a serious injury to a player or umpire occurs.

(iii) he leaves his normal position for consultation.

(iv) one or both bails fall from the striker's wicket before he has the opportunity of playing the ball.

(v) he is satisfied that for an adequate reason the striker is not ready for the delivery of the ball and, if the ball is delivered, makes no attempt to play it.

(vi) the striker is distracted by any noise or movement or in any other way while he is preparing to receive or receiving a delivery. This shall apply whether the source of the distraction is within the game or outside it. Note, however, the provisions of Law 42.4

(Deliberate attempt to distract the striker).

The ball shall not count as one of the over.

(vii) the bowler drops the ball accidentally before delivery.

(viii) the ball does not leave the bowler's hand for any reason other than an attempt to run out the non-striker before entering his delivery stride. See Law 42.15 (Bowler attempting to run out non-striker before delivery).

(ix) he is required to do so under any of the Laws.

On occasions, an umpire is required to intervene and stop play. When doing so he must call and signal Dead ball. On most occasions it is the bowler's end umpire who does this but sometimes the striker's end umpire will make the call.

Either umpire shall call and signal Dead ball when:

I) HE WISHES TO INTERVENE DUE TO ANY ACT OF UNFAIR PLAY

Although covered fully under the relevant Laws, an example would be the obstruction of a batsman when running.

*II) THERE IS A **SERIOUS** INJURY TO A PLAYER OR UMPIRE*

Serious injury to a player

Often, it is not easy to decide what is serious in the split second in which an injury occurs. If, in the umpire's judgement, the injury is serious then attention must be given to the player concerned as soon as possible and Dead ball must be called. However, before doing so the umpire must take stock of what is going on around him, and where the ball is.

EXAMPLE 4

The ball has been hit into the outfield and the fielder, in attempting to stop it, falls and is in obvious pain through a serious injury.

Before calling Dead ball, the umpire should look to see if the ball is continuing towards the boundary. If it is and it will reach the boundary almost immediately, he would not call Dead ball as once the ball crosses the boundary it is going to be dead anyway. By delaying the call he will neither be depriving the batting side of a boundary nor unnecessarily delaying getting attention to the stricken fielder.

EXAMPLE 5

The same scenario as above except this time the ball stops and there is no other fielder close enough to field it.

In this case a delayed call of Dead ball may well affect the well-being of the stricken fielder so the umpire must step in without delay and stop the game.

EXAMPLE 6

In trying to hook the ball the striker only succeeds in getting a top edge and the ball hits him full in the face. As he yells in pain and sinks to the ground outside his ground a fielder runs in to attempt a run out.

The umpire should immediately call Dead ball to save the batsman from being run out, and also to get first aid to him quickly.

Serious injury to an umpire

The umpire is there to adjudicate on affairs and if he is injured to such an extent that he cannot perform this duty then his colleague should immediately call and signal Dead ball in order to get attention to him as soon as possible.

III) THE UMPIRE(S) LEAVE THEIR POSITIONS TO CONSULT

Most consultation between umpires can be achieved by the use of discreet signals. However, there are occasions when they do need to discuss an incident before arriving at a decision. At these times it is important that the ball is dead while they hold their discussion. If, when they wish to leave their positions, the ball is in play one of them must call and signal Dead ball to ensure that no action takes place while their discussion is taking place. If, when they wish to leave their positions, the ball is already dead a call of Dead ball announces the fact that something unusual is about to happen.

IV) ONE OR BOTH BAILS FALL FROM THE STRIKER'S WICKET BEFORE THE STRIKER RECEIVES THE BALL

The umpire is only required to call and signal Dead ball if a bail falls from the striker's wicket, not if it falls from the non-striker's wicket. If the bowler knocks the bails off the non-striker's wicket as he delivers the ball play continues and Dead ball is not called. Any fielder may replace the bails, however the umpire will only do so when the ball becomes dead.

The striker's wicket must be intact for the duration of the delivery and if the bails are blown off prior to the striker receiving the ball either umpire must step in and stop the game by calling and signalling Dead ball. The striker's end umpire must then replace the bails.

V) THE STRIKER IS NOT READY TO RECEIVE THE DELIVERY

The striker may indicate that he is not ready to receive the delivery and step away from his wicket. Provided that the umpire is satisfied that the reason for doing this is acceptable then he will call and signal Dead ball. If, having stepped back, or signified that he is not ready to receive the delivery, the striker then attempts to play the ball, he negates his initial action and is deemed to have accepted the delivery.

VI) THE STRIKER IS DISTRACTED BY NOISE/MOVEMENT WHILE PREPARING TO RECEIVE THE DELIVERY

Similar to the previous example, this provides for noises or movement that distract the striker. This distraction is not limited to events within the game itself but can also come from outside it, such as when people are walking behind the bowler's arm.

VII) THE BOWLER ACCIDENTALLY DROPS THE BALL DURING HIS RUN UP

As the ball has come into play, if the bowler drops it either umpire must call and signal Dead ball.

VIII) THE BALL DOES NOT LEAVE THE BOWLER'S HAND (EXCEPT WHEN ATTEMPTING TO RUN OUT THE NON-STRIKER SEE LAW 42.15)

Once the ball comes into play the bowler would, normally, be expected to deliver it to the striker. However, there are two unusual scenarios that have to be considered:

- If the bowler attempts to run out the non-striker, before reaching his delivery stride, he may do so by holding on to the ball and breaking the wicket. Although the ball has not left his hand the umpire would not call and signal Dead ball at that point in time. The bowler is allowed to attempt the run out and the umpire will allow the attempt to be made. Dead ball will be called if the attempt fails.
- If the bowler makes no attempt to run out the non-striker but does not release the ball the umpire will call and signal Dead ball immediately. This usually happens when the bowler has misjudged his run up and either stops in mid run up or runs through the popping crease without releasing the ball. The umpire would call and signal Dead ball in these or similar circumstances.

IX) WHEN HE IS REQUIRED TO DO SO UNDER ANY OF THE LAWS

There are several times when the Laws state that the umpire must intervene and call and signal Dead ball. This must be done where stipulated.

4. BALL CEASES TO BE DEAD

The ball ceases to be dead – that is, it comes into play – when the bowler starts his run up or, if he has no run up, his bowling action.

This definition is used in several Laws and is of particular relevance to all umpires. If a bowler does not have a run up then his bowling action starts with the first movement of his feet or arm which signifies that he is about to bowl.

5. ACTION ON CALL OF DEAD BALL

(a) A ball is not to count as one of the over if it becomes dead or is to be considered dead before the striker has had an opportunity to play it.

(b) If the ball becomes dead or is to be considered dead after the striker has had an opportunity to play the ball, except in the circumstances of 3(vi) above and Law 42.4 (Deliberate attempt to distract striker), no additional delivery shall be allowed unless No ball or Wide has been called.

In cases where the umpire has called and signalled Dead ball, the answers to:

- whether or not the delivery is counted as one in the over, and
- whether or not the striker has received the ball

will depend on when the call was made. If the call was made **prior** to the striker receiving the ball, it will not count as a ball bowled or received. The scorers may or may not need to make an entry in the scoring record. If, however, the call is made **after** the striker has received the ball, the delivery will count as one in the over. This always presupposes that it was not a No ball or a Wide, when, as detailed in Laws 24 and 25, another ball will be allowed in the over because of the illegality of such deliveries.

Law 24 No ball

1. MODE OF DELIVERY

(a) The umpire shall ascertain whether the bowler intends to bowl right handed or left handed, over or round the wicket, and shall so inform the striker.
It is unfair if the bowler fails to notify the umpire of a change in his mode of delivery. In this case, the umpire shall call and signal No ball.
(b) Underarm bowling shall not be permitted except by special agreement before the match.

The striker has the right to know where the ball is to be delivered from; if the bowler is right-handed or left-handed; if over the wicket or round the wicket. This is called the **mode of delivery**.

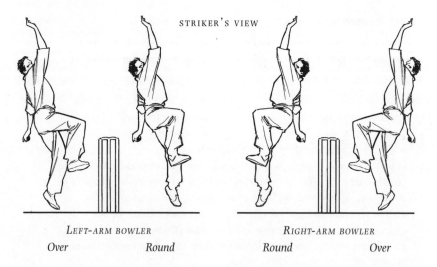

STRIKER'S VIEW

| *LEFT-ARM BOWLER* | | *RIGHT-ARM BOWLER* | |
| *Over* | *Round* | *Round* | *Over* |

When a bowler comes on to bowl the umpire must find out what his intended mode of delivery is and inform the striker. If the bowler subsequently wishes to change this mode of delivery he is quite entitled to do so and may do so as often as he likes. However, each time he changes he must inform the umpire who will pass the information on to the batsmen. If the bowler changes his mode of delivery without prior warning to the umpire, the umpire must call and signal No ball as soon as the ball is delivered. It is important that the umpire and bowler realise their responsibilities:

- It is the **umpire's responsibility** to ascertain a bowler's mode of delivery when the bowler starts his spell
- It is the **bowler's responsibility** to tell the umpire if he wishes to change his mode of delivery during that spell

When there are right- and left-handed batsmen at the wicket, the bowler needs to inform each batsman only once of his intended bowling action. Provided that the bowler does not change his mode of delivery to the batsman concerned, the umpire does not need to keep calling the change of action each time the batsmen change ends.

Having stated that he will bowl right arm over the wicket the question arises as to how far across the front of the wicket the bowler is allowed to run before delivering the ball. It would be possible for a bowler to run up to the correct side of the wicket (e.g. to the umpire's left) and, once past the wicket, cut in front of the stumps and bowl from, effectively, round the wicket.

It is permitted for the bowler to deliver the ball when his feet are at any point between the return crease and the wicket. It is unfair if the bowler delivers the ball when his front foot is markedly further across the line of the wicket than this. It is for the umpire to judge what is 'markedly further'.

Underarm bowling is not permitted in any grade of cricket except by special agreement made before the match. While some junior grades may permit underarm bowling, the Law is clear and concise. Should a bowler inform the umpire that he proposes to bowl underarm, he must be advised that this is contrary to Law and is not permitted; and that any underarm delivery will attract the call and signal of No ball. In addition to the No ball, the incident would be reported to the captain and, because the bowler had failed to comply with the instructions of an umpire, the appropriate action, as laid down in Law 42.18, would be taken.

2. FAIR DELIVERY – THE ARM

For a delivery to be fair in respect of the arm the ball must not be thrown. See 3 below.

Although it is the primary responsibility of the striker's end umpire to ensure the fairness of a delivery in this respect, there is nothing in this Law to debar the bowler's end umpire from calling and signalling No ball if he considers that the ball has been thrown.

(a) If, in the opinion of either umpire, the ball has been thrown, he shall

(i) call and signal No ball.

(ii) caution the bowler, when the ball is dead. This caution shall apply throughout the innings.

(iii) inform the other umpire, the batsmen at the wicket, the captain of the fielding side and, as soon as practicable, the captain of the batting side of what has occurred.

(b) If either umpire considers that after such caution a further delivery by the same bowler in that innings is thrown, the umpire concerned shall repeat the procedure set out in (a) above, indicating to the bowler that this is a final warning. This warning shall also apply throughout the innings.

(c) If either umpire considers that a further delivery by the same bowler in that innings is thrown,

(i)   the umpire concerned shall call and signal No ball. When the ball is dead he shall inform the other umpire, the batsmen at the wicket and, as soon as practicable, the captain of the batting side of what has occurred.

(ii) the umpire at the bowler's end shall direct the captain of the fielding side to take the bowler off forthwith. The over shall be completed by another bowler, who shall neither have bowled the previous over nor be allowed to bowl the next over.

The bowler thus taken off shall not bowl again in that innings.

(iii) the umpires together shall report the occurrence as soon as possible to the Executive of the fielding side and any Governing Body responsible for the match, who shall take such action as is considered appropriate against the captain and bowler concerned.

This clause details the action to be taken by either umpire should they decide that a bowler has thrown the ball as opposed to bowling it. The definition of a throw is dealt with under clause 3 of this Law. Although either umpire can take the following action, in practice it is likely to be the striker's end umpire who has the best opportunity to watch the arm action as the ball is delivered.

If either umpire considers that the ball has been thrown, the following will take place:

Fair delivery – the arm

On the FIRST occurrence of a throw either umpire will:	
Action	Inform
• Call and signal no ball.	• Colleague.
• **Caution** the bowler.	• Batsmen at the crease.
• This caution applies throughout the innings.	• Fielding captain.
	During the next interval when players leave the field:
• It applies whichever end the bowler bowls from.	• Batting captain.

If there is a further occurrence of a throw by the same bowler in the same innings, the following will take place:

Fair delivery – the arm

On the SECOND occurrence of a throw, by same bowler, either umpire will:	
Action	Inform
• Call and signal No ball.	• Colleague.
• Issue bowler with his **Final Warning.**	• Batsmen at the crease.
• This final warning applies throughout the innings.	• Fielding captain.
	During the next interval when players leave the field:
• It applies whichever end the bowler bowls from.	• Batting captain.

Should there be occasion for either umpire to act again on this matter in the same innings then the following will take place:

Fair delivery – the arm

On the THIRD occurrence of a throw, by same bowler, either umpire will:	
Action	Inform
• Call and signal No ball	• Colleague
• Tell the captain that the bowler is **barred from bowling** with immediate effect.	• Batsmen at the crease
	During the next interval when players leave the field:
• Bowler concerned cannot bowl again in that innings.	• Batting captain.
	As soon as possible, report the incident to:
• If applicable, complete over with another bowler.	• The Executive of the fielding side.
	• The Governing body responsible for the match.

3. DEFINITION OF FAIR DELIVERY – THE ARM

A ball is fairly delivered in respect of the arm if, once the bowler's arm has reached the level of the shoulder in the delivery swing, the elbow joint is not straightened partially or completely from that point until the ball has left the hand.

This definition shall not debar a bowler from flexing or rotating the wrist in the delivery swing.

This clause defines a fair delivery. It does not define an unfair delivery. If a delivery fails to meet these criteria it is unfair, and the umpire must call and signal No ball. The time frame for judging the fairness starts as the arm reaches shoulder height in the delivery swing and continues until the ball is released.

• During this part of the delivery swing the elbow joint must not straighten either partially or to its full extent. The arm may be bent at the elbow and may remain bent to that same degree throughout the delivery and that will be fair. However, any change in the angle of the elbow joint that causes the arm to become straighter is not acceptable and will constitute an unfair delivery action.

- For the umpire to be satisfied that the ball has been thrown he must be satisfied that the angle of the elbow has changed during the delivery swing in such a way as to straighten the arm, partially or completely.
- The wrist may be flexed during the delivery swing and this is not unfair. Movement in the wrist can often suggest that the ball is being thrown and umpires must take care in distinguishing between the unfair and fair movements.

The bowler's end umpire will be watching the feet for their placement and so it is generally the striker's end umpire who will watch the bowler's action. This is an occasion when the umpire may move from the leg side to the off side to obtain a better view of the arm. It is sometimes easier for the bowler's end umpire to determine if an action is unfair. Providing the umpire is satisfied with the placing of the feet he may observe the bowling action and is within his rights to take action should he decide that the action is indeed unfair.

Umpires must never shirk from taking action under this Law. It is particularly important in junior cricket as the early identification of problems can assist in corrective action being taken.

4. BOWLER THROWING TOWARDS STRIKER'S END BEFORE DELIVERY

If the bowler throws the ball towards the striker's end before entering his delivery stride, either umpire shall call and signal No ball. See Law 42.16 (Batsmen stealing a run). However, the procedure stated in 2 above of caution, informing, final warning, action against the bowler and reporting shall not apply.

This may be attempted because the striker is a long way out of his ground, or is giving the bowler 'the charge', and the bowler thinks he stands a chance of a run out by throwing the ball at the striker's wicket. However, the umpire is not required to guess the reason for the throw. Provided that the ball is thrown **before the bowler enters his delivery stride** then it is permitted and, apart from the 1 run penalty for the No ball, no action will be taken against him.

As soon as he throws the ball, in his attempt, either umpire will call and signal No ball – for an illegal arm action, a throw. The striker is quite at liberty to hit the ball and if he does then it will be treated exactly the same way as any other No ball that he receives during the course of the game. If he misses the ball and it hits his wicket he will be run out.

EXAMPLE 1
The bowler has not entered his delivery stride and throws the ball towards the striker's wicket (No ball).
The ball hits the wicket direct.

Striker is out of his ground (the reason is immaterial).
The striker is **not out** – Bowled (it was a No ball).
The striker is **out** – Run out (striker is out of his ground).

EXAMPLE 2
The bowler has not entered his delivery stride and throws the ball towards the striker's wicket (No ball).
Striker is out of his ground but not attempting a run.
Wicket-keeper takes ball and fairly breaks the wicket.
Striker is **not out** – Stumped (it was a No ball).
Striker is **not out** – Run out (from a No ball, the wicket-keeper, acting alone, cannot run out striker if he is not attempting a run).

EXAMPLE 3
The bowler has not entered his delivery stride and throws the ball towards the striker's wicket (No ball).
Striker is out of his ground attempting a run.
Wicket-keeper takes ball and fairly breaks the wicket.
Striker is **not out** – Stumped (it was a No ball).
Striker is **out** – Run out (from a No ball, the wicket-keeper, acting alone, can run out striker, provided the striker is running).

To summarise these three examples:
- a direct run out of the striker, by the bowler, is only possible if he has not entered his delivery stride
- if the bowler throws the ball to the wicket-keeper a run out will only be possible if a run is being attempted.

Lastly, even though it was a throw, the disciplinary procedures, as detailed above, are not enforced.

5. FAIR DELIVERY – THE FEET

For a delivery to be fair in respect of the feet, in the delivery stride
(i) the bowler's back foot must land within and not touching the return crease.
(ii) the bowler's front foot must land with some part of the foot, whether grounded or raised, behind the popping crease.
If the umpire at the bowler's end is not satisfied that both these conditions have been met, he shall call and signal No ball.

In order for a delivery to be considered fair the umpire must be fully satisfied that the feet are placed within certain bounds as laid down under this Law. If he has any doubts as to the correct placement of the feet the umpire must call and signal No ball as soon as the ball is delivered.

These bounds are clearly defined and are applied when the bowler's feet land for the final time prior to the ball being delivered. This landing of the feet prior to delivery is known as the **delivery stride** and all judgements about the legality of the feet positions are made at that point in time. Any subsequent movement or slipping of the feet after this first impact are ignored.

The Law is quite succinct in the wording used to describe these bounds but the Law is best explained by use of illustrations.

BACK FOOT

The back foot must land within and not touching the return crease.

Fair ball
Back foot has landed within the return crease.

No ball
Back foot has landed on the return crease.

No ball
Back foot has landed outside the return crease.

Fair ball The back foot has complied with the Law and, even though it is overhanging the return crease, it has landed 'within' it and is not 'touching' it. If this foot subsequently drops down on to the crease it would still be a fair delivery – the reason being that in the delivery stride (when the foot actually landed) it was not touching the return crease. The subsequent dropping of the foot is ignored.

Fair ball Here the foot has landed before it has reached the return crease marking. However, the Law regarding 'landing within and not touching the return crease' still applies. The return crease extends all the way back to the boundary and so the foot still has to be within it even though there is no actual line to indicate where the crease is.

FRONT FOOT

The front foot must land with some part of it, whether grounded or raised, behind
the popping crease.

Fair ball
Front foot has landed
behind the popping
crease.

Fair ball
Part of the front foot, the
heel, has landed behind
the popping crease.

Fair ball
The heel is behind the
popping crease even
though it is raised.

No ball Here the foot is on the line
and that does not comply with the
Law. It is the back edge of the
popping crease marking that is the
actual crease and some part of the
foot has to be behind the back edge
of the marking.

No ball This is clearly a No ball since
no part of the foot is behind the
popping crease.

Foot lands   then slides

These two pictures are part of the same piece of action. The foot has landed as in the
picture on the left and has subsequently slipped forward and as the ball is delivered is

as shown in the picture on the right. This is a fair delivery because the foot has landed with some part of it behind the popping crease – any subsequent movement after that is ignored.

In these two pictures the front foot has landed outside the return crease. This is of no consequence since it is only the popping crease that governs the placement of the front foot. In the picture on the left the front foot is grounded behind the popping crease and in the picture on the right, although raised, part of the foot is behind the popping crease. Each picture illustrates a fair delivery.

BOWLING FROM BEHIND THE UMPIRE

In order for a delivery to be considered fair the umpire must be fully satisfied that the feet are placed within certain bounds as laid down under this Law. If he has any doubts as to the correct placement of the feet the umpire must call and signal No ball as soon as the ball is delivered.

The act of bowling from behind the umpire is, in itself, not illegal. It is quite permissible for a bowler to bowl from 23-24 yards in order to try to deceive the striker with the change in flight of a delivery. However, the umpire must be satisfied that the back foot was within the return crease. Since he may not have seen it land he would be perfectly within his rights, and the Law, to call and signal No ball.

Before doing so, it would be worth considering the flight of the ball. If the ball was travelling towards the striker in a straight line down the pitch, wicket to wicket, he could reasonably assume that the bowler's feet were legally placed. It would be almost impossible to have achieved such a straight flight if the feet were outside the return crease. If, however, the ball was travelling towards the striker at any sort of angle, it would be more than likely that the back foot was not within its set boundary. In either case, the umpire must be fully satisfied that the back foot was legally placed and if he has any doubts at all he must call and signal No ball.

The other consideration that the umpire has to be aware of is that the ball might have been thrown. However, neither umpire can call and signal No ball because of a suspicion of throwing – they have to be certain.

6. BALL BOUNCING MORE THAN TWICE OR ROLLING ALONG THE GROUND

**The umpire at the bowler's end shall call and signal No ball if a ball
which he considers to have been delivered, without having previously
touched the bat or person of the striker,
either (i) bounces more than twice
or   (ii) rolls along the ground
before it reaches the popping crease.**

This clause simply states what happens should the ball bounce three times or more or roll along the ground before it reaches the popping crease. This rolling or bouncing has to occur before any contact is made by the bat or striker's person, otherwise it does not apply. So, if the striker moves forward and touches the ball, thus causing it to roll along the ground, even though it does so in front of the popping crease, this Law will not apply. The Law is specifically designed to cater for the ball that does either of these things without help/contact from the striker.

7. BALL COMING TO REST IN FRONT OF STRIKER'S WICKET

**If a ball delivered by the bowler comes to rest in front of the line of
the striker's wicket, without having touched the bat or person of the
striker, the umpire shall call and signal No ball and immediately call
and signal Dead ball.**

This clause caters for the delivery that, although correctly delivered, does not have enough force behind it to reach the striker. It might bounce or roll along the pitch but, because of its lack of momentum, stops in front of the striker. In this case the bowler's end umpire must:

• call and signal No ball, then immediately
• call and signal Dead ball.

The striker is not given the opportunity to hit it. The delivery will not count as one of the over.

8. CALL OF NO BALL FOR INFRINGEMENT OF OTHER LAWS

**In addition to the instances above, an umpire shall call and signal
No ball as required by the following Laws.
Law 40.3 – Position of wicket-keeper
Law 41.5 – Limitation of on side fielders
Law 41.6 – Fielders not to encroach on the pitch
Law 42.6 – Dangerous and unfair bowling
Law 42.7 – Dangerous and unfair bowling – action by the umpire
Law 42.8 – Deliberate bowling of high full pitched balls.**

See individual clauses for further details.

9. REVOKING A CALL OF NO BALL

An umpire shall revoke the call of No ball if the ball does not leave the bowler's hand for any reason.

The bowler's end umpire, in calling and signalling No ball for a foot fault, may be unaware that the bowler has not released the ball. On realising what has happened, the umpire must immediately call and signal Dead ball and revoke the No ball call. In reality he will, in fact, simply repeat the Dead ball signal to the scorers, because his repeated No ball signal will not be made. The scorers will therefore not record the No ball because it was never signalled to them.

10. NO BALL TO OVER-RIDE WIDE

**A call of No ball shall over-ride the call of Wide ball at any time.
See Law 25.1 (Judging a Wide) and 25.3 (Call and signal of Wide ball).**

Whenever a No ball is called, whatever subsequently happens to that ball in terms of its width and the ability of the batsman to hit it will be ignored. A No ball will always take precedence over a Wide.

11. BALL NOT DEAD

The ball does not become dead on the call of No ball.

Just because a No ball is called it does not mean that the ball becomes dead. Umpires must keep their eyes and attention firmly fixed on the play since runs can still be scored and certain dismissals effected. Only when the ball becomes dead should the umpire repeat the No ball signal, followed by any other appropriate signals, to the scorers and await acknowledgement of each one.

12. PENALTY FOR A NO BALL

A penalty of one run shall be awarded instantly on the call of No ball. Unless the call is revoked, this penalty shall stand even if a batsman is dismissed. It shall be in addition to any other runs scored, any boundary allowance and any other penalties awarded.

13. RUNS RESULTING FROM A NO BALL – HOW SCORED

The one run penalty for a No ball shall be scored as a No ball extra. If other penalty runs have been awarded to either side, these shall be scored as in Law 42.17 (Penalty runs). Any runs completed by the batsmen or a boundary allowance shall be credited to the striker if the ball has been struck by the bat; otherwise they also shall be scored as No ball extras.

Apart from any award of a 5 run penalty, all runs resulting from a No ball, whether as No ball extras or credited to the striker, shall be debited against the bowler.

14. NO BALL NOT TO COUNT

A No ball shall not count as one of the over. See Law 22.4 (Balls not to count in the over).

15. OUT FROM A NO BALL

When No ball has been called, neither batsman shall be out under any of the Laws except 33 (Handled the ball), 34 (Hit the ball twice), 37 (Obstructing the field) or 38 (Run out).

Since a No ball is an illegal delivery the bowler will be penalised as follows:

- a one run penalty will be added to the score the instant the No ball is called and will be debited against the bowler's analysis
- the bowler cannot be credited with any of the following forms of dismissal: LBW, Caught, Bowled, Stumped or Hit wicket. The only ways that the fielding side can dismiss a batsman when a No ball has been bowled are: Run out, Obstructing the field, Hit the ball twice and Handled the ball
- since the ball is an illegal delivery it does not count as one of the six legal deliveries in the over.

The 1 run penalty is automatic and will stand no matter what else happens from that delivery, even the dismissal of a batsman where other runs may be disallowed. Any further runs that are scored will be added to this 1 run penalty to give the total scored from that delivery.

- the 1 run penalty for the No ball will be scored as No ball extras
- if the striker hits the ball and runs/scores a boundary those runs will be credited to him
- if the striker does not hit the ball but runs are scored they will also be recorded as No ball extras
- any other penalty runs awarded by the umpire will be recorded in the penalty run section of the scoring record.

How recorded

EXAMPLE 4

A No ball is delivered	1 No ball extra
The striker hits the ball and completes 3 runs	3 to the striker
Total runs recorded	4
All debited against the bowler	

EXAMPLE 5

A No ball is delivered	1 No ball extra
The striker misses it, runs and crosses on 3rd run	3 No ball extras
The ball is illegally fielded	5 penalty runs
Total runs recorded	9

The 4 No ball extras are debited against the bowler
The 5 penalty runs are not debited against the bowler

EXAMPLE 6

A No ball is delivered	1 No ball extra
The striker tries to hit it but does	
not make contact with the bat, but	
the ball hits his leg and reaches the boundary	4 No ball extras
Total runs recorded	5

In Example 6 the umpire has to convey to the scorers that the 4 runs for the boundary are not to be credited to the striker – he did not hit the ball with the bat. The way to do this is to use the Bye signal. Even though the ball hit the striker's leg they cannot be Leg byes because Leg byes can only be scored from a fair delivery. The use of the Bye signal in this case is simply to tell the scorers that the ball was not hit by the striker and that the runs have to be scored as No ball extras.

The sequence of signals to the scorers would therefore be: No ball, Bye, Boundary 4, with each one being acknowledged separately by the scorers.

Law 25 Wide ball

1. JUDGING A WIDE

(a) If the bowler bowls a ball, not being a No ball, the umpire shall adjudge it a Wide if according to the definition in (b) below, in his opinion, the ball passes wide of the striker where he is standing and would also have passed wide of him standing in a normal guard position.

(b) The ball will be considered as passing wide of the striker unless it is sufficiently within his reach for him to be able to hit it with his bat by means of a normal cricket stroke.

2. DELIVERY NOT A WIDE

The umpire shall not adjudge a delivery as being a Wide
(a) if the striker, by moving,

    either (i) causes the ball to pass wide of him, as defined
             in 1(b) above,

    or   (ii) brings the ball sufficiently within his reach to be able
             to hit it with his bat by means of a normal cricket stroke.

(b) if the ball touches the striker's bat or person.

This is one of the Laws that is often modified to cater for limited-overs competitions and, because of this, various interpretations as to what constitutes a Wide abound throughout the world of cricket. This section will not be dealing with such interpretations.

Before entering into the criteria which the Law lays down for judging a Wide it must be clearly understood that **should the batsman make contact with the ball at any stage during the delivery** – be that contact with the bat or his person – **the ball cannot be judged as Wide**. The following explanation of how the umpire judges a Wide always presupposes that no contact with the ball is made.

A Wide is defined in Law as a ball that passes wide of the striker so that he is unable to hit it with his bat by means of **a normal cricket stroke**. This criterion has to be applied both from **where he is standing when attempting to hit the ball** AND from **where he would be standing in a normal guard position**.

(a) *'a normal cricket stroke'*
This does not have to be a classic textbook stroke but simply means that he should be able to hit the ball with a reasonable amount of control. So if, for example, the only contact he could make was on the toe end of the bat, that cannot be deemed to be a normal cricket stroke since there would be very little control over the direction in which the ball would be hit.

The bowler's end umpire must judge each delivery on its own merits. There is no defined distance down the bat, or a specified place on the bat, which, if the ball passes beyond it, would cause the umpire to deem the delivery a Wide. It is a judgement solely for the umpire to make.

(b) *'where he is standing when attempting to hit the ball'*
Batsmen often move from their normal guard position to try to hit the ball – it is a natural reflex action. However, this action is a crucial factor in the umpire's decision as to whether the ball is to be considered a Wide or not. The criterion defining 'a normal cricket stroke' has to be applied from the position the batsman is in when he tries to hit the ball.

(c) *'where he would be standing in a normal guard position'*
The significant word here is 'a' – it should not be defined as that particular striker's normal guard position. The phrase 'a normal guard position' is meant as a general guard position that would be taken under normal circumstances – a leg-stump guard; a middle-and-leg-stump guard; a middle/centre-stump guard. Any exaggerated, unusual guard positions must be ignored, and judgement is made from where it would normally be expected that the striker would stand.

For example, if the striker takes a guard so far outside leg stump that he is unable to reach a normal delivery that would otherwise bowl him, he cannot claim that the delivery was one that prohibited him from playing a 'normal cricket stroke'. Had he been in a normal guard position he could easily have hit the ball.

It is important that the umpire makes his judgement in (a) above, using the two positions explained in (b) and (c). If only one of these criteria applies the delivery cannot be called a Wide.

EXAMPLE 1

The ball is delivered outside the off stump. The striker does not move his feet and waves the bat at the ball. The ball passes over the bat near the toe end.

This is clearly a Wide since he cannot hit it by means of a normal cricket stroke, and he cannot do so from both positions (b) and (c) above. The striker is under no obligation to move in order to try to hit the ball. He is quite entitled to stand in his guard position and let the ball pass. Provided that he is unable to hit it within the criteria laid down then it will be a Wide. It is the bowler's responsibility to bowl the ball in such a place that the striker can reach it.

EXAMPLE 2

Similar delivery as above but this time the striker moves from his guard position towards the ball thus bringing it within a distance from which he could play a normal cricket stroke. He decides, however, to let the ball pass through to the wicket-keeper.

This is clearly **not** a Wide because although he could not play a normal cricket stroke from his (c) guard position he has moved and put himself in a position where it is possible to play a normal cricket stroke, thus negating the criterion laid down in (b). (Had he tried to hit the ball and missed, it is still not a Wide. He has moved into a position where it is possible to play a normal cricket stroke – his inability to make contact with the ball is not the bowler's fault and therefore he cannot be penalised by the umpire calling Wide ball.)

EXAMPLE 3

The ball is delivered outside the off stump well within reach of the striker. The striker, in order to give himself a little more room, takes a step backwards towards square leg, plays at the ball and misses.

This is **not** a Wide because had he stayed in a normal guard position he would have been in a position to hit the ball. By moving backwards he has voluntarily moved into a position where he could not reach it. Again, this is not the bowler's fault and he should not be penalised. The striker cannot move in such a manner and 'create' a Wide.

Two further points must be considered when deciding whether or not the batsman can play the ball:

THE STATURE OF THE STRIKER
Every batsman is of a different height and tall batsmen can reach much further than short ones. It follows therefore that a delivery deemed a Wide to a short striker may not necessarily be so to a taller one.

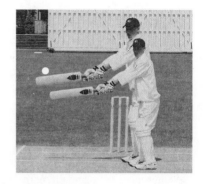

THE HEIGHT AT WHICH THE BALL REACHED THE STRIKER
The lower the ball, the harder it is to hit. As the height of the ball rises so it becomes easier to hit. The picture shows the natural arc the bat makes as it is raised and lowered and the extent to which the height of the ball will affect the strikers' ability to play a normal stroke at it. It is clear that the ball at (B) is, laterally, the same distance away from the striker as ball (A), but because it is lower it is not in a position where the striker can hit it by means of a normal cricket stroke. Therefore delivery (B) is a Wide and delivery (A) is not.

These variables must form part of the umpire's assessment when deciding to call a delivery a Wide ball, irrespective of whether the ball is on the off side or the leg side. However, when a ball is directed down the leg side its height and the reach of the batsman become even more crucial. If the striker retains his position and does not move his feet, his reach on the leg side is more restricted. While the ball may be nearer to the striker, its height and distance are factors the umpire must consider when calling Wide ball.

DELIVERIES OVER HEAD HEIGHT

If a delivery pitches (bounces) and passes, or would have passed, over the batsman's head then it is not a Wide, even though the criteria for a Wide may well have been met. It is a No ball that is called and signalled by the bowler's end umpire. Details of this are to be found in Law 42.6

CONSISTENCY OF INTERPRETATION

The umpire must, of course, be certain of what the Law says and what it means. This, however, is not enough. The practicality of umpiring is that the umpire must make judgements based on what he sees and hears as well as what he knows. In applying this to Wides, whether they be the so-called One-day Wide or not, a most important quality is consistency of interpretaton. Players will not tolerate inconsistency. They are entitled to expect that the umpires will maintain a constant judgement of wide deliveries throughout the game, no matter what stage the match is at.

At no time should an umpire change his judgement of what width a delivery has to be in order for him to call it a Wide. Just because the match situation has become tight and runs are at a premium there is no justification for the umpire to change his interpretation regarding what is acceptable and what isn't. Once the umpire has set out his standard – and this will be done very early in the game – he should not veer from it for the rest of the game.

Many competition regulations state how strict the umpires should be for a particular match and umpires are advised to ensure that they not only adhere to these criteria but also that they advise the captains what is expected of their bowlers. The captains do not usually mind how strict the umpires are in this respect provided that they are consistent and apply the same standards throughout the whole game, to both sides.

It is also advisable that umpires remember that this consistency applies not only to themselves, as individuals, but also that both umpires are consistent with each other. It is wrong for one umpire to apply one set of criteria only for his colleague to apply a different set during the same game.

Similarly, where the match forms part of a competition/tournament all the umpires involved in that tournament should discuss the matter and come to a common interpretation that they will all follow. By doing this the theme of consistency will be applied in three ways: each umpire will be consistent with himself, with his colleague and with the needs of the tournament.

Umpires should remember that **inconsistency** breeds frustration and resentment, while **consistency** leads to tolerance and acceptance.

3. CALL AND SIGNAL OF WIDE BALL

(a) **If the umpire adjudges a delivery to be a Wide he shall call and signal Wide ball as soon as the ball passes the striker's wicket. It shall, however, be considered to have been a Wide from the instant** of delivery, even though it cannot be called Wide until it passes the striker's wicket.

(b) The umpire shall revoke the call of Wide ball if there is then any contact between the ball and the striker's bat or person.

(c) The umpire shall revoke the call of Wide ball if a delivery is called a No ball. See Law 24.10 (No ball to over-ride Wide).

Four points are made in this clause:

1. The bowler's end umpire must make the call and signal of Wide ball when the ball passes the striker's wicket – this is for the benefit of the participants on the field. When the ball is dead he will repeat the signal to the scorers and await their acknowledgement.

2. Even though a call and signal of Wide ball is not made until the ball passes the striker's wicket, that delivery is deemed to be a Wide the instant it leaves the bowler's hand. See Example 4. This interpretation has a significant influence on other Laws.

EXAMPLE 4

The batting side need 1 run to win and only have 1 wicket left. A Wide is delivered from which the striker is stumped.

The result of the game is that the batting side have won by 1 wicket. The Wide is deemed to have been bowled as soon as it left the bowler's hand, so it means that the batting side have scored the run needed to win, and at that point the match is over. The 'stumping' happens after the match is over and is not relevant to the action.

3. If the ball makes contact with the striker's bat or person and the umpire inadvertently calls and signals Wide ball, when the ball becomes dead the umpire must revoke that signal of Wide ball using the Revoke signal described in Law 3.

4. The call of No ball overrides the call of Wide ball. Whenever a No ball is called, whatever subsequently happens to that ball in terms of its width and the ability of the batsman to hit it will be ignored. The width of the delivery is immaterial since a No ball overrides a Wide.

4. BALL NOT DEAD

The ball does not become dead on the call of Wide ball.

On the call of Wide ball, the ball remains in play and runs can be scored and a dismissal effected.

Only when the ball becomes dead should the umpires repeat the signal to the scorers and await acknowledgement. Scorers should note that the first call and signal is for the benefit of the players and no acknowledgement is required or expected until the signal is repeated for them.

5. PENALTY FOR A WIDE

A penalty of one run shall be awarded instantly on the call of Wide ball. Unless the call is revoked (see 3 above), this penalty shall stand even if a batsman is dismissed, and shall be in addition to any other runs scored, any boundary allowance and any other penalties awarded.

6. RUNS RESULTING FROM A WIDE – HOW SCORED

All runs completed by the batsmen or a boundary allowance, together with the penalty for the Wide, shall be scored as Wide balls. Apart from any award of a 5 run penalty, all runs resulting from a Wide shall be debited against the bowler.

7. WIDE NOT TO COUNT

A Wide shall not count as one of the over. See Law 22.4 (Balls not to count in the over).

8. OUT FROM A WIDE

When Wide ball has been called, neither batsman shall be out under any of the Laws except 33 (Handled the ball), 35 (Hit wicket), 37 (Obstructing the field), 38 (Run out) or 39 (Stumped).

Since a Wide is not a fair delivery the bowler is penalised as follows:
- a 1 run penalty will be added to the score the instant it is called and will be debited against the bowler's analysis
- the striker cannot be out in any of the following ways: Bowled, LBW, Caught. However, the bowler can dismiss the striker and gain credit for Hit wicket and Stumped and either batsman can be dismissed Handled the ball, Obstructing the field, and Run out.

The 1 run penalty is automatic and will stand no matter what else happens from that delivery. Even if a batsman is dismissed the 1 run penalty remains.

Any further runs scored by the batsmen running or the ball reaching the boundary are added to this 1 run penalty to give the total from that delivery, as follows:
- the 1 run penalty is scored as a Wide
- any runs scored are also recorded as Wides
- any other penalty runs awarded by the umpire will be recorded in the penalty run section of the scoring record.

How recorded
EXAMPLE 5

A Wide is delivered	1 Wide
The batsmen complete 3 runs	3 Wides
Total runs recorded	4 Wides
All debited against the bowler	

EXAMPLE 6

A Wide is delivered	1 Wide
The batsmen cross on their 3rd run	3 Wides
The ball is illegally fielded	5 penalty runs
Total runs	9 runs

The 4 Wides are debited against the bowler

The 5 penalty runs are not debited against the bowler

As a Wide is not a fair delivery it is not counted as one of the six legal deliveries of the over. A Wide is not considered to be a ball received by the striker and is not counted as a ball faced in his innings, even though scorers may record it in his details.

Law 26 Bye and Leg bye

I. BYES

If the ball, not being a No ball or a Wide, passes the striker without touching his bat or person, any runs completed by the batsmen or a boundary allowance shall be credited as Byes to the batting side.

Byes are the runs scored from a **fair** delivery that does not touch the striker's bat, person or equipment.

It is not necessary for the striker to make an attempt to hit the ball with his bat in order for Byes to be scored. If the opportunity arises, runs can be scored provided that the ball does not touch him, his bat or equipment.

Byes are not debited against the bowler in his analysis.

If a No ball is delivered and the striker fails to make contact with it – with his bat, person or equipment – any runs completed are recorded as No ball extras.

If a Wide is delivered any runs scored are always recorded as Wides.

2. LEG BYES

(a) **If a ball delivered by the bowler first strikes the person of the striker, runs shall be scored only if the umpire is satisfied that the striker has**
either (i) attempted to play the ball with his bat,
or   (ii) tried to avoid being hit by the ball.
If the umpire is satisfied that either of these conditions has been met, and the ball makes no subsequent contact with the bat, runs completed by the batsmen or a boundary allowance shall be credited to the batting side as in (b). Note, however, the provisions of Laws 34.3 (Ball lawfully struck more than once) and 34.4 (Runs permitted from ball lawfully struck more than once)
(b) **The runs in (a) above shall,**
   (i) if the delivery is not a No Ball, be scored as Leg byes.

(ii) if **No ball** has been called, be scored together with the penalty for the **No ball** as **No ball** extras.

3. LEG BYES NOT TO BE AWARDED

If in the circumstances of 2(a) above the umpire considers that neither of the conditions (i) and (ii) therein has been met, then **Leg** byes will not be awarded. The batting side shall not be credited with any runs from that delivery apart from the one run penalty for a **No ball** if applicable. Moreover, no other penalties shall be awarded to the batting side when the ball is dead. See Law 42.17 (Penalty runs). The following procedure shall be adopted.

(a) If no run is attempted but the ball reaches the boundary, the umpire shall call and signal Dead ball, and disallow the boundary.

(b) If runs are attempted and if

(i) neither batsman is dismissed and the ball does not become dead for any other reason, the umpire shall call and signal Dead ball as soon as one run is completed or the ball reaches the boundary. The batsmen shall return to their original ends. The run or boundary shall be disallowed.

(ii) before one run is completed or the ball reaches the boundary, a batsman is dismissed, or the ball becomes dead for any other reason, all the provisions of the Laws will apply, except that no runs and no penalties shall be credited to the batting side, other than the penalty for a **No ball** if applicable.

A Leg bye is scored when the ball does not touch the bat, but is **unintentionally** deflected by the striker's person with the batsmen then completing runs or the ball reaching the boundary.

Leg byes can only be scored from a fair delivery. If a No ball is bowled, and the ball is then unintentionally deflected, any runs will be recorded as No ball extras and not Leg byes. It is impossible to score Leg byes off a Wide.

In order for Leg byes to be allowed the striker must comply with one of the following criteria:

• the striker must make a **genuine** attempt to hit the ball with the bat or

• the striker must make a legitimate attempt to avoid being hit by the ball.

THE STRIKER MUST MAKE A
GENUINE ATTEMPT TO HIT THE BALL
WITH THE BAT
This is not always easy to determine.

• The striker may well 'play a shot' at the
ball but by the timing of such a stroke it

may be doubtful that he actually intends to try and hit it. The Law is very clear that there must be a genuine attempt to play the ball with the bat – not simply to play a shot. Photo 1 clearly shows a genuine attempt to hit the ball with the bat.

- If the striker brings his bat down after the ball has made contact with his pads, the umpire must consider if the attempt was genuine. Similarly, if the striker plays a shot by tucking his bat behind the pad, doubts must be raised as to whether he was genuinely trying to hit the ball. If doubt exists that a genuine attempt to hit the ball with the bat was made then the umpire must disallow any runs scored. Photo 2 would indicate that the striker, although playing a shot, had no intention of hitting the ball with the bat.
- If, as in Photo 3, the striker 'shoulders arms' to the delivery and it subsequently hits him, that cannot be considered as a genuine attempt.

The umpire must always bear these conditions in mind when deciding if Leg byes are to be allowed – the deflection must be **unintentional**, and the attempt to play at the ball must be **genuine**. It must be stressed that the umpire must be consistent throughout the game.

THE STRIKER MUST MAKE A LEGITIMATE ATTEMPT TO AVOID
BEING HIT BY THE BALL

Provided that the umpire is satisfied that the action the striker is making is a genuine one to prevent the ball from hitting him, then Leg byes will be allowed. This movement may be a pronounced movement or it could be a slight movement of the body or head – however, it is for the umpire to decide if it was made with the sole intention of avoiding being hit by the ball.

If one of the above criteria has been fulfilled, Leg byes will be allowed. If neither of the above criteria apply, the bowler's end umpire should initially allow the batsmen to run and complete one run, then:

- call and signal Dead ball
- disallow that run
- return the batsmen to their original ends
- repeat the Dead ball signal to the scorers
- await the scorers' acknowledgement
- ensure that the scorers understand that no runs are to be recorded from that delivery.

Waiting until one run is completed allows the fielding side a chance to run out one of the batsmen. If they achieve this the dismissal stands and there is no need for the umpire to call Dead ball or disallow the run.

If there is no run out attempt, or it is unsuccessful, the umpire should immediately call and signal Dead ball on completion of the run.

If the ball is travelling so fast that it reaches the boundary before the batsmen are able to complete one run, as soon as the ball reaches the boundary the bowler's end umpire must follow the bulleted procedures outlined above for one run.

The object of this Law is to ensure that under no circumstances can the batting side gain a benefit from scoring runs where Leg byes are not allowed.

NO BALL IS DELIVERED

If a No ball is bowled the 1 run penalty will still be awarded but any runs that are subsequently run will be disallowed if the ball has been **deliberately deflected**.

The criteria for scoring extras from a No ball are exactly the same as for a fair delivery. The striker is required to make either a genuine attempt to hit the ball with his bat or a genuine attempt to avoid injury. If he is doing neither, any 'extras' attempted must be disallowed.

If in the umpire's opinion the ball was unintentionally deflected by the batsman any runs scored are recorded as No ball extras, not as Leg byes. (Leg byes can only be scored from a fair delivery.)

The correct signals to the scorers are:

- No ball signal, followed by
- Bye signal.

The Bye signal is used (not the Leg bye signal) to inform the scorers that the striker did not hit the ball with his bat and he must not be credited with any runs. The umpire cannot give the Leg bye signal since these runs are not Leg byes, they are No ball extras.

If the ball subsequently reaches the boundary the signals are:

- No ball signal, followed by
- Bye signal, followed by
- Boundary 4 signal.

Each signal must be acknowledged separately thus ensuring that the scorers fully understand the umpire's instructions. (Incidentally, it is not possible to score a boundary 6 as Leg byes or No ball extras because a boundary 6 can only be scored if the ball comes off the bat.) Leg byes are not debited against the bowler in his analysis.

Law 27 Appeals

1. UMPIRE NOT TO GIVE BATSMAN OUT WITHOUT AN APPEAL

Neither umpire shall give a batsman out, even though he may be out under the Laws, unless appealed to by the fielding side. This shall not debar a batsman who is out under any of the Laws from leaving his wicket without an appeal having been made. Note however, the provisions of 7 below.

2. BATSMAN DISMISSED

A batsman is dismissed if
either (a) he is given out by an umpire, on appeal
or   (b) he is out under any of the Laws and leaves his wicket as in 1 above.

An umpire cannot dismiss a batsman unless there is an appeal. The batsman is quite within his rights to remain at his crease until an appeal is made and the umpire gives his decision. Even though the umpire may know that the batsman is out he cannot give him out until requested to do so by the fielding side. If there is no appeal, the umpire has no decision to make.

It is acceptable for a batsman to 'walk' knowing he is out even though the fielding side has not appealed and/or the umpire has not dismissed him. This usually happens in cases of Bowled or Caught where the batsman knows he is out and does not bother to wait for either the appeal or the umpire's decision – he simply 'walks'. 'Walking' in such circumstances is acceptable, and should be encouraged, so long as he is walking for a legitimate form of dismissal. If he 'walks' and the umpire knows that he is not out under any of the Laws then he must be recalled – see clause 7 below.

3. TIMING OF APPEALS

For an appeal to be valid it must be made before the bowler begins his run up or, if he has no run up, his bowling action to deliver the next ball, and before Time has been called.
The call of Over does not invalidate an appeal made prior to the start of the following over provided Time has not been called. See Laws 16.2 (Call of Time) and 22.2 (Start of an over).

4. APPEAL 'HOW'S THAT?'

An appeal 'How's That?' covers all ways of being out.

In Law, there are several restrictions placed on the fielding side as to when they can appeal.

TIMING

The appeal must be made before the bowler begins his run up, or bowling action, for the next delivery. Once this act takes place, any appeal for an event that took place on the previous delivery will not be valid and will not be considered by the umpire.

The call of Over does not invalidate an appeal. If no immediate appeal is made from the action resulting from the last ball of the over, an appeal would still be valid up until the next bowler starts his run up (or bowling action) for the first ball of the next over. The umpire must answer any appeal made during this time.

The call of Time, however, does invalidate an appeal. Any such appeal will not be considered by the umpire – for example, an appeal cannot be made or answered during an interval.

WHAT CONSTITUTES AN APPEAL?

Any form of question that asks the umpire to give a verdict is acceptable. The normal question is 'How's that?' However, any variation of 'How's that?' is sufficient for the umpire to deem that a question has been asked and he is required to give an answer.

5. ANSWERING APPEALS

The umpire at the bowler's end shall answer all appeals except those arising out of any of Laws 35 (Hit wicket), 39 (Stumped) or 38 (Run out) when this occurs at the striker's wicket. A decision Not out by one umpire shall not prevent the other umpire from giving a decision, provided that each is considering only matters within his jurisdiction. When a batsman has been given Not out, either umpire may, within his jurisdiction, answer a further appeal provided that it is made in accordance with 3 above.

6. CONSULTATION BY UMPIRES

Each umpire shall answer appeals on matters within his own jurisdiction. If an umpire is doubtful about any point that the other umpire may have been in a better position to see, he shall consult the latter on this point of fact and shall then give his decision. If, after consultation, there is still doubt remaining the decision shall be Not out.

When a member of the fielding side makes an appeal it is deemed to be a **general** appeal which:

• covers all possible methods of dismissal, and
• is directed at both umpires.

Both umpires must consider the action that has instigated the appeal and must answer it for dismissals within their jurisdiction.

If the appeal is turned down the relevant umpire must call Not out. He may also shake his head to confirm the decision – this would be done where the noise from the crowd may drown the call of Not out – but it is not acceptable to shake the head without saying Not out. The fielding side have asked the umpire a question and it is totally unacceptable for the umpire to shake his head or turn away without giving the correct verbal response. Where the response is made in the affirmative, the umpire must give the correct Out signal. This may be accompanied by a nod of the head but the important gesture is that of the raised finger – not the nod of the head.

It is important to note that the fielding side cannot make a specific appeal against one batsman in order to dismiss only him, thus 'protecting' the other batsman.

EXAMPLE 1

The striker is a tail-ender, struggling to score runs, and the other batsman has been scoring freely. The striker hits the ball in the air and runs. A fielder catches the ball and throws it to the wicket-keeper who runs out the non-striker. The fielding side appeal specifically for the run out in order to dismiss the free-hitting batsman.

This is totally unacceptable and the appeal for the catch must take precedence.

Each umpire has jurisdiction for specific dismissals:

Bowler's end

Law 30	Bowled
Law 32	Caught
Law 33	Handled the ball
Law 34	Hit the ball twice
Law 36	LBW
Law 37	Obstructing the field
Law 31	Timed out (while not required in Law, consultation with the striker's end umpire is desirable)

Striker's end

Law 35	Hit wicket
Law 39	Stumped

Relevant end

Law 38	Run out

An umpire can only answer appeals under his jurisdiction and may not instigate, or attempt to interfere, in the decision of his colleague. However, an umpire may consult his colleague on any decision if he was in a better position to see the event and be able to give factual advice.

If an umpire is incapacitated, and is not in a position to give a decision, he may seek help from his colleague. He will then make his decision based on the information his colleague has proffered.

EXAMPLE 2
The ground is damp and the worn ends of an adjoining pitch are a little slippery. The umpire, in moving into position to judge a run out, slips and falls over. The wicket is broken at his end and there is an appeal for a run out.

If the umpire did not see the incident he must consult his colleague who will give him whatever information he has that will help. The decision, however, remains with the umpire who fell over. If he is not absolutely certain about any of the facts the appeal must be declined.

If the action is such that there could be more than one type of dismissal, if one is turned down the other must be considered.

EXAMPLE 3
The wicket-keeper 'catches' the striker and then 'stumps' him.

If the catch is declined by the bowler's end umpire, the appeal for the stumping must be answered by the striker's end umpire. If both methods of dismissal are valid, the striker would be dismissed Caught, since a catch takes precedence over every other dismissal other than bowled.

EXAMPLE 4
The ball hits the striker on the pads and rolls out to first slip. The bowler appeals (for LBW) and the batsman stands outside his popping crease awaiting the verdict. Meanwhile, the fielder throws the ball at the wicket in an attempt to run out the striker.

If the appeal for LBW is declined by the bowler's end umpire, the appeal for run out must still be considered by the striker's end umpire. If both methods of dismissal are valid then LBW takes precedence as it occurred first. (It should be noted that if a batsman is bowled then that takes precedence over all other forms of dismissal, including LBW. If the batsman would have been given out LBW but the ball travelled on to hit the stumps he is Bowled.)

CONSULTATION OF UMPIRES
Umpires must always remember that they are a team and must work together. By doing so, they demonstrate their unity to both teams and should be able to help each other in times of doubt.

EXAMPLE 5
The ball is deflected off the edge of the bat and is travelling low towards second slip. Just as it is about to be caught the bowler, in his follow-through, blocks the umpire's view of the catch. There is an appeal but, because of his view being blocked, the bowler's end umpire does not see the ball caught cleanly.

It would be wrong to turn down the appeal simply because he had not seen all the action. Consultation is imperative, and if the striker's end umpire is able to see and confirm that the ball carried and was caught, the bowler's end umpire must give the striker out. If the striker's end umpire is unable to confirm the catch, the appeal must be declined.

Consultation does not mean that the umpires actually have to talk – discreet signals between umpires often suffice. Provided the correct answers are communicated, how this is done is of no consequence.

An umpire should never seek confirmation from a member of the fielding side, irrespective of his status. They have already demonstrated their position by appealing. The umpire's duty is to adjudicate in a neutral manner and asking the fielding side their opinion is not the way to achieve this.

In all cases where consultation between umpires takes place, the decision is still the umpire's concerned – he cannot delegate the decision to his colleague. If there is ever any doubt about a dismissal, the batsman must always receive the benefit of such a doubt.

7. BATSMAN LEAVING HIS WICKET UNDER A MISAPPREHENSION

An umpire shall intervene if satisfied that a batsman, not having been given out, has left his wicket under a misapprehension that he is out. The umpire intervening shall call and signal Dead ball to prevent any further action by the fielding side and shall recall the batsman.

There are occasions when a batsman will leave his ground believing that he has been fairly dismissed when, in fact, he has not. This is referred to as: 'leaving his wicket under a misapprehension'. If this happens the umpire must:
• call and signal Dead ball (to protect him from a run out attempt)
• recall him to the wicket to continue his innings.
If he fails to return, the umpires must inform the scorers to record him as Retired Out, not the method of dismissal that the batsman thought was the case.

EXAMPLE 6
The batsman hits the ball and it hits the fielder standing at short leg on the helmet. The ball pops up into the air and the fielder catches it.
This is not out, since a 'catch' cannot be made when the ball makes contact with the helmet being worn by a fielder. If the batsman 'walks', thinking the catch was valid, he must be recalled.

EXAMPLE 7
The batsman does not hear the call of No ball and leaves his ground when the ball is 'caught'.
Since he cannot be caught from a No ball he must be recalled.

EXAMPLE 8
The striker, in playing forward, is out of his ground when the wicket-keeper attempts a

stumping and the striker 'walks'. However, the striker's end umpire is not satisfied that the wicket-keeper broke the wicket correctly – the ball was not in his hands.
The striker must be recalled.

EXAMPLE 9
The batsmen run for a quick single and the non-striker is short of his ground when the ball is thrown in to the wicket-keeper. The wicket-keeper breaks the wicket with his gloves before taking the ball. The batsman 'walks'.
The non-striker must be recalled.

There is a clear difference between the batsman 'walking' and leaving his wicket under the misapprehension that he is properly dismissed. Umpires may only permit a batsman to 'walk' if he has been properly dismissed – see clause 1 above.

8. WITHDRAWAL OF AN APPEAL

The captain of the fielding side may withdraw an appeal only with the consent of the umpire within whose jurisdiction the appeal falls and before the outgoing batsman has left the field of play. If such consent is given the umpire concerned shall, if applicable, revoke his decision and recall the batsman.

It is permissible for a captain to request that an appeal be withdrawn. The request must be made before the batsman leaves the field of play – therefore, by inference, should be done promptly. It must be stressed that the captain can only **request** permission to withdraw the appeal, it is the umpires' decision as to whether or not that request is granted. If permission to withdraw is granted the batsman may resume his innings. If not, the original dismissal must stand.

9. UMPIRE'S DECISION

An umpire may alter his decision provided that such alteration is made promptly. This apart, an umpire's decision, once made, is final.

The umpire's decision is final on all matters and no appeal or challenge is permitted at the time or at any later stage. However, the umpire is permitted to change his mind on any decision he has made in error, but he must do so promptly and without undue delay.

A prudent umpire will always take a moment or two to consider the facts before him. No shame is attached to an umpire changing his mind if, in the final analysis, the decision is a correct one.

TECHNIQUES FOR UMPIRES
- Never be swayed or intimidated by constant appealing or by loud 'chorus' appealing by a team. Remain calm and give an honest answer based on the events before you.

- Give a firm, considered reply to the appeal. Wait until the appeal has died down before answering so that you have time to consider the action. This is particularly true in the case of LBW appeals, where there is a lot to consider before a decision can be made. An appeal leads to disappointment to one side or the other and if the player(s) concerned have seen that you have at least spent a little time thinking about the decision they will more readily accept it.
- A quiet appeal must be considered with the same care as a vociferous one.
- You will decline more appeals than you uphold. You are there to offer unbiased adjudication, irrespective of how that affects your 'popularity'.
- Answer all appeals, frivolous or real. Never answer an appeal with just a nod or shake of the head. Always respond to an appeal giving a polite, but firm, reply.
- Never turn away from an appeal, which is extremely ill-mannered – the ball may still be in play so any subsequent action will need to be monitored.
- When giving a batsman out, there is no need to say anything. Comments such as 'That's out' are not necessary – the raised finger says it all.
- Remain calm at all times. Never lose your temper or show signs of being perturbed by the appeal. If you appear ruffled, some players will attempt to exploit that.
- Never rely on a batsman 'walking' – it is good if they do, but it is your job to make the decision, and you must not shirk from it.
- Never ask a batsman or fielder for his opinion on any matter or decision. It shows lack of confidence and may appear that you have ceased to be neutral.

Umpires who show firmness, fairness and consistency
gain the respect of the players.
Umpires who exhibit uncertainty, hesitancy or officiousness
gain nothing but a bad reputation.

Law 28 The wicket is down

I. WICKET PUT DOWN

(a) **The wicket is put down if a bail is completely removed from the top of the stumps, or a stump is struck out of the ground by**
   (i) the ball.
   (ii) the striker's bat, whether he is holding it or has let go of it.
   (iii) the striker's person or by any part of his clothing or equipment becoming detached from his person.
   (iv) a fielder, with his hand or arm, providing that the ball is held in the hand or hands so used, or in the hand of the arm so used.
   The wicket is also put down if a fielder pulls a stump out of the ground in the same manner.
(b) **The disturbance of a bail, whether temporary or not, shall not constitute its complete removal from the top of the stumps, but if**

a bail in falling lodges between two of the stumps this shall be regarded as complete removal.

The key element of a wicket being down or broken is the permanent removal of one of the bails from the top of the stumps while the ball is in play. It is not necessary for both bails to be removed – the removal of one bail is sufficient for the wicket to be down.

Wicket not broken
Because the bail is not completely removed.

Wicket not broken
Because the bail is not completely removed.

Wicket broken
Because the left bail is completely removed from the top of the stumps.

During play, a bail may be temporarily knocked out of its groove and fall back into place. This is not a permanent removal and the wicket cannot be considered broken.

For the wicket to be broken legally the bail must be removed by one of the following:
• the ball
• the striker's bat, whether he is holding it or not
• the striker; his person or equipment (whether he is wearing it or not)
• a fielder by his hand, providing the ball is in the hand used
• a fielder by his arm, provided the ball is in the hand of the arm used.

The contact causing the removal of the bail may be on the bail itself or by the disturbance of the stumps.

The *ball* may remove a bail.

The *fielder with the ball in the hand* may remove a bail.

The *arm* (within the green line) *of a fielder* may be used to remove a bail, providing the ball is in the hand of that arm.

The ball does not always become dead because a bail has been removed; play may continue with a broken wicket. If both bails are removed, there are four ways in which the wicket can be properly broken:

- a fielder may pull a stump out of the ground **provided that the ball is in the hand or hands used**
- a fielder may knock a stump out of the ground with his arm provided that the ball is **in the hand of the arm used**
- the ball may be thrown with sufficient force to strike a stump **completely out of the ground**. When struck out of the ground the stump must be completely removed from the ground as shown
- a fielder may replace one or both bails and then remove one of them in the afore-mentioned manner.

HOW NOT TO BREAK THE WICKET

The fielder on the left has pulled a stump out of the ground **but not** with the ball in the hand used, it is in his other hand. On the right the fielder has the ball in hand but has used his knee to break the wicket. He has not used the arm of the hand holding the ball. Neither of these is correct.

2. ONE BAIL OFF

If one bail is off, it shall be sufficient for the purpose of putting the wicket down to remove the remaining bail, or to strike or pull any of the three stumps out of the ground, in any of the ways stated in I above.

Should one bail be removed and the ball remains in play, one bail in place on top of the stumps in its grooves is deemed to be a complete wicket. Should that remaining bail be removed in a fashion described above, the wicket is considered broken.

3. REMAKING THE WICKET

If the wicket is broken or put down while the ball is in play, the umpire shall not remake the wicket until the ball is dead. See Law 23 (Dead ball). Any fielder, however, may
(i) replace a bail or bails on top of the stumps
(ii) put back one or more stumps into the ground where the wicket
originally stood.

Should the wicket be broken and the ball remains in play, the umpire must not attempt to remake the wicket. Both umpires must continue to watch the play for further action.

While the ball remains in play, any member of the fielding side may remake the wicket by:
• replacing one or more of the bails, in the grooves on top of the stumps, or by
• replacing a stump in one of the holes where the wicket originally stood.

The wicket subsequently remade in this fashion is considered complete even if only one stump or only one bail is in place.

Only when the ball becomes dead should the umpire remake the wicket.

4. DISPENSING WITH BAILS

If the umpires have agreed to dispense with bails, in accordance with Law 8.5 (Dispensing with bails), the decision as to whether the wicket has been put down is one for the umpire concerned to decide.
(a) After a decision to play without bails, the wicket has been put down
if the umpire concerned is satisfied that the wicket has been struck
by the ball, by the striker's bat, person, or items of his clothing or
equipment separated from his person as described in 1(a)(ii) or
1(a)(iii) above, or by a fielder with the hand holding the ball or with
the arm of the hand holding the ball.
(b) If the wicket has already been broken or put down, (a) above shall
apply to any stump or stumps still in the ground. Any fielder may
replace a stump or stumps, in accordance with 3 above, in order to
have an opportunity of putting the wicket down.

PLAYING WITHOUT BAILS

The umpires make the decision to play without bails and they should not do so lightly, as additional considerations become necessary. Dispensing with bails should only occur during extreme windy conditions (a pair of heavy bails is usually sufficient to prevent bails blowing off in windy conditions) and then only for as long as necessary. As soon as conditions permit, both sets of bails must be replaced.

When it becomes necessary for the umpires to dispense with bails, the bails must be removed from the stumps at both ends of the pitch. It is not permissible to remove one set and leave the other in place.

In this situation, the decision as to when the wicket is broken is purely one for the umpire to make. All he has to be satisfied with is that the ball has hit the wicket. Provided that he sees the ball hit the wicket, that wicket is deemed to have been broken – he does not have to consider whether the force of the ball hitting the stumps was sufficient to remove the bails.

If the wicket has been disturbed during some previous action – for example, an unsuccessful run out attempt – and the fielding side wish to break the wicket again to effect a subsequent run out, they only have to hit a stump which is still in its original hole. They can do this by any of the methods described in clause 1. It does not matter if the stump(s) concerned are not upright – provided that the stump that is hit is in its original hole then the ball hitting it will be enough for the wicket to be deemed as broken.

Where the bails have been dispensed with there is never a requirement that a stump has to be completely removed from the ground.

Law 29 Batsman out of his ground

1. WHEN OUT OF HIS GROUND

A batsman shall be considered to be out of his ground unless his bat or some part of his person is grounded behind the popping crease at that end.

The clause is concise – some part of the batsman, or his bat in hand, must be grounded behind the popping crease at that end. If not, he is out of his ground.

The foot is grounded behind the popping crease.

The bat is grounded behind the popping crease.

2. WHICH IS A BATSMAN'S GROUND

(a) If only one batsman is within a ground
    (i) it is his ground.
    (ii) it remains his ground even if he is later joined there by the other batsman.

(b) If both batsmen are in the same ground and one of them subsequently leaves it, (a)(i) above applies.

(c) If there is no batsman in either ground, then each ground belongs to whichever of the batsmen is nearer to it, or, if the batsmen are level, to whichever was nearer to it immediately prior to their drawing level.

(d) If a ground belongs to one batsman then, unless there is a striker with a runner, the other ground belongs to the other batsman irrespective of his position.

(e) When a batsman with a runner is striker, his ground is always that at the wicket-keeper's end. However, (a), (b), (c) and (d) above will still apply, but only to the runner and the non-striker, so that that ground will also belong to either the non-striker or the runner, as the case may be.

The ground referred to in this Law is the field of play behind the popping crease, (from boundary to boundary). Specific examples best demonstrate the principal requirements of this Law.

EXAMPLE 1

The batsmen do not run and stay in their ground.

The striker's ground is at the wicket-keeper's end, and the non-striker's ground is at the bowler's end.

EXAMPLE 2

The batsmen run and complete two runs.

The striker's ground is at the wicket-keeper's end and the non-striker's ground is at the bowler's end.

EXAMPLE 3

The batsmen run and complete one run.

The striker's ground is now at the bowler's end and the non-striker's ground is at the wicket-keeper's end.

EXAMPLE 4

The two batsmen are running on their first run – and have not yet crossed.

The striker's ground is still at the wicket-keeper's end and the non -striker's ground is still at the bowler's end.

EXAMPLE 5

The two batsmen are running on their first run – and have crossed.

The striker's ground is now at the bowler's end and the non-striker's ground is at the wicket-keeper's end.

The overriding principle is that a batsman's ground is either:

- the one he is **occupying**, or
- when running, the one he is **nearest to**.

If the batsmen are alongside each other, they have not crossed – the act of crossing **changes the end** they are nearest to.

Some specific match examples:

EXAMPLE 6
The striker remains in his ground and the non-striker runs and joins him.
The striker's ground is still at the wicket-keeper's end (he has not left it) and the non-striker's ground is at the bowler's end. The non-striker is out of his ground.

EXAMPLE 7
The striker runs to the bowler's end but the non-striker does not move out of his ground.
The non-striker's ground is still at the bowler's end (he has not left it) and the striker's ground is still at the wicket-keeper's end. The striker is out of his ground.

EXAMPLE 8
Both batsmen set off on their first run. After several paces the striker turns and runs back to the wicket-keeper's end. The non-striker continues to run towards that end.
The ground at the wicket-keeper's end belongs either to:

- the one who reaches it first, or
- the one who is nearest to it, if/when, the wicket is broken.

The bowler's end ground belongs to whichever batsman does not claim the ground at the wicket-keeper's end.

EXAMPLE 9
Both batsmen are at the wicket-keeper's end when one of them decides to run back to the bowler's end.
The batsman who stays at the wicket-keeper's end retains it and the running batsman assumes the bowler's end. If the wicket is put down at the bowler's end with the running batsman out of his ground, on appeal, the running batsman is out.

If an injured batsman has a **runner** acting for him, these provisions of ownership do not apply to him, as the only safe ground the injured striker has is at the wicket-keeper's end. If, while he is the striker and while the ball is in play, he leaves that ground for any reason, he is out of his ground and will suffer the consequences of being stumped or run out if that wicket is legally put down. The runner assumes the running role for his injured colleague; should the runner be out of his ground when the wicket is put down, he becomes subject to the same criteria as any normal batsman.

3. POSITION OF NON-STRIKER

The non-striker, when standing at the bowler's end, should be positioned on the opposite side of the wicket to that from which the ball is being delivered, unless a request to do otherwise is granted by the umpire.

The non-striker is required to stand where he is not going to interfere with the bowler during his run-up or follow-through. This is usually on the opposite side of the wicket to that from where the bowler is delivering the ball. However, it could be that by doing so he will be in the way of a fielder; or a fielder may be in his path when running; or, following a delay for rain, the ground on the bowler's side is more suitable for the non-striker to run on.

Under any such reasonable circumstances a request for him to stand on the same side as the bowler would be granted, provided that it does not inconvenience the fielding side.

Law 30 Bowled

I. OUT BOWLED

(a) The striker is out Bowled if his wicket is put down by a ball delivered by the bowler, not being a No ball, even if it first touches his bat or person.

(b) Notwithstanding (a) above he shall not be out Bowled if before striking the wicket the ball has been in contact with any other player or with an umpire. He will, however, be subject to Laws 33 (Handled the ball), 37 (Obstructing the field), 38 (Run out) and 39 (Stumped).

2. BOWLED TO TAKE PRECEDENCE

The striker is out Bowled if his wicket is put down as in I above, even though a decision against him for any other method of dismissal would be justified.

A striker can be out Bowled only from a fair delivery, he cannot be bowled from a No ball or a Wide.

Very simply, if the bowler delivers a fair delivery and in playing at it or not, the striker either

• misses it and it goes on to hit the wicket, or
• he deflects it on to his wicket with either his person or equipment

he will be out – Bowled.

The second instance is commonly referred to as 'played on'. However, as there is no such dismissal as 'played on', it is recorded as Bowled.

If the striker is attempting to guard his wicket by, legally, hitting the ball a second time and, in doing so, hits the ball on to his own wicket he is out – Bowled.

If the ball subsequently touches, or is touched by, any other person on the field of play the striker cannot be recorded as Bowled. Notwithstanding this, another form of dismissal may be valid, for example run out or stumped.

The striker is vulnerable to being bowled from the moment the ball leaves the bowler's hand until it comes into contact with any other player or an umpire. Even though there may be a time lapse from when the striker first receives the ball until it actually breaks his wicket, he remains vulnerable under this Law.

Bowled takes precedence over all other forms of dismissal.

EXAMPLE 1

A fair delivery hits the striker in such a way that an LBW decision would be valid and the ball goes on to break the wicket.

The striker will be out Bowled, not LBW.

EXAMPLE 2

A fair delivery hits the striker's pad and it goes on to remove one bail from the stumps. In an instant, the wicket-keeper, standing close to the stumps, gathers the ball and correctly removes the other bail.

On appeal, the correct dismissal is Bowled, not Stumped.

A dismissal of Bowled is credited to the bowler.

Law 31 Timed out

1. OUT TIMED OUT

(a) Unless Time has been called, the incoming batsman must be in position to take guard or for his partner to be ready to receive the next ball within 3 minutes of the fall of the previous wicket. If this requirement is not met, the incoming batsman will be out, Timed out.

(b) In the event of protracted delay in which no batsman comes to the wicket, the umpires shall adopt the procedure of Law 21.3 (Umpires awarding a match). For the purposes of that Law the start of the action shall be taken as the expiry of the 3 minutes referred to above.

This Law is to prevent the batting side from gaining any advantage by wasting time when a batsman has been dismissed. Without this Law, a match could be reduced to a farce. When a batsman is dismissed, the incoming batsman must take his place on the field without undue delay.

The Law states that the incoming batsman has 3 minutes from the fall of the wicket in which to be in a position either to take guard or for his partner to receive the next delivery. If the incoming batsman is not in either of these positions then, on appeal, he will be timed out. The umpires are not required to investigate the reason for any delay – only to be satisfied that the incoming batsman has exceeded his allotted maximum of 3 minutes and that there is an appeal.

This stipulation means, in effect, that the incoming and outgoing batsmen should cross on the field of play and, provided that they do not spend more than a moment talking, the possibility of a valid appeal is unlikely.

Before answering an appeal for Timed out there has to be someone on the field for the umpire to dismiss if that is the decision. It is only when the incoming batsman crosses the boundary, and therefore his innings has commenced, that the umpire can dismiss him.

Having said, above, that the umpires are not required to investigate the reasons for any late arrival of a batsman, the Law does detail what they should do if there is a **protracted delay**. A delay can be considered as protracted if the incoming batsman has not appeared by the time the 3 minutes has elapsed. If the umpires decide that a protracted delay has occurred they will:

- call Time
- leave the field
- investigate the reason(s) for the delay
- together decide if the delay constitutes a refusal to play.

If they decide it was a **refusal to play** the umpires must follow the provisions of Law 21.3:

- inform the batting captain of this decision and explain the penalty should the delay continue
- if the captain fails to act, or if his action is ineffective, then award the match to the fielding side.

No appeal is necessary – it is for the umpires alone to decide. While not a requirement in Law, prudent umpires will report their decision to the Governing Body responsible for the match.

If the umpires decide that the reason(s) for the delay do not constitute a refusal to play, the following procedure should be adopted:

- calculate the time lost in the match due to this investigation (the time lost will be from when the 3 minutes expired until play resumes)
- add the time lost to the end of the day's play and reschedule the close of play accordingly
- adjust the time of the last hour (if applicable)

EXAMPLE 1

The close of the day's play is scheduled for 6.30 p.m. – the last hour to start at 5.30 p.m. During the day, 5 minutes' play is lost because of an investigation.

The scheduled time for the end of the day's play must be adjusted. Close of play is rescheduled to 6.35 p.m. with the last hour starting at 5.35 p.m.

If the delay occurs during the last hour of the match, the minimum number of overs is not adjusted, however the close of play time is.

EXAMPLE 2

The close of the day's play is scheduled for 6.30 p.m. – the last hour to start at 5.30 p.m. At 6.00 p.m. there is an investigation that takes 7 minutes to resolve. 9.2 overs have been bowled at this time.

The 7 minutes are added to the close of play time which now becomes 6.37 p.m. When play resumes at 6.07 p.m. there would still be a minimum of 10.4 overs left to bowl, however if they are bowled before 6.37 p.m. play will continue until a result is achieved or the remaining time is used up.

Is anyone out when there is a protracted delay?

The answer to this question depends entirely on the action taken by the fielding side before the umpire calls Time in order to carry out their investigation.

If the fielding side **do not appeal** before Time is called, no one can be dismissed. Even though there is a delay and the incoming batsman takes longer than his allotted 3 minutes because there is no appeal, **before** the umpire calls Time no one can be given out.

If the fielding side **do appeal** before Time is called, a batsman is dismissed. The problem arises as to which batsman is out. Since no one has stepped foot on to the field of play the umpires have no way of knowing who the next man is. In this situation the captain of the batting side nominates the batsman who is to suffer this fate.

Obviously, the question of a dismissal will not be applicable if the umpires award the match where they decide that the delay does constitute a refusal to play.

Should there be an interval or interruption **immediately** following a dismissal, this Law does not apply. It only applies when play is taking place. At an interval or interruption Time is called immediately following the dismissal, so the 3-minute stipulation cannot apply.

Should there be an interval or interruption immediately following a dismissal, Time will have been called. After the interval the two batsmen must enter the field of play in time for the session to start at the scheduled time. Any delay by the batsmen will be subject to the Laws regarding time-wasting and refusal to play.

2. BOWLER DOES NOT GET CREDIT

The bowler does not get credit for the wicket.

A dismissal of Timed out is not credited to the bowler. As the dismissed batsman did not face a delivery, there are no balls to record.

Law 32 Caught

1. OUT CAUGHT

The striker is out Caught if a ball delivered by the bowler, not being a
No ball touches his bat without having previously been in contact with
any member of the fielding side and is subsequently held by a fielder as
a fair catch before it touches the ground.

2. CAUGHT TO TAKE PRECEDENCE

If the criteria of 1 above are met and the striker is not out Bowled,
then he is out Caught, even though a decision against either batsman
for another method of dismissal would be justified. Runs completed
by the batsmen before the completion of the catch will not be
scored. Note also Laws 21.6 (Winning hit or extras) and 42.17(b)
(Penalty runs).

3. A FAIR CATCH

A catch shall be considered to have been fairly made if
(a) throughout the act of making the catch
  (i) any fielder in contact with the ball is within the field of play.
  See 4 below.
  (ii) the ball is at no time in contact with any object grounded
  beyond the boundary.
  The act of making the catch shall start from the time when
  a fielder first handles the ball and shall end when a fielder
  obtains complete control both over the ball and over his own
  movement.
(b) the ball is hugged to the body of the catcher or accidentally lodges
  in his clothing or, in the case of the wicket-keeper, in his pads.
  However, it is not a fair catch if the ball lodges in a protective
  helmet worn by a fielder. See Law 23 (Dead ball).
(c) the ball does not touch the ground, even though the hand holding it
  does so in effecting the catch.
(d) a fielder catches the ball after it has been lawfully struck more than
  once by the striker, but only if the ball has not touched the ground
  since first being struck.
(e) a fielder catches the ball after it has touched an umpire, another
  fielder or the other batsman. However, it is not a fair catch if the
  ball has touched a protective helmet worn by a fielder, although the
  ball remains in play.
(f) a fielder catches the ball in the air after it has crossed the boundary
  provided that
  (i) he has no part of his person touching, or grounded beyond, the
  boundary at any time when he is in contact with the ball.

(ii) the ball has not been grounded beyond the boundary.
See Law 19.3 (Scoring a boundary).

(g) the ball is caught off an obstruction within the boundary, provided it has not previously been decided to regard the obstruction as a boundary.

4. FIELDER WITHIN THE FIELD OF PLAY

(a) A fielder is not within the field of play if he touches the boundary or has any part of his person grounded beyond the boundary. See Law 19.3 (Scoring a boundary).

(b) 6 runs shall be scored if a fielder
(i) has any part of his person touching, or grounded beyond, the boundary when he catches the ball.
(ii) catches the ball and subsequently touches the boundary or grounds some part of his person over the boundary while carrying the ball but before completing the catch.
See Laws 19.3 (Scoring a boundary) and 19.4 (Runs allowed for boundaries).

5. NO RUNS TO BE SCORED

If the striker is dismissed Caught, runs from that delivery completed by the batsmen before the completion of the catch shall not be scored, but any penalties awarded to either side when the ball is dead, if applicable, will stand. Law 18.12(a) (Batsman returning to wicket he has left) shall apply from the instant of the catch.

The Law outlines the basic requirements for a batsman to be out Caught:

*   A striker can be out Caught only from a fair delivery.
*   A striker cannot be caught from a No ball, or a Wide.
*   In order for a catch to be claimed the ball must have come off the bat. The bat is defined as:
    the bat itself and includes the glove which is on the hand holding the bat. Provided that the ball has hit any part of this area then it will be possible for the striker to be caught.
*   The ball must not have touched the ground at any time prior to it being caught.

Having established the above the Law goes on to explain how the act of a catch is defined. The act of making a catch:
*   **starts** when the fielder first touches the ball and
*   **ends** when he has complete control over both
    the ball and
    his own movement.

The first part is self-explanatory. It is the end of the catch that needs looking at.

'. . . COMPLETE CONTROL OVER THE BALL'

It is usually fairly obvious if the fielder is in control of the ball or not. If he is juggling with it then it is clear that he does not have control over it. However, if he is able to throw the ball high into the air, even though he had it in his hands for only a second, he has shown sufficient control over it for the catch to be valid. There is no time limit laid down as to how long the ball has to be in the hand(s) – the only criterion is that the fielder has to have control over it.

'. . . COMPLETE CONTROL OVER HIS OWN MOVEMENT'

The Law also stipulates that, having controlled the ball, the fielder must be in control of his own movement. This is more difficult for the umpire to determine because if the fielder is running the umpire has to decide whether the natural momentum of the fielder is under his control or not. The basic requirement is that the fielder is in full control of all his movements.

This aspect of the Law is particularly applicable when a catch is taken near the boundary and the fielder ends up stepping on or over the boundary. The umpire has to decide whether:

- it was the fielder's momentum which carried him over the boundary – a case of the fielder not being in control of his own movements or
- the fielder deliberately ran over the boundary as part of his celebrations – a case where the catch would be valid since the fielder had full control over where he wanted to go.

It is possible within the Law for a fielder to leave the field of play during the act of taking a catch and return to complete it. Provided that he is not in contact with the ball while he is grounded over the boundary then the catch will be valid.

EXAMPLE 1

Having 'caught' the ball the fielder realises that his momentum is going to carry him over the boundary before he has the chance to control his movement. While on the field of play he throws the ball into the air. His momentum carries him over the boundary where he recovers his control and returns to the field and catches the ball before it touches the ground. This will be a fair catch because the fielder fulfilled the criteria of the Law and at no time was he in contact with the ball while outside the field of play.

It will be a fair catch if the ball:

- is hugged to the body of the fielder – it does not have to be caught in the hand
- accidentally lodges in the clothing of a fielder
- is caught or lodges accidentally in the wicket-keeper's pads – the ball does not have to be caught with the hands. Provided that the control elements are present then the catch will be valid
- rebounds off an umpire or either batsman – the ball is still in play when this happens and the catch will be valid

- is in the hand and the hand touches the ground – provided that the ball doesn't touch the ground then the hand can do so without it invalidating the catch
- is caught while in the air even though the ball is beyond the boundary. Provided that neither the ball nor the fielder are grounded on or over the boundary it will be a fair catch (Photo 1)
- is caught after having hit an obstacle within the field of play, provided that the obstacle in question has not been agreed as a boundary.

However, it will **not** be a fair catch:

- if the ball lodges in the fielder's helmet – in this case the ball is dead
- if the ball rebounds from a fielder's helmet and is subsequently 'caught'. In this case the ball is still in play and although a catch cannot be claimed a run out could still be attempted (provided that the ball does not rebound directly on to the wicket)
- if a fielder, with the ball in hand, comes in contact with the boundary (Photo 2) – 6 runs are scored

- if the fielder completes a catch but steadies himself against a boundary fence or advertising board (Photo 3) – 6 runs are scored
- if the fielder completes the catch but carries the ball over the boundary (Photo 4) – 6 runs are scored. As in photos 2, 3 and 4, the Law is specific that 6 runs are scored no matter what the agreed boundary allowance

- if, in attempting a catch, the ball is deflected over the boundary the appropriate boundary allowance is scored, usually 4 or 6, depending on whether the ball touches the ground inside the boundary first.

HIT THE BALL TWICE

In Law 34 it is detailed that a striker may legally hit the ball a second time in defence of his wicket. If this is done then he will not be given out – Hit the ball twice. However, if he hits the ball a second time, and it is then caught, he will be given out Caught, provided that the ball has not touched the ground between the first and second hit. This always presupposes that at least one of the 'hits' was off the bat! If the ball touches the ground at any time after the first hit, the catch is invalid.

RUNS – AND THE FINAL POSITION OF THE NON-STRIKER

If a catch is successfully taken, no runs are scored by the batsmen even though they may have had time to complete one or more. However, any penalty runs awarded by the umpires will be added to the score.

Umpires should note the positions of the two running batsmen at the moment of completion of the catch as this determines at which end the not-out batsman is to be for the next delivery. If the batsmen had crossed on the run in progress, the not-out batsman will go to the end to which he was running or will remain at the end he had reached. If they had not crossed, the not-out batsman must be directed back to the end from which he came. The striker's end umpire should bear the responsibility for seeing that this is done as the bowler's end umpire will be concentrating more on whether the catch was legally made. If he is unsure it will be necessary for him to consult with his colleague and together the umpires will decide which end the non-striker should be.

A catch takes precedence over all other dismissals other than Bowled.

EXAMPLE 2

The ball is hit firmly back towards the bowler who, in his attempt to catch it, only manages to deflect it on to the wicket at his end. The non-striker is backing up and is out of his ground. The ball ricochets from the stumps into the hands of mid-off.

On appeal the striker is out – Caught. Even though the run out of the non-striker happened first, the catch takes precedence and the striker is the one given out.

A dismissal of Caught is credited to the bowler.

Law 33 Handled the ball

1. OUT HANDLED THE BALL

Either batsman is out Handled the ball if he wilfully touches the ball while in play with a hand or hands not holding the bat unless he does so with the consent of the opposing side.

2. NOT OUT HANDLED THE BALL

Notwithstanding 1 above, a batsman will not be out under this Law if
(i) he handles the ball in order to avoid injury.
(ii) he uses his hand or hands to return the ball to any member of
the fielding side without the consent of that side. Note, however, the
provisions of Law 37.4 (Returning the ball to a member of the
fielding side).

3. RUNS SCORED

If either batsman is dismissed under this Law, any runs completed
before the offence, together with any penalty extras and the penalty
for a No ball or Wide, if applicable, shall be scored. See Laws 18.10
(Runs scored when a batsman is dismissed) and 42.17 (Penalty runs).

4. BOWLER DOES NOT GET CREDIT

The bowler does not get credit for the wicket.

Either batsman can be dismissed Handled the ball from a fair delivery, a No ball, or a Wide.

If the ball is in play, and either batsman **wilfully** handles the ball without the consent of a member of the fielding side, that batsman is at risk of dismissal. If consent is given or implied by any member of the fielding side the batsman is not out. If consent is not given or implied the batsman will be given out.

If the batsman handles the ball while it is dead then he cannot be given out under this Law.

Law 34 describes how the striker may legally hit the ball a second time in defence of his wicket, using his bat or some part of his body. However he is not permitted to use his hand. If he offends in this way, he is at risk of dismissal.

EXAMPLE 1
A fair delivery is deflected off the striker's bat into the air and it falls towards his stumps. In an endeavour to prevent this, the striker uses his hand to deflect the ball.
On appeal, the striker must be dismissed Handled the ball.

This Law uses the word 'wilfully'. That means the umpire must be satisfied that the handling of the ball is deliberate. Having decided that an act was wilful the umpire will, if he has any doubt that the ball was handled, call Dead ball and consult with his colleague. If his colleague confirms the handling, the offending batsman will be dismissed under this Law. If a batsman uses his hand to prevent injury, real or perceived, this is not deemed to be a wilful act – it is an instinctive reaction that is not punished. Any wilful act of handling the ball should be considered an act that prevents or might prevent the fielding side from fulfilling their obligations and/or could create a situation whereby the batting side gain an unfair advantage.

The Law also states that should a batsman use his hands to return a ball that is in play to the fielding side (without first having gained their consent) then, although it is a wilful act, it is not punished by dismissal under this Law. However, an appeal would be justified under Law 37 (Obstructing the field) and the batsman would be dismissed under that Law.

Runs can be scored when a batsman is given out Handled the ball. The runs scored would be any completed runs scored prior to the act of handling; plus any penalty runs for a No ball or Wide delivery; plus any penalty runs given away by the fielding side.

EXAMPLE 2

The batsmen are running their 3rd run when the non-striker **wilfully** *deflects the returning ball with his hand.*

On appeal, the offending non-striker must be dismissed. The 2 completed runs are scored, but the 3rd run, during which the offence takes place, is not, even if the batsmen have crossed. The striker must be directed to the end to which he is closest at the moment the handling took place.

A dismissal of Handled the ball is not credited to the bowler.

Law 34 Hit the ball twice

1. OUT HIT THE BALL TWICE

(a) The striker is out Hit the ball twice if, while the ball is in play, it strikes any part of his person or is struck by his bat and, before the ball has been touched by a fielder, he wilfully strikes it again with his bat or person, other than a hand not holding the bat, except for the sole purpose of guarding his wicket. See 3 below and Laws 33 (Handled the ball) and 37 (Obstructing the field).

(b) For the purpose of this Law, 'struck' or 'strike' shall include contact with the person of the striker.

2. NOT OUT HIT THE BALL TWICE

Notwithstanding 1(a) above, the striker will not be out under this Law if
(i) he makes a second or subsequent stroke in order to return the ball to any member of the fielding side. Note, however, the provisions of Law 37.4 (Returning the ball to a member of the fielding side).
(ii) he wilfully strikes the ball after it has touched a fielder. Note, however, the provisions of Law 37.1 (Out Obstructing the field).

3. BALL LAWFULLY STRUCK MORE THAN ONCE

Solely in order to guard his wicket and before the ball has been touched by a fielder, the striker may lawfully strike the ball more than once with his bat or with any part of his person other than a hand not holding the bat.

Notwithstanding this provision, the striker may not prevent the ball from being caught by making more than one stroke in defence of his wicket. See Law 37.3 (Obstructing a ball from being caught).

4. RUNS PERMITTED FROM BALL LAWFULLY STRUCK MORE THAN ONCE

When the ball is lawfully struck more than once, as permitted in 3 above, only the first strike is to be considered in determining whether runs are to be allowed and how they are to be scored.

(a) If on the first strike the umpire is satisfied that

either (i)   the ball first struck the bat

or   (ii) the striker attempted to play the ball with his bat

or   (iii) the striker tried to avoid being hit by the ball

then any penalties to the batting side that are applicable shall be allowed.

(b) If the conditions in (a) above are met then, if they result from overthrows, and only if they result from overthrows, runs completed by the batsmen or a boundary will be allowed in addition to any penalties that are applicable. They shall be credited to the striker if the first strike was with the bat. If the first strike was on the person of the striker they shall be scored as Leg byes or No ball extras, as appropriate. See Law 26.2 (Leg byes).

(c) If the conditions of (a) above are met and there is no overthrow until after the batsmen have started to run, but before one run is completed,

(i)   only subsequent completed runs or a boundary shall be allowed. The first run shall count as a completed run for this purpose only if the batsmen have not crossed at the instant of the throw.

(ii) if in these circumstances the ball goes to the boundary from the throw then, notwithstanding the provisions of Law 19.6 (Overthrow or wilful act of fielder), only the boundary allowance shall be scored.

(iii) if the ball goes to the boundary as the result of a further overthrow, then runs completed by the batsmen after the first throw and before this final throw shall be added to the boundary allowance. The run in progress at the first throw will count only if they have not crossed at that moment; the run in progress at the final throw shall count only if they have crossed at that moment. Law 18.12 (Batsman returning to wicket he has left) shall apply as from the moment of the final throw.

(d) If, in the opinion of the umpire, none of the conditions in (a) above have been met then, whether there is an overthrow or not, the batting side shall not be credited with any runs from that delivery apart from the penalty for a No ball if applicable. Moreover, no other penalties shall be awarded to the batting side when the ball is dead. See Law 42.17 (Penalty runs).

5. BALL LAWFULLY STRUCK MORE THAN ONCE – ACTION BY THE UMPIRE

If no runs are to be allowed, either in the circumstances of 4(d) above, or because there has been no overthrow and

(a) if no run is attempted but the ball reaches the boundary, the umpire shall call and signal Dead ball and disallow the boundary.

(b) if the batsmen run and

(i) neither batsman is dismissed and the ball does not become dead for any other reason, the umpire shall call and signal Dead ball as soon as one run is completed or the ball reaches the boundary. The batsmen shall return to their original ends. The run or boundary shall be disallowed.

(ii) a batsman is dismissed, or if for any other reason the ball becomes dead before one run is completed or the ball reaches the boundary, all the provisions of the Laws will apply except that the award of penalties to the batting side shall be as laid down in 4(a) or 4(d) above as appropriate.

6. BOWLER DOES NOT GET CREDIT

The bowler does not get credit for the wicket.

This Law affects only the striker. A striker can be out Hit the ball twice off a fair delivery and a No ball, but not off a Wide.

It is important to establish exactly what the Law means by the phrase 'hit the ball twice'. There are basically three situations in which a ball can be hit twice – two that are permissible and not subject to dismissal, with the third being the one that this Law is intended to prevent.

The phrase 'hit the ball twice' does not require the ball to be hit twice by the bat. It can be any combination of bat and the striker's person, so can be with:

• bat, then bat
• bat, then person
• person, then bat
• person, then person.

The following are examples of the ball being hit twice, only the third one being illegal.

ACCIDENTAL SECOND HIT

The striker is permitted to make a second contact with the ball while trying to hit it, provided that the second contact is made while executing the **same stroke**. This is not punished. This is a comparatively common event: the ball being deflected off the pad or foot on to the bat or vice-versa; or the ball making two contacts with the bat while the striker is in the process of executing a hook shot.

WILFUL SECOND HIT (IN DEFENCE OF HIS WICKET)

The striker is permitted a second **separate** contact provided it is made for **the sole purpose of guarding his wicket**. The striker is permitted to use his bat or person (but not his hand) to protect his wicket and this is not punished, provided he does not prevent a catch in the process. So if the ball, after being hit with the bat, rolls towards his wicket, the striker is permitted to knock it away with his bat, foot, or person (other than the hand) without fear of being dismissed. If, however, by doing this he prevents a catch from being taken, he will be guilty of Obstructing the field and will be given out for this offence – not for hitting the ball a second time.

If **No ball** is called and the striker legally hits the ball a second time in defence of his wicket he cannot be dismissed – even though, technically, his wicket was not at risk. Since it was a No ball, there was no danger of the striker being bowled and therefore it would not be necessary for him to try to prevent the ball from hitting the stumps. However, the Law allows for the instinctive reaction of the striker to be taken into account and therefore does not punish the striker for this natural reaction to the situation.

WILFUL SECOND HIT (ILLEGAL)

The striker is not permitted a second **separate** hit if he is not attempting to protect his wicket. It is this third example that the Law legislates for, intended as it is to prevent the batsman from 'teeing up' the ball by using the first hit to stop the ball, or slow it down, then hitting it again to score runs. Though rarely encountered, were it not covered in the Laws there would be no action that the umpires could take if it happened during a match.

Should a batsman hit the ball a second time to return it to the fielding side (without first having gained their consent), the striker is given out under Law 37 Obstructing the field. By doing this he is going to be given out – it is only the way that it is recorded that needs to be understood.

RUNS SCORED

The situation regarding runs scored (or not scored) when this act takes place requires careful consideration since it can get rather complicated.

The striker has the right to hit the ball a second time to guard his wicket but he is not permitted to gain any further advantage by scoring runs. The current passage of play is complete and unless something happens to reactivate it, the action from that delivery is at an end and the ball is effectively dead.

It follows therefore that the only runs that can be scored from the delivery – provided nothing else happens – are penalty runs given away by the fielding side i.e. No balls and penalty awards. This is quite logical since penalty runs are runs given to the batting side by the fielding side as opposed to runs being scored as a result of actions by the batsmen. If the fielding side are careless in their fielding of the ball and subsequent throwing of it, the batsmen are allowed to score runs resulting from such carelessness – overthrows. Remember, however, that for this Law, runs can be scored from overthrows only if the first strike is by the bat or, if by the striker's person, provided he has tried to hit the ball with the bat or has tried to avoid being hit by the ball.

Given that **prior** to an act of overthrows, or if overthrows do not occur, the batting side cannot score runs from running, what happens if they do attempt to score runs before the overthrow occurs? In these circumstances, the umpire should wait to see what the fielding side wish to do about it before taking any action. The fielding side have two options:

Option 1

They can do nothing and just watch the batsmen run. The umpire must wait until the batsmen have completed their first run and then:
- call and signal Dead ball
- disallow that run
- return the batsmen to their original ends.

Option 2

They can attempt to run out either batsman. If they are successful in the attempt then one batsman is run out. If they are not successful the umpires must decide how many runs are to be scored following the overthrow, which will depend upon where the batsmen are when the ball is actually thrown.

Two scenarios are applicable here:

1. The batsmen set off for a run and have crossed before the fielder throws the ball, i.e. before the instant of the overthrow.

Since the batsmen have tried to score a run before they are legally allowed to do so, the first run (the one they are running when the ball is thrown) does not count. The fact that the batsmen have crossed on this first run means that they have gained too much of an advantage and so the run is not counted. Any other runs completed after this first one will be counted.

EXAMPLE 1

The batsmen set off for a run and have crossed before the fielder throws the ball. They complete 1 run before the ball becomes dead.

Since the batsmen have crossed before the ball is thrown, the first – and only – run is not counted.

RUNS SCORED: = 0.

The batsmen are not returned to their original ends. Only when a run is disallowed are batsmen returned to their original ends – here, the run is, simply, not counted.

EXAMPLE 2

The batsmen set off for a run and have crossed before the fielder throws the ball. They complete 3 runs before the ball becomes dead.

Since the batsmen have crossed before the ball is thrown the first run is not counted, but the subsequent runs are since they occurred after the throw.

RUNS SCORED: = 2.

The batsmen remain at the ends at which they finished. Although only 2 runs are scored, the batsmen do not revert to their original positions. They stay where they are.

2. The batsmen set off for a run and have not crossed when the fielder throws the ball, i.e. before the instant of the overthrow.

Even though the batsmen have set off for a run before they are legally allowed to do so, the first run (the one they are on when the ball was thrown) is counted. The fact that the batsmen have not crossed on this first run means that they have not gained too much of an advantage. Therefore, in this scenario, all runs are counted.

EXAMPLE 3

The batsmen set off for a run and have not crossed when the fielder throws the ball. They complete 1 run before the ball becomes dead.

Since the batsmen have not crossed before the ball is thrown the one – and only – run is counted.

RUNS SCORED: Runs scored = 1.

EXAMPLE 4

The batsmen set off for a run and have not crossed when the fielder throws the ball. They complete 3 runs before the ball becomes dead.

Since the batsmen have not crossed before the ball is thrown all completed runs are counted.

RUNS SCORED: Runs scored = 3.

The relevant point in the above examples is whether or not the batsmen had crossed before the overthrow:

• if they had crossed then they cannot gain credit for the run in progress
• if they had not crossed they do gain credit for the run started.

(This is the reverse of other occasions in the Laws where crossing on a run usually means that the run in progress will count – e.g. illegal fielding and normal overthrows.)

If the ball reaches the boundary from the original overthrow, only the boundary will count. The above matter of when the batsmen had crossed, in relation to the throw, will not be applicable.

The reason for this is that, as runs become legitimate because of the throw, it follows that runs before the throw cannot be counted. Therefore, in line with a normal overthrow situation, the runs to be added to the score will be the boundary allowance of 4 runs plus the runs accrued before the throw – in this situation, none.

EXAMPLE 5

The batsmen start to run after the fielder throws the ball – quite legal.

The batsmen cross on their 2nd run when the ball reaches the boundary.

Only the boundary is scored.

RUNS SCORED: Runs scored = 4.

If there is a series of overthrows which result in the ball finally reaching the boundary, only the final overthrow will be considered. Any runs completed prior to the last throw, and the run in progress provided the batsmen had crossed, will be added to the boundary allowance. This is normal overthrow procedure.

EXAMPLE 6

The batsmen start to run after the fielder throws the ball – quite legal.

The first attempt at the run out fails and the ball runs into the outfield. The batsmen complete their 2nd run while it is being retrieved – 2 scored.

The second throw is wild and also misses the stumps. At the moment the second throw takes place the batsmen have crossed on their 3rd run.

This run will count (because they have crossed before the throw took place – a normal overthrow situation) – 3 scored in total up to this moment.

The ball goes on to reach the boundary from this second throw – 4.

RUNS SCORED: Total runs scored = 3 + 4 = 7.

Any runs scored from overthrows are credited to the striker providing the ball hit the bat before any second contact. If the first hit was not with the bat the runs are recorded as extras, either No balls or Leg byes. Due to the various permutations and the complicated nature of this Law, the umpires will almost always need to confer in order to calculate the number of runs scored and then confirm this to the scorers.

A dismissal of Hit the ball twice is not credited to the bowler.

When a batsman is out Hit the ball twice no runs are scored – except, where applicable, the 1 run penalty for a No ball.

Law 35 Hit wicket

1. OUT HIT WICKET

(a) **The striker is out Hit wicket if, after the bowler has entered his delivery stride and while the ball is in play, his wicket is put down either by the striker's bat or by his person as described in Law 28.1(a)(ii) and (iii) (Wicket put down)**

    either (i) in the course of any action taken by him in preparing to receive or in receiving a delivery,

    or   (ii) in setting off for his first run immediately after playing, or playing at, the ball,

or (iii) if he makes no attempt to play the ball, in setting off for
his first run, providing that in the opinion of the umpire this is
immediately after he has had the opportunity of playing the ball,

or (iv) in lawfully making a second or further stroke for the
purpose of guarding his wicket within the provisions of Law 34.3
(Ball lawfully struck more than once).

(b) If the striker puts his wicket down in any of the ways described in
Law 28.1(a)(ii) and (iii) (Wicket put down) before the bowler has
entered his delivery stride, either umpire shall call and signal
Dead ball.

2. NOT OUT HIT WICKET

Notwithstanding 1 above, the batsman is not out under this Law should
his wicket be put down in any of the ways referred to in 1 above if

(a) it occurs after he has completed any action in receiving the
delivery, other than as in 1(a)(ii), (iii) or (iv) above.

(b) it occurs when he is in the act of running, other than in setting off
immediately for his first run.

(c) it occurs when he is trying to avoid being run out or stumped.

(d) it occurs while he is trying to avoid a throw-in at any time.

(e) the bowler after starting his run up, or his bowling action if he has
no run up, does not deliver the ball. In this case either umpire shall
immediately call and signal Dead ball. See Law 23.3 (Umpire calling
and signalling Dead ball).

(f) the delivery is a No ball.

A striker can be out Hit wicket off a fair delivery or a wide. He cannot be out Hit
wicket off a No ball.

This Law deals with the case(s) where the striker's person or equipment breaks the
wicket. If, at any time, the ball breaks the wicket, even though the striker may have
kicked or hit it on to the wicket, that dismissal is Bowled – not Hit wicket.

The dismissal Hit wicket is confined to a specific, limited time frame. The striker is
vulnerable to dismissal:

• from the moment the bowler enters his delivery stride
• until, and including, him setting off for his first run immediately after playing at,
or attempting to play at, the ball.

If the striker breaks his wicket before the bowler enters his delivery stride the umpire
will call and signal Dead ball and the striker cannot be out. Once the bowler has
reached his delivery stride the striker is vulnerable to dismissal, and if he breaks his
wicket while undertaking any of the following he is liable to dismissal:

• preparing to receive the ball – this includes movements such as the backlift of
his bat
• playing at the ball while receiving it
• any follow-through of the bat after the ball has been received

- any other action that occurs prior to his setting off for his first run.

This setting off for the first run, again, has a specific and important time frame surrounding it. It is defined as being **immediately** after playing at the ball. If there is any delay between playing at the ball and setting off for the first run, that delay will negate any Hit wicket dismissal.

EXAMPLE 1

Having played at the ball the striker waits for a second or two to see if the ball has evaded the fielder and then sets off for a run. In doing so, he slips and breaks his wicket.

The striker cannot be dismissed because there was a delay in his setting off on that first run – it was not immediately after playing at the ball. The ball remains in play following that appeal. The striker's end umpire must watch the action and decide when the action of playing the ball is complete and if the act of commencing his first run is immediate.

The striker is also vulnerable to being dismissed if he hits his wicket while legally attempting to hit the ball a second time while trying to protect his wicket.

It is stated at the beginning of this Law that it could be either the striker's person that breaks the wicket or his equipment. This includes such things as his bat, his pads, his hat or helmet falling on to the wicket and provided that it occurs within that limited time frame he must be dismissed Hit wicket.

EXAMPLE 2

Having played a late cut at the delivery, the striker steps back on to his stumps removing a bail. There is an appeal and he retains his ground.

The umpire must decide if the action occurred during the time frame. Since it clearly did so, the striker's end umpire must give the striker out – Hit wicket.

EXAMPLE 3

As the striker attempts to play at the ball, his cap is dislodged and falls on to his stumps removing a bail. The striker does not wait for an appeal and 'walks'.

The dismissal of Hit wicket is valid.

Other things that may occur causing the striker to hit his wicket could include:

- moving quickly to avoid a throw in and stepping on to his wicket
- running back to avoid being stumped or run out
- running into the wicket while in pursuit of runs.

If any of these incidents occur, the striker cannot be dismissed Hit wicket because they would have occurred after the specific time frame.

An appeal for dismissal Hit wicket is one of the appeals to be answered by the striker's end umpire.

A dismissal of Hit wicket is credited to the bowler.

Law 36 Leg before wicket

1. OUT LBW

The striker is out **LBW** in the circumstances set out below.

(a) The bowler delivers a ball, not being a No ball,

and (b) the ball, if it is not intercepted full pitch, pitches in line between wicket and wicket or on the off side of the striker's wicket,

and (c) the ball not having previously touched his bat, the striker intercepts the ball, either full-pitch or after pitching, with any part of his person,

and (d) the point of impact, even if above the level of the bails

either (i) is between wicket and wicket,

or   (ii) is either between wicket and wicket or outside the line of the off stump if the striker has made no genuine attempt to play the ball with his bat,

and (e) but for the interception, the ball would have hit the wicket.

2. INTERCEPTION OF THE BALL

(a) In assessing points (c), (d) and (e) in 1 above only the first interception is to be considered.

(b) In assessing point (e) in 1 above, it is to be assumed that the path of the ball before interception would have continued after interception, irrespective of whether it might have pitched subsequently or not.

3. OFF SIDE OF WICKET

The off side of the striker's wicket shall be determined by the striker's stance at the moment the ball comes into play for that delivery.

SUMMARY

In order for the striker to be out LBW all of the following must have happened:

- the ball must have been a fair delivery
- the ball must have pitched or have been intercepted full pitch between wicket and wicket or on the off side of the wicket
- the first interception must have been the striker's person or equipment and not the bat
- where the striker **has** made a genuine attempt to hit the ball with the bat, that interception must have been between wicket and wicket

  or

  where the striker has **not** made a genuine attempt to hit the ball with the bat, that interception must have been between wicket and wicket or on the off side
- but for that interception the ball must have been going to hit the wicket.

EXPLANATION

When dealing with LBW the umpire must consider four questions and, in order to give the striker out, must answer them all in the affirmative. It is easier to deal with each question as it happens on the field thus ending up with a logical approach to the appeal. For ease it is assumed that the delivery was fair (the striker cannot be out LBW from a no ball).

1. Did the ball pitch between wicket and wicket or on the off side?

In the example above the only deliveries which are able to get the striker out LBW are the ones in the green sector i.e. balls 2 and 3 and the one outside the off stump, ball 1. The green sector is the area between wicket and wicket. Provided the ball pitches somewhere in either of these sectors, the striker is possibly going to be given out. The final decision will depend on the answers to the other three questions that the umpire will consider in turn.

If the ball pitches **outside the leg stump** (ball 4) the striker **must not** be given out LBW.

A ball pitching in line with leg stump (ball 3) has pitched between wicket and wicket and therefore would fall into the green sector.

Provided the answer to this question is Yes, the umpire can proceed to the next question. If the answer is No then the striker is not out and no further considerations need be made.

2. Was the first point of interception the striker's person or equipment and not the bat?

This simply means that the umpire must be sure that the first contact that the ball made was on the person or equipment of the striker. If the ball first made contact with the bat, or the hand (including the glove on the hand) holding the bat, and subsequently made contact with the striker's person or equipment then he cannot be given out LBW.

Any contact with the bat before the ball hits the person or equipment means that the answer to this question is No and the striker is not out LBW.

If the umpire is sure that the first contact was the person or equipment then the answer to this question is Yes and the striker is still vulnerable to being given out (again, depending on the answers to the next two questions).

The next question is divided into two parts and the answer depends on what action the striker takes when dealing with the delivery. He has two options:

- he can make a genuine attempt to hit the ball using his bat or
- he can decide to ignore the bat and simply play the ball with his person or equipment.

Option 1 Where the striker **does** make a genuine attempt to hit the ball with the bat but misses it.

3a. Was that first interception (in question 2) between wicket and wicket?

Provided that the striker has attempted to hit the ball using his bat then the interception that took place in question 2 has to be between wicket and wicket. If this happens the answer to the question is Yes and the umpire progresses to the last question.

Where the striker **does** make a genuine attempt to hit the ball with the bat, the umpire must be very careful to pinpoint the striker's position when the interception took place. The striker will be moving as the attempt to play the ball is made and if the movement is such that the interception takes place outside the off stump then the striker cannot be out LBW. The umpire must be sure that the interception took place between wicket and wicket before he can answer this question with a Yes.

Option 2 Where the striker makes no attempt to hit the ball with his bat but simply uses his person or equipment to stop/deflect the ball.

3b. Was that first interception (in question 2) between wicket and wicket or on the off side?

In the photograph opposite, because the striker has not attempted to use his bat his area of vulnerability is larger. As in the previous instance he is still liable to be given out from the ball (1) which has been intercepted between wicket and wicket, but this time he is also vulnerable from the ball (2) that has hit him outside the off stump.

In the illustration above, the answer to the question is Yes on both occasions and the umpire has to progress to the last question to see if the striker is going to be given out.

The umpire should easily answer the first three questions because they are events that actually happened. Provided that the umpire is concentrating then he should not make an error with the facts that he saw. The final question is not a question of fact but of opinion and needs careful consideration by the umpire.

4. Had the ball not been intercepted, in the umpire's opinion, would it have gone on to hit the wicket?

In order for the umpire to make this judgement there are certain pieces of information that he has been given that will help him with his final decision.

FLIGHT OF THE BALL

The umpire should be aware that information regarding the flight of the ball, as it travels towards the striker, begins as soon as the ball leaves the bowler's hand. The umpire should not dwell too long on the bowler's feet during the delivery stride so that he is late in picking up the flight of the ball. The decision regarding the placement of the bowler's feet should be made as soon as possible so as to allow the eyes to be diverted to the ball as it travels down the pitch. This is of particular importance should the delivery be intercepted on the full.

TRAVELLING DISTANCE

What happens to the ball between pitching and making contact with the batsman is probably the most significant piece of information when deciding an LBW decision. The distance from where the ball pitched in front of the striker to where it actually makes contact with him is known as travelling distance (indicated by the line in the photograph). This will vary from delivery to delivery. The reason it is important is that during this distance the umpire needs to be certain of the ball's path after pitching and before interception.

Was the path that the ball was taking straight? Did it spin? If so, to what degree? Did it deviate off the seam? Again, to what degree? Seeing any such movement or deviation helps the umpire decide on the ball's future path.

After any spin, swing or movement that was detected, the ball would have carried on along that same path, but for the interception. So all the umpire has to do is envisage where that path would have taken the ball in relation to the wicket.

The travelling distance will vary. The closer the ball pitches to the striker – in other words the shorter the travelling distance – the harder it is for the umpire to make a judgement as to the ball's future path. Also, the faster the ball is travelling the quicker it will cover this distance. So, the faster the delivery the more travelling distance the umpire needs.

The amount of time that the umpire has to watch the ball will dictate how accurately he can estimate its future path. The more time he has, and therefore the greater the travelling distance, the easier this prediction becomes.

There are no statutory travelling distances for any given speeds of bowling. The umpire must be satisfied that he has had enough time to see what path the ball was taking after it pitched and before it was intercepted. Each umpire's experience and abilities are different and any judgement made in this area will depend on an umpire's own personal aptitude.

It must always be remembered that, from the bowler's end, the umpire gets a foreshortened view of the striker, ball and wicket at the striker's end. This foreshortening of distances can be very deceptive and can lead to misinterpretation of facts if not borne in mind.

The picture on the left shows exactly what this means. It is the same situation as the one above and clearly shows the dangers that this foreshortened view can give.

POINT OF INTERCEPTION

There is another factor for the umpire to consider in connection with the delivery. At the point where the ball was intercepted, how much further did it have to travel in order for it to reach the wicket? The further this distance, the more difficult it is for the umpire to be certain that the ball would have gone on to hit the wicket.

Playing forward

By playing forward the striker (see photograph, next page) has his front foot some 6–7 ft (2–2.25 m) in front of the wicket. The umpire has to monitor the path of the ball as it travels towards the wicket and must try to ignore the fact that it has been interrupted on its journey. He has to try to predict whether the path it was taking

would, but for the interception, have taken it on to the stumps. A distance such as this makes it very difficult for him to judge whether or not it would have hit the wicket – particularly if there had been any spin or movement off the seam. Having said this, many a batsman has been given out 'on the front foot' and that is perfectly correct if the umpire is quite happy that, from what he has seen, the ball would have gone on to hit the wicket.

Playing back

When the batsman is playing back to a delivery, the judgement of the ball's future path becomes much easier. In this illustration the striker is standing a little way back from the popping crease when he intercepts the ball which means that the ball would only have 3-4 ft (1.25 m) to travel to reach the wicket. As in the previous example the umpire has to assume that the path the ball took, after pitching and before interception, would have been the same had it not hit the striker's pad, but the shorter distance makes it a much easier judgement to make – and of course, if it was spinning towards leg or the off side then the judgement may well be that it would have missed the wicket.

HOW HIGH WAS THE INTERCEPTION?

So far all the points made have been concentrated on any spin, swing or movement off the seam – i.e. any lateral or sideways movement the ball has taken. While this is important, the umpire must also consider the height at which the ball was

intercepted. Using the above example we can see that the height at which the ball is intercepted will also determine whether or not it would hit the stumps.

In each of the examples considered above it has been assumed that the ball was on its way up as it struck the striker. However, if it was a slow delivery and dropping down as it hit him, different judgements may well be made.

The illustration above depicts a ball that has pitched (ball 1) and has been intercepted by the striker's pads in three separate areas (balls 2-4). Since the striker is playing back it could be judged that the top ball (4) might well be going over the stumps. If the ball was rising as it hit the striker then that assumption would be correct. However, if the ball was a slow delivery which had reached the height of its trajectory and was on its way down when it was intercepted the ball may well have gone on to hit the wicket.

Remember: the ball can be intercepted anywhere on the body, even to the extent of it being intercepted above the level of the stumps, and still be going on to hit them provided that it is dropping. So if a batsman is down on one knee playing a sweep shot, misses the ball, and is hit when the ball is above the level of the stumps, this does not debar him from being out LBW: if the ball is dropping, or is going to drop before it reaches the stumps, the umpire may well decide that the ball would have hit the wicket.

The whole point about height is that it must be considered in addition to all the other aspects that have been discussed. The amount of spin, swing or movement off the seam plus the height at which the ball was intercepted must all be considered together.

FULL TOSS

When the ball is intercepted on the full the four questions referred to on pages 226 to 229 are dealt with in the following way:

Question 1 can be disregarded because the ball did not pitch before it was intercepted.

Question 2 is still relevant because it is vital that the **first** interception was the striker's person or equipment and not his bat.

Question 3 is still relevant because the action the striker takes when receiving the delivery still has a bearing on where it has to be intercepted in order to fulfil the criteria laid down in the law.

Question 4 still applies.

Since the ball never pitches the most significant information that the umpire receives about this type of delivery is the flight of the ball (see page 229 for further details). So, if the ball were travelling in a straight line before it was intercepted, the umpire would expect that it would have kept going straight had it not been interrupted in its journey towards the wicket. Similarly, a swinging ball would have continued to swing along its same path had it not been stopped from doing so by the interception.

In the illustration on page 234, the ball is swinging to leg and is intercepted on the full in front of the stumps. So far it has met all the criteria for a 'full toss' LBW: the first interception was the striker's person; that interception was between wicket and wicket; and the striker was attempting to hit it. But, had it not been intercepted, the ball would have continued to swing along the same path that it was already taking, which would take it past the leg stump. So the striker cannot be out since the ball would not have hit the wicket.

In this example the path of the ball, before interception, was straight. Therefore, had the striker's foot not stopped it, the umpire has to assume that the ball would have continued along that same straight line and would have hit the wicket.

The fact that the ball *would/may* have pitched on the ground and *may* have taken some deviation through spin, or the roughness of the ground, due to that pitching **is of no interest** to the umpire. He does not have to guess the amount of deviation that the ball *may* have taken due to this *imaginary* pitching. All the umpire is concerned with is the path of the ball before it was intercepted and then mentally extend that path to judge whether it would have taken the ball on to the wicket.

Note, however, that when dealing with full tosses those other factors discussed in relation to a ball that pitches still apply:

• how far had the ball to travel in order to reach the wicket? If the interception took place a long way in front of the popping crease then the decision as to whether or not the ball would have hit the wicket would still be a difficult one to make.

• how high was the interception? The umpire still has to make the judgement with regards to the height of the interception and whether or not the ball would be above the height of the stumps when it reached the wicket.

3. OFF SIDE OF WICKET

The off side of the striker's wicket shall be determined by the striker's stance at the moment the ball comes into play for that delivery.

This is put into the Law to clarify at what stage the leg side and off side are determined for each delivery.

A batsman may take any action in order to play the delivery and that may mean turning his body so that he is adopting a different stance from when the bowler started his run-up. The reverse sweep is a good example of a batsman changing the position of the leg side after the bowler has delivered the ball. Another would be when a right-handed batsman switches hands, and therefore his stance, to play the ball left handed (after the bowler has started his run-up) – quite legitimate but it could cause confusion when deciding what is the leg side after any such movement.

The Law stipulates that, once the ball comes into play for that delivery i.e. the bowler starts his run-up or (where he has no run-up) his delivery action, the off side and leg side are determined by the striker's stance at that point in time. Any subsequent movement by the striker does not alter the position of the leg or off side for that delivery.

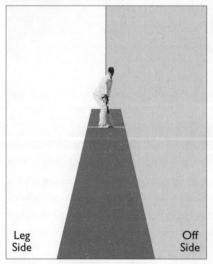

| Leg Side | Off Side | Off Side | Leg Side |

A left-handed striker's off side is to the umpire's right – the shaded zone.

A right-handed striker's off side is to the umpire's left – the shaded zone.

No runs are scored when a batsman is out LBW.

Penalty runs can be awarded and scored following the delivery but these are not credited to the striker or debited against the bowler.

A dismissal of LBW is credited to the bowler.

Law 37 Obstructing the field

I. OUT OBSTRUCTING THE FIELD

Either batsman is out Obstructing the field if he wilfully obstructs or distracts the opposing side by word or action. It shall be regarded as obstruction if either batsman wilfully, and without the consent of the fielding side, strikes the ball with his bat or person, other than a hand not holding the bat, after the ball has touched a fielder. See 4 below.

2. ACCIDENTAL OBSTRUCTION

It is for either umpire to decide whether any obstruction or distraction is wilful or not. He shall consult the other umpire if he has any doubt.

- Either batsman can be out Obstructing the field off a fair delivery, a No ball, or a Wide.
- The batsmen are vulnerable only while the ball is in play – if the ball is dead then no part of this Law applies.
- The batting side are not allowed to deliberately obstruct the fielding side from performing their role of fielding the ball.

If either umpire considers that either batsman has unfairly hindered the fielding side then he will uphold the appeal for Obstructing the field. However, he must be very careful to distinguish between what is an accidental act and one that is wilful i.e. deliberate. There are often cases of accidental obstruction and these must not be punished by the batsman being dismissed. The umpire must be sure that the obstruction was deliberate and it may be necessary to consult with his colleague before making his final decision.

The Law makes it clear that obstruction can be caused through **word** or **action.** There may be occasions when a batsman:

- deliberately uses his bat to deflect the ball away from the wicket he is running towards; or
- deliberately shouts as the fielder is about to field the ball; or
- deliberately shouts or physically obstructs the fielder from taking a catch.

While these examples may appear obvious, a prudent umpire may wish to consult with his colleague before giving his final decision

It must be fully understood which batsman is given out when such deliberate obstruction takes place. Under normal conditions, he who obstructs is dismissed – and quite rightly so – since the one who causes the obstruction is at fault and should face the consequences. However, clause 3 below also needs to be taken into account before a final decision is made.

3. OBSTRUCTING A BALL FROM BEING CAUGHT

The striker is out should wilful obstruction or distraction by either batsman prevent a catch being made.

This shall apply even though the striker causes the obstruction in lawfully guarding his wicket under the provisions of Law 34.3 (Ball lawfully struck more than once).

If the deliberate obstruction prevents a catch from being made it is always the striker who is dismissed, even though he may not have caused the obstruction. Had the obstruction not taken place, and the catch had been held, the striker would be dismissed so it follows that it should still be the striker who is out.

The degree of difficulty of the catch is not the umpire's concern. Provided that the umpire considers that it was a situation where a catch could have been effected then any wilful obstruction of that catch is punished.

On such occasions, the umpire may need to explain his decision, particularly if the wrong batsman starts to leave the field.

Law 34 deals with the case where a striker legally hits a ball a second time in defence of his wicket. If that act prevents a catch, on appeal, the striker must be dismissed Obstructing the field.

4. RETURNING THE BALL TO A MEMBER OF THE FIELDING SIDE

Either batsman is out under this Law if, without the consent of the fielding side and while the ball is in play, he uses his bat or person to return the ball to any member of that side.

While the ball is in play the batsman is not allowed to return the ball to the fielding side by using his bat or any part of his person unless he has permission from the fielding side.

Should a batsman use his hand to return the ball he will not be dismissed for handling the ball, although that is what he has done, but he will be guilty of deliberate obstruction and will be dismissed Obstructing the field. However, if he picks up the ball and throws it away from the fielding side's reach he will be dismissed because he has Handled the ball and will be recorded as such in the scoring record.

Once the fielding side has given the batsman permission to return the ball, either verbally or by a signal, the batsman cannot be dismissed.

5. RUNS SCORED

If a batsman is dismissed under this Law, runs completed by the batsmen before the offence shall be scored, together with the penalty for a No ball or a Wide, if applicable. Other penalties that may be awarded to either side when the ball is dead shall also stand. See Law 42.17(b) (Penalty runs).

If, however, the obstruction prevents a catch from being made, runs completed by the batsmen before the offence shall not be scored, but other penalties that may be awarded to either side when the ball is dead shall stand. See Law 42.17(b) (Penalty runs).

Runs are allowed if a batsman is given out under this Law. The number of runs scored will depend on how many the batsmen have completed before the act took place.

All completed runs which are scored before the act are recorded but the run in progress at the time of the act is not – since the run in progress was not completed it cannot be allowed to stand. Penalty runs awarded by the umpires or the penalty for a No ball or Wide ball are scored.

However, if the obstruction prevents a catch from being taken no runs are scored. This is consistent with Law 32 that states that where a catch is made no runs are scored. Prevention of a catch falls under the same heading.

Penalty runs awarded by the umpires will stand because they are runs awarded for an offence by the fielding team, as opposed to those being scored through the actions of the batsmen in running.

The umpires should ensure that the correct number of runs are recorded and they may need to confer with the scorers at the next interval.

6. BOWLER DOES NOT GET CREDIT
The bowler does not get credit for the wicket.

A dismissal of Obstructing the field is not credited to the bowler.

Law 38 Run out

1. OUT RUN OUT
(a) **Either batsman is out Run out, except as in 2 below, if at any time while the ball is in play**
  (i) **he is out of his ground**
  and (ii) **his wicket is fairly put down by the opposing side.**
(b) **(a) above shall apply even though No ball has been called and whether or not a run is being attempted, except in the circumstances of Law 39.3(b) (Not out Stumped).**

2. BATSMAN NOT RUN OUT
Notwithstanding 1 above, a batsman is not out Run out if
(a) **he has been within his ground and has subsequently left it to avoid injury, when the wicket is put down.**
(b) **the ball has not subsequently been touched again by a fielder, after the bowler has entered his delivery stride, before the wicket is put down.**
(c) **the ball, having been played by the striker, or having come off his person, directly strikes a helmet worn by a fielder and without**

further contact with him or any other fielder rebounds directly on
to the wicket. However, the ball remains in play and either batsman
may be Run out in the circumstances of 1 above if a wicket is
subsequently put down.

(d) he is out Stumped. See Law 39.1(b) (Out Stumped).

**(e) he is out of his ground, not attempting a run and his wicket is fairly
put down by the wicket-keeper without the intervention of
another member of the fielding side, if No ball has been called.
See Law 39.3(b) (Not out Stumped).**

Either batsman can be run out off a fair delivery, a no ball, or a wide. In simple terms
a batsman will be run out if, while the ball is in play, he is out of his ground, and his
wicket is put down.

All the component parts of this Law are detailed in other Laws so there is no need
to dwell on them here:

- Law 23 Dead ball: while the **ball is in play** – it is **not** dead
- Law 29 Batsman out of his ground: no part of his **person** or **bat in hand** is
  grounded behind the **popping crease**
- Law 28 The Wicket is down: provided this is done correctly.

This Law also details the occasions when a batsman **cannot** be run out, following
certain incidents:

- **The striker**: if the action falls in line with Law 39 Stumped.
- **Either batsman**: if a batsman **makes good his ground** and then subsequently
  leaves it to avoid being hit or injured by the ball.
  In such an event, he cannot be dismissed if his wicket is immediately broken by
  the fielding side. The crucial point here for umpires to watch for is that the batsman **does** makes good his ground **before** leaving it. It is only **provided** that the batsman fulfills this part of his obligations that he is saved from being run out.
- **Either batsman**: if the ball **directly** strikes and then rebounds **directly** back on to
  the wicket off a helmet worn by a fielder.
  In these circumstances, the ball remains in play, and a further run out attempt can
  be made. While the fielding side are allowed to wear helmets for protection they
  cannot be allowed to use that extra protection to their advantage in this situation.
- **Non-striker**: if the ball is hit **directly** back on to the wicket at the bowler's end.
  In order to effect a valid run out the ball must be touched by a member of the fielding
  side before it breaks the wicket. The umpire must be particularly observant when
  the ball is hit directly down the pitch towards him, not only to get out of its way,
  but also because the bowler may make an attempt to field the ball and/or divert it
  on to the wicket. Should the bowler make the slightest contact with the ball before
  it breaks the stumps, on appeal – the non-striker must be dismissed, provided he
  was out of his ground at that instant. These actions often occur rapidly requiring
  a split-second reaction from the umpire.

- **The striker**: if a **No ball** has been delivered, and provided the **striker does not attempt a run**, he **cannot** be run out if the wicket-keeper breaks the wicket when acting entirely on his own.

  When a No ball has been delivered a run out can only be effected by: a fielder or combination of fielders; a fielder/wicket-keeper combination; but **never** by a wicket-keeper acting entirely on his own.

3. WHICH BATSMAN IS OUT

The batsman out in the circumstances of 1 above is the one whose ground is at the end where the wicket is put down. See Laws 2.8 (Transgression of the Laws by a batsman who has a runner) and 29.2 (Which is a batsman's ground).

So, when the wicket is broken and the batsmen are running, who is out? It is the batsman who is nearest the wicket that is broken. Law 29 details the specific requirements concerning a batsman's ground, and a few simple examples should suffice to illustrate how that Law, and this one, work in practice.

EXAMPLE 1

The two batsmen are running a single. They cross and the wicket is broken at the bowler's end with both batsmen short of their ground.
The striker is run out.

EXAMPLE 2

Same scenario as Example 1 with the wicket being broken at the wicket-keeper's end.
The non-striker is run out.

EXAMPLE 3

The two batsmen attempt 3 runs but on the third 3rd run, because of a misunderstanding, find themselves both running towards the wicket-keeper's end; the wicket is broken at that end.
Whoever is nearest that wicket when it is broken is run out, i.e. the batsman **leading** the race to that end.

EXAMPLE 4

Same scenario as Example 3 with the wicket being broken at the bowler's end.
Whoever is nearest the bowler's end wicket is run out, i.e. the batsman **losing** the race towards the wicket-keeper's end.

EXAMPLE 5

The striker plays the ball and calls for a run. He changes his mind and goes back into his ground at the wicket-keeper's end and does not leave it again. The non-striker continues to run and joins him there behind the popping crease. The wicket is then broken at the wicket-keeper's end.
No one is out since the striker has made good his ground.

EXAMPLE 6

Same scenario as Example 5 with the wicket being broken at the bowler's end.

The non-striker is run out because he was out of his ground at the bowler's end. The ground at the wicket-keeper's end belongs to the striker, so the only ground available to the non-striker is at the bowler's end – and he is nowhere near it.

4. RUNS SCORED

If a batsman is dismissed Run out, the batting side shall score the runs completed before the dismissal, together with the penalty for a No ball or a Wide, if applicable. Other penalties to either side that may be awarded when the ball is dead shall also stand. See Law 42.17 (Penalty runs).

If, however, a striker with a runner is himself dismissed Run out, runs completed by the runner and the other batsman before the dismissal shall not be scored. The penalty for a No ball or a Wide and any other penalties to either side that may be awarded when the ball is dead shall stand. See Laws 2.8 (Transgression of the Laws by a batsman who has a runner) and 42.17(b) (Penalty runs).

Any runs **completed** prior to the dismissal are scored and since the current run is incomplete it cannot be scored.

The one **exception** to this is when the striker, who has a runner acting for him, is responsible for his own dismissal, by being run out. Should this occur, no runs are scored even though the runner and non-striker may have otherwise completed one or more runs. Having gained consent to have a runner, the 'contract' (detailed in Law 2.8) does not permit the injured batsman to run.

In all cases, penalty runs awarded for a No ball or a Wide are scored in addition to any runs credited to the striker. In all cases, penalty runs awarded by the umpire for fielding infringements will also be added to the batting side's total.

5. BOWLER DOES NOT GET CREDIT

The bowler does not get credit for the wicket.

A dismissal of Run out is not credited to the bowler.

It is becoming common practice for scorers to record (in brackets) the name of the fielder making the throw that led to the dismissal.

Law 39 Stumped

1. OUT STUMPED

(a)   The striker is out Stumped if
(i) he is out of his ground
and (ii) he is receiving a ball which is not a No ball
and (iii) he is not attempting a run
and (iv) his wicket is fairly put down by the wicket-keeper
without the intervention of another member
of the fielding side. Note Law 40.3 (Position of wicket-keeper).

(b)   The striker is out Stumped if all the conditions of (a) above are
satisfied, even though a decision of Run out would be justified.

2. BALL REBOUNDING FROM WICKET-KEEPER'S PERSON

(a)   If the wicket is put down by the ball, it shall be regarded as having
been put down by the wicket-keeper if the ball
(i) rebounds on to the stumps from any part of his person
or equipment, other than a protective helmet
or   (ii) has been kicked or thrown on to the stumps by the
wicket-keeper.

(b)   If the ball touches a helmet worn by the wicket-keeper, the ball
is still in play but the striker shall not be out Stumped. He will,
however, be liable to be Run out in these circumstances if there
is subsequent contact between the ball and any member of the
fielding side. Note, however, 3 below.

3. NOT OUT STUMPED

(a)   If the striker is not out Stumped, he is liable to be out Run out
if the conditions of Law 38 (Run out) apply, except as set out in
(b) below.

(b)   The striker shall not be out Run out if he is out of his ground,
not attempting a run, and his wicket is fairly put down by the
wicket-keeper without the intervention of another member
of the fielding side, if No ball has been called.

A striker can be stumped off a fair delivery or a Wide. He cannot be stumped off a
No ball.

Only the wicket-keeper can effect this dismissal – a fielder can never stump
anyone. The striker can be out Stumped only if there has been no intervention by
another member of the fielding side. If a fielder fields the ball and throws it to the
wicket-keeper who removes the bails with the striker out of his ground, the dismissal
is Run out, even though the striker may not be physically attempting a run. Once a
fielder makes contact with the ball an appeal for stumped becomes invalid.

Provided the striker is not attempting a run, the ball does not have to be in the hands of the wicket-keeper in order for a stumping to be achieved. Each of the following will be sufficient:

- a rebound off his pads or person – but not off his helmet
- a throw at the wicket
- the ball being kicked on to the wicket.

If the ball rebounds on to the stumps **directly** from the wicket-keeper's helmet then the striker **cannot** be stumped. (This is consistent with other Laws preventing the fielding side gaining an advantage because a protective helmet is worn by one of its members.) Should this occur, the ball remains in play and a subsequent run out attempt may be made.

If the striker starts to run and the wicket-keeper puts the wicket down, the dismissal is **Run out**, even though no other fielder may have touched the ball; the act of running negates the stumping. The umpire must be very clear in his mind whether or not the striker has actually commenced a run or is merely advancing towards the ball in order to reach it earlier than he would had he stayed in his guard position. The difference between the two may be marginal but very important when deciding if the striker is out Stumped or Run out.

The umpire may need to clarify the method of dismissal with the scorers either at the time or during the next interval.

The wicket-keeper can come **in front** of the wicket to stump the striker only **after** the ball has first come in contact with the striker's bat, or person. If the wicket-keeper does so **before** the ball has made this contact or **before the ball passes his stumps**, the striker's end umpire must call and signal No ball.

The striker's end umpire makes the decision for this dismissal. When the wicket-keeper stands close to the stumps, it is good practice for the striker's end umpire to stand a little nearer to the wicket, endeavouring to be in a position where he can clearly see the wicket-keeper, the striker and the popping crease.

If the umpire has any doubt over whether the wicket was broken correctly, his answer to an appeal must always be Not out.

A dismissal of Stumped is credited to the bowler.

Law 40 The wicket-keeper

1. PROTECTIVE EQUIPMENT

**The wicket-keeper is the only member of the fielding side permitted
to wear gloves and external leg guards. If he does so, these are to be
regarded as part of his person for the purposes of Law 41.2 (Fielding
the ball). If by his actions and positioning it is apparent to the umpires
that he will not be able to discharge his duties as a wicket-keeper, he
shall forfeit this right and also the right to be recognised as a wicket-
keeper for the purposes of Laws 32.3 (A fair catch), 39 (Stumped),
41.1 (Protective equipment), 41.5 (Limitation of on side fielders) and
41.6 (Fielders not to encroach on the pitch).**

The wicket-keeper is the only member of the fielding side permitted to wear **external**
protection in the form of pads and gloves. When doing so, these items are considered
part of his person.

He may also wear a helmet, however, the striker cannot be out Caught if the ball
strikes the helmet before the catch is completed, nor can he be out Run out or
Stumped if the ball, in play, ricochets **directly** from his helmet on to the wicket. The
ball remains in play after making contact with the helmet, but another fielding
action must occur to effect a valid dismissal.

Having granted the wicket-keeper the right to wear gloves and pads it is expected
that he will, prior to the ball coming into play, take up a position consistent with the
role of wicket-keeper. If he wishes to field in a position that is not consistent with that
role then he must remove his gloves and pads. If he does not wish to remove these
items of protection then he must be advised to resume a traditional wicket-keeping
position. The umpires should advise the captain of these options and also advise him
of the consequences if he does not comply with the advice – that is if the wicket-
keeper touches the ball when in play with his gloves or pads he will be guilty of illegally
fielding the ball and 5 penalty runs will be awarded to the batting side.

2. GLOVES

**If, as permitted under 1 above, the wicket-keeper wears gloves, they
shall have no webbing between the fingers except joining index finger
and thumb, where webbing may be inserted as a means of support. If
used, the webbing shall be**

**(a) a single piece of non-stretch material which, although it may have
facing material attached, shall have no reinforcement or tucks.**

(b) such that the top edge of the webbing

    **(i) does not protrude beyond the straight line joining the top of the
index finger to the top of the thumb.**

    (ii) is taut when a hand wearing the glove has the thumb fully extended.

See Appendix C.

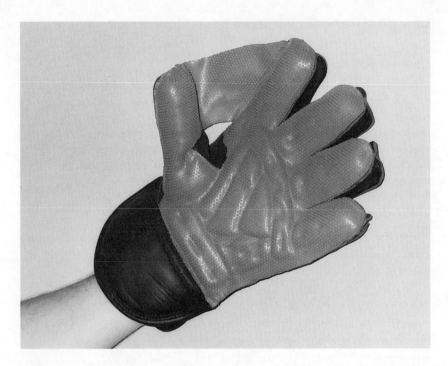

This clause clearly establishes the style of glove acceptable within the game. This photograph and the ones in Appendix C show examples of the type of glove that is allowed and should be viewed in conjunction with the above definition. Should a player wear gloves that do not conform to these specifications the umpire must insist that they be changed for gloves that do conform.

3. POSITION OF WICKET-KEEPER

The wicket-keeper shall remain wholly behind the wicket at the striker's end from the moment the ball comes into play until
    (a) a ball delivered by the bowler
        either (i) touches the bat or person of the striker
        or   (ii) passes the wicket at the striker's end
or (b) the striker attempts a run.
In the event of the wicket-keeper contravening this Law, the umpire at the striker's end shall call and signal No ball as soon as possible after the delivery of the ball.

This restriction of the wicket-keeper's positioning is effective from the moment the bowler starts his run-up or, where he has no run-up, his bowling action, until:
- the ball hits the striker, or
- the striker hits the ball with his bat, or
- the ball passes the striker's wicket, or
- the striker attempts a run.

Until one of these four events occurs, the wicket-keeper may not venture in front of his stumps. Should he do so, the striker's end umpire must call and signal No ball.

If the wicket-keeper encroaches in front of the wicket **during the bowler's run-up** the striker's end umpire must wait until the ball has been delivered before calling and signalling the No ball. Even though the wicket-keeper may withdraw the offending part of his person or equipment before the ball is actually delivered, the fact that he had encroached during the run-up is still deemed unfair and must attract the call and signal of No ball.

If the infringement takes place after the ball has been delivered, and before one of the four things above have occurred, the call of No ball must be made the moment the infringement happens.

Note that this Law specifically states 'wholly behind the wicket' – as shown by the green line in this photograph. It does not state 'behind the bowling crease' – a fine line but a significant difference nonetheless. The phrase 'wholly behind' means just that. No part of the wicket-keeper's person or equipment is allowed to be in front of the wicket and if the wicket-keeper does not conform to this the umpire will call and signal No ball.

4. MOVEMENT BY WICKET-KEEPER

It is unfair if the wicket-keeper standing back makes a significant movement towards the wicket after the ball comes into play and before it reaches the striker. In the event of such unfair movement by the wicket-keeper, either umpire shall call and signal Dead ball. It will not be considered a significant movement if the wicket-keeper moves a few paces forward for a slower delivery.

The striker is entitled to know where the fielders are stationed before the ball comes into play and he will make himself familiar with the position of the wicket-keeper. Should the wicket-keeper make any significant forward movement after the ball has come into play, this is deemed to be unfair and either umpire must immediately call and signal Dead ball.

When the wicket-keeper is standing back to a fast bowler, it is quite permissible for him to take a step or two forward, to take up a new position, if the bowler wishes to bowl a slower delivery. He is not permitted to make any significant movement forward towards the wicket as the bowler is running in, so that, when the ball is delivered, he is significantly closer to the stumps. This is unfair on the striker who is quite entitled to assume that the wicket-keeper is standing in his original position.

Should a call of Dead ball be made in these circumstances, an explanation to the captain of the fielding side and the batsmen at the wicket may be necessary.

Once the ball has made contact with the striker, or his bat, or has passed his stumps, or the striker attempts to run, there are no restrictions placed on the movement of the wicket-keeper.

5. RESTRICTION ON ACTIONS OF WICKET-KEEPER

If, in the opinion of either umpire, the wicket-keeper interferes with the striker's right to play the ball and to guard his wicket, Law 23.3(b)(vi) (Umpire calling and signalling Dead ball) shall apply.

If, however, the umpire concerned considers that the interference by the wicket-keeper was wilful, then Law 42.4 (Deliberate attempt to distract striker) shall apply.

The striker has the right to play at a delivery and to protect his wicket unhindered by word or deed from any member of the fielding team. This permits him to play any stroke of his choosing, even if the ball may have passed the line of his wicket. This right to play the ball after it has passed the wicket is unusual and would only apply should the striker wish to play a late cut or similar stroke. Any later attempt to hit the ball must be disallowed.

Should the wicket-keeper infringe upon the striker's right to have this free access to hit the ball, the striker should not suffer dismissal from that interference.

If the wicket-keeper does interfere with the striker's right to play the ball the only ways in which the striker can be out are:

- Handled the ball, or
- Hit the ball twice, or
- Obstructing the field, or
- Run out.

6. INTERFERENCE WITH WICKET-KEEPER BY STRIKER

If, in playing at the ball or in the legitimate defence of his wicket, the striker interferes with the wicket-keeper, he shall not be out, except as provided for in Law 37.3 (Obstructing a ball from being caught).

Having said that the striker has every right to play at the ball unhindered by the wicket-keeper, it follows that any attempt to guard his wicket, by legally hitting the ball again, must be permitted. This **cannot** be considered as interference with the wicket-keeper, and the striker would not be dismissed for doing so. However, there is one exception to this:

- if, in legally protecting his wicket by hitting the ball again, the striker prevents a catch, he will be out Obstructing the field.

EXAMPLE 1

The ball is struck into the air, causing the wicket-keeper to run forward in an attempt to take the catch. The striker, seeing that the ball is about to drop on to his wicket, knocks it away.
On appeal, the striker is given out Obstructing the field.

EXAMPLE 2

After coming into contact with the striker the ball rolls along the ground towards the stumps. The striker, in legally hitting the ball away, prevents the wicket-keeper from attempting to field the ball.

The striker is not out. He was legally protecting his wicket.

Law 41 The fielder

1. PROTECTIVE EQUIPMENT

No member of the fielding side other than the wicket-keeper shall be permitted to wear gloves or external leg guards. In addition, protection for the hand or fingers may be worn only with the consent of the umpires.

Any member of the fielding team may wear a helmet but no other **external** protective equipment is permitted. A helmet worn by a fielder is considered part of his person. However, a striker cannot be out Caught if the ball in play is caught after hitting the helmet. Other protective equipment may be worn, provided it is inside a player's normal clothing and is thus covered and invisible.

If a fielder wishes to have some part of his hand or fingers taped for protection, he may do so but, only with the consent of the umpires. Both umpires should consider the legitimacy of the protection and if they suspect it is worn for any other reason, they should ask for it to be removed. Such protection may be tape or plasters but does not extend to gloves of any type. If consent is given, the opposing captain has no right of objection.

2. FIELDING THE BALL

A fielder may field the ball with any part of his person but if, while the ball is in play he wilfully fields it otherwise,
(a) the ball shall become dead and 5 penalty runs shall be awarded to the batting side. See Law 42.17 (Penalty runs). The ball shall not count as one of the over.
(b) the umpire shall inform the other umpire, the captain of the fielding side, the batsmen and, as soon as practicable, the captain of the batting side of what has occurred.
(c) the umpires together shall report the occurrence as soon as possible to the Executive of the fielding side and any Governing Body responsible for the match who shall take such action as is considered appropriate against the captain and player concerned.

There are no restrictions regarding how a fielder can field the ball provided that he uses his person to do so (see Appendix D for a definition of what constitutes his person). It is when he uses any other article to field the ball that he is penalised.

This penalty will always be the awarding of 5 penalty runs to the batting side and will usually, but not always, be accompanied by the umpires reporting the event. Whether or not the report is made depends on the circumstances surrounding the act that led to the illegal fielding. If the act is **deliberate**, the report is made; if accidental, the report is not made.

EXAMPLE 1

A fielder using the wicket-keeper's discarded glove.

In this instance the fielder has deliberately picked up the glove and used it to catch/field the ball. This is a case of illegal fielding and 5 penalty runs will be awarded to the batting side and a report made (because the act leading to the illegal fielding was deliberate). The ball does not count as one of the over.

EXAMPLE 2

Fielding the ball by using a cap, hat or helmet.

The deliberate use of a fielder's cap/hat/helmet to stop the ball is illegal. As soon as the headgear makes contact with the ball the ball becomes dead and the penalty provisions must be invoked. The headgear does not have to stop the ball – the mere fact that it has made contact with the ball is sufficient for the penalty provisions to be invoked. In this case 5 penalty runs would be awarded to the batting side and a report made. It is worth noting that throwing the hat etc. at the ball is not illegal. It is any subsequent contact by the headgear with the ball that is punished. If the headgear is thrown and misses the ball, that is not illegal and the game continues uninterrupted. The ball does not count as one of the over.

EXAMPLE 3

The fielder uses clothing he is wearing to field the ball.

If the ball accidentally comes into contact with clothing worn by the fielder it is not considered illegal. The fielder is permitted to clutch the ball to his body to effect a catch or while retrieving the ball without fear of punishment. It is, however, illegal if he uses his clothing to gain an advantage e.g. a fielder pulling out the bottom of his sweater to form a pouch in which to catch the ball. The catch would not be allowed as it would be classed as illegal fielding invoking the penalty provisions. In this case 5 penalty runs would be awarded and a report made (because the act leading to the illegal fielding was a deliberate one). The ball does not count as one of the over.

EXAMPLE 4

The ball hits a cap, hat or helmet that has been thrown to the ground by a fielder.

In this case the fielder has discarded his cap while he chases after the ball. As the ball is being returned to the wicket it accidentally hits the headgear. In this case 5 penalty runs would be awarded to the batting side but no report is made (because the act of the ball hitting the headgear was not done deliberately).

EXAMPLE 5

The ball hits any discarded item within the field of play.

It is not often that this happens but the umpire must be wary of players removing pullovers, caps etc. and placing them on the ground while they are not required. This is not a very advisable thing to do because if the ball hits any such discarded item 5 penalty runs are awarded to the batting side – but no report is made (because the act of the ball hitting the discarded item was accidental).

It is worth mentioning at this point that the generally accepted items that an umpire is expected to hold for the players are the bowler's pullover, hat or cap and sunglasses etc. Anything else, such as protective boxes, arm guards, shin guards and helmets are not acceptable items for them to carry around. If any other player wishes to dispense with an item of clothing or protection, this should be done at the end of an over or when a wicket falls and should be promptly removed to outside the boundary. Umpires should not permit themselves to become coat hangers!

The only item of player equipment permitted to be placed on the ground is a **fielder's helmet**. This must be placed behind the wicket-keeper in line with the two wickets. (It is permissible to have two or more helmets placed in this position.) Umpires must not allow any other item whatsoever to be placed on the ground within the field of play.

This permission does not extend to a batsman's helmet which, when not in use, should be removed from the field of play.

EXAMPLE 6

Wicket-keeper's discarded glove lying on the ground.

In this case the glove has been thrown on the ground and when the ball is thrown back to the wicket accidentally hits the discarded glove. This is a case of illegal fielding and 5 penalty runs will be awarded to the batting side but a report is not made (because the act of the ball hitting the glove was not deliberate.)

EXAMPLE 7

The ball hits a cap or hat that blows off the fielder's head.

In this case the headgear has blown off in the natural course of events, i.e. the fielder did not help it in any way. If the ball in play hits this headgear no penalty runs are awarded, neither is a report made. Play continues as though nothing had happened.

When there is a case of illegal fielding **the ball becomes automatically dead**. However, a prudent umpire may wish to call and signal Dead ball, simply to bring that fact to the players' attention. Under the Law it is not necessary to do this, but it will go a long way to clarifying the situation for the players on the field. The umpire should then award to the batting side **5 penalty runs** which are added to any **completed** runs that have been made and to the run in progress if the batsmen have crossed **before** the illegal act took place.

EXAMPLE 8

The batsmen have crossed on their third run when a fielder illegally fields the ball.

RUNS SCORED: 2 (completed) + 1 (in progress) + 5 penalty runs = 8.

EXAMPLE 9

The batsmen have just turned for the second run and the illegal fielding takes place.

RUNS SCORED: 1 (completed) + 5 penalty runs = 6.

In this instance the second run will not be scored because the act of illegal fielding took place before the batsmen had crossed.

Whenever illegal fielding occurs, the two umpires will almost certainly have to consult with each other to agree how many runs should be recorded. Both must be aware of what has happened so that they can help each other. After consultation, the bowler's end umpire must signal to the scorers the appropriate number of runs to be recorded. The umpires should also note the incident for confirmation with the scorers during the next interval. They should also ensure that the batsmen are at the correct ends before permitting play to resume. This can be determined by ignoring the 5 penalty runs and treating the batsmen's running in the normal way.

The 5 penalty runs are recorded in the penalty runs section of the scoring record. This is standard practice for all cases where 5 penalty runs are awarded. The runs scored by the batsmen are recorded in the normal fashion i.e. to the striker, if he had hit the ball, or to the appropriate extras, if he did not.

When illegal fielding takes place after **No ball** or **Wide ball** has been called there is a **double penalty** involved:

• the penalty for illegal fielding (always signalled first)
• the penalty for a No ball or a Wide (always signalled next).

EXAMPLE 10

The striker misses a No ball and the batsmen complete 3 runs after which the ball is illegally fielded.

RUNS SCORED: 4 No ball extras (1 for the No ball + 3 No ball extras for the runs completed by the batsmen before the illegal act) + 5 penalty runs = 9.

EXAMPLE 11

The bowler delivers a Wide and the batsmen complete 2 runs when the ball is illegally fielded.

RUNS SCORED: 3 Wide extras (1 for the Wide + 2 runs completed by the batsmen before the illegal act) + 5 penalty runs = 8.

When an act of illegal fielding takes place the following procedure must be followed by the bowler's end umpire:

Illegal fielding

ANY occurrence – by ANY fielder

Action	Inform
• Ball becomes automatically dead.	• Colleague.
• Award 5 penalty runs to the batting side.	• Fielding captain.
	• Batsmen at the crease.
• Ensure the scorers understand how many runs are to be recorded.	*During the next interval when the players leave the field:*
	• Batting captain.
• Ensure the batsman take the correct ends.	*Where applicable, report the incident to:*
	• The Executive of the fielding side.
• Ball does not count as one of the over	• The Governing Body responsible for the match

3. PROTECTIVE HELMETS BELONGING TO THE FIELDING SIDE

Protective helmets, when not in use by fielders, shall only be placed, if above the surface, on the ground behind the wicket-keeper and in line with both sets of stumps. If a helmet belonging to the fielding side is on the ground within the field of play, and the ball while in play strikes it, the ball shall become dead. 5 penalty runs shall then be awarded to the batting side. See Laws 18.11 (Runs scored when ball becomes dead) and 42.17 (Penalty runs).

The only safe place for the helmet is on the fielder's head. If the ball hits the helmet, when it is being worn, then no penalty is incurred When not in use the helmet should be taken from the field of play altogether, but if it is only temporarily out of use then it must be placed behind the wicket-keeper in line with the wickets. This does not mean that it is safe from the penalty should the ball hit it, but it is at least in a place where it is less likely to be hit.

In this case, there will be an award of 5 penalty runs to the batting side, but no report is to be made.

If the ball hits the helmet, correctly positioned behind the wicket-keeper, the following procedure must be followed by the bowler's end umpire:

Ball in play making contact with a helmet
correctly placed on the ground behind the wicket-keeper

ANY occurrence

Action	Inform
• Ball becomes automatically dead.	• Not required.
• Award 5 penalty runs to the batting side.	
• Ensure the scorers understand how many runs are scored.	
• Ensure the batsman take the correct ends.	

4. PENALTY RUNS NOT TO BE AWARDED

Notwithstanding 2 and 3 above, if from the delivery by the bowler the ball first struck the person of the striker and if, in the opinion of the umpire, the striker
neither (i) attempted to play the ball with his bat,
nor (ii) tried to avoid being hit by the ball,
then no award of 5 penalty runs shall be made and no other runs or penalties shall be credited to the batting side except the penalty for a No ball if applicable. See Law 26.3 (Leg byes not to be awarded).

This clause cross-refers to the relevant clause in Law 26. If the striker makes no attempt to play at a delivery or fails to attempt to avoid injury, the batting team cannot claim an advantage of scoring leg byes. This is well documented under Law 26. Thus, if legitimate leg byes are not allowed the batting team cannot be credited with penalty runs for any illegal act immediately following the ball's deflection off the striker.

5. LIMITATION OF ON SIDE FIELDERS

At the instant of the bowler's delivery there shall not be more than two fielders, other than the wicket-keeper, behind the popping crease on the on side. A fielder will be considered to be behind the popping crease unless the whole of his person, whether grounded or in the air, is in front of this line.

In the event of infringement of this Law by the fielding side, the umpire at the striker's end shall call and signal No ball.

It is illegal for there to be more than two fielders behind the popping crease on the on side (leg side) as shown by the green area at the instant of delivery.

This means that if there are already two leg-side fielders behind the popping crease and a third fielder then places any part of his person behind the popping crease as the ball is delivered, an infringement occurs. It is also not necessary for the third fielder to have his person grounded behind the popping crease – an arm, or foot, in the air is sufficient for the law to be broken.

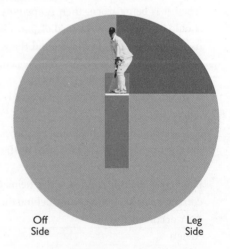

Off
Side

Leg
Side

It may be difficult for the striker's end umpire to see the infringement from where he is normally standing because the third fielder may well be behind him at deep square leg. If this is the case the umpire should move to the off side to obtain a clearer view of any possible third fielder in that restricted zone.

If this Law is infringed, the **striker's end umpire** must call and signal No ball at the instant of delivery or as soon as possible thereafter.

Note that it is the job of the striker's end umpire to call and signal the No ball, not the bowler's end umpire. If the bowler's end umpire notices an infringement has occurred but his colleague does not call it, he cannot make the call himself as it is outside his jurisdiction: the delivery must be considered legal.

If a fielder is stationed behind the line of the popping crease and, during the bowler's run-up, moves out of the area in question **before the ball is delivered**, no offence under this clause has occurred. However, if this movement is **significant** – as described in clauses 7 and 8 below – the umpire will take the appropriate action. No action is necessary should the adjustment be minor.

6. FIELDERS NOT TO ENCROACH ON THE PITCH

While the ball is in play and until the ball has made contact with the bat or person of the striker, or has passed the striker's bat, no fielder, other than the bowler, may have any part of his person grounded on or extended over the pitch.

In the event of infringement of this Law by any fielder other than the wicket-keeper, the umpire at the bowler's end shall call and signal No ball as soon as possible after the delivery of the ball. Note, however, Law 40.3 (Position of wicket-keeper).

Law 7 defines the width of the pitch as 10 ft (3.05 m) and this clause states that, while the ball is in play, no fielder, other than the bowler, is allowed to have any part of his person **grounded on** or **extended over** the pitch until the ball has:

- hit the striker's bat, or
- hit the striker's person, or
- passed the striker's bat.

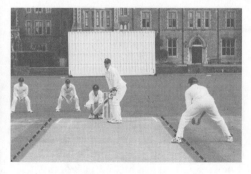

Fielder's foot on the pitch

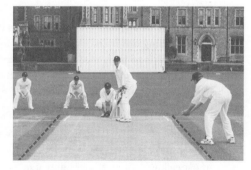

Fielder's hands extended over the pitch

The fielder has to remain off the pitch from the time the ball comes into play until one of the above has occurred. Any part of a fielder grounded on the pitch, or in the air over it, is in contravention of this Law, as illustrated above. The striker must be assured of a free and unrestricted right to attempt to hit the ball without interference by any close fielder.

If a fielder violates this law No ball must be called and signalled by the bowler's end umpire.

Even if the pitch has been mowed incorrectly, either too narrow or too wide, the 10 ft (3.05 m) restriction still applies. As part of the umpires' pre-match inspections, such matters must be noted and discussed with both captains before the toss.

A question often asked is: What about a fielder's **shadow**? A fielder's shadow does not constitute 'part of his person' and, as such, is not penalised under this Law.

The fielder must ensure that his shadow does not move during the period between the bowler starting his run-up and the striker's attempt to play the ball. If the fielder, and hence his shadow, moves and becomes a distraction the umpire must request the captain of the fielding side to ensure the movement of the fielder's shadow is not a distraction to the striker. If this instruction is complied with no further action is necessary. However, if the request is not complied with, the umpire can impose sanctions under whichever of the following Laws is most appropriate: i) Law 42.4 (Deliberate attempt to distract striker) or ii) Law 42.18 (Players' conduct).

In either event, it is not a No ball offence.

7. MOVEMENT BY FIELDERS

Any significant movement by any fielder after the ball comes into play and before the ball reaches the striker is unfair. In the event of such unfair movement, either umpire shall call and signal Dead ball. Note also the provisions of Law 42.4 (Deliberate attempt to distract striker).

8. DEFINITION OF SIGNIFICANT MOVEMENT

(a) For close fielders anything other than minor adjustments to stance or position in relation to the striker is significant.

(b) In the outfield, fielders are permitted to move in towards the striker or striker's wicket, provided that 5 above is not contravened. Anything other than slight movement off line or away from the striker is to be considered significant.

(c) For restrictions on movement by the wicket-keeper see Law 40.4 (Movement by wicket-keeper).

The striker is entitled to know where the fielders are stationed before the ball comes into play, and he may make himself familiar with the positions of each. Should any fielder make any **significant** movement (as defined in these clauses), either umpire must call and signal Dead ball as soon as the movement is apparent. This Law does not apply to the wicket-keeper, who is restricted in his movements under Law 40.

The Law distinguishes between the movements of two types of fielder:

• **Close fielders** are permitted to make only minor movements to stance or position. Anything else is considered **significant**.

- **Outfielders** may only move in a **straight line** towards the striker or his wicket. They may not move sideways or away from the striker's wicket.

If any fielder moves in such a way that either umpire deems it **significant** he must immediately call and signal Dead ball. The offending fielder must be instructed to take the position he wishes to adopt and conform to the requirements of the Law. Repetition of these offences attracts only the call of Dead ball. No other cautions or penalties are administered. Since the offence occurs before the striker has received the delivery the ball does not count as one in the over.

Law 42 Fair and unfair play

1. FAIR AND UNFAIR PLAY – RESPONSIBILITY OF CAPTAINS

The responsibility lies with the captains for ensuring that play is conducted within the spirit and traditions of the game, as described in The Preamble – The Spirit of Cricket, as well as within the Laws.

2. FAIR AND UNFAIR PLAY – RESPONSIBILITY OF UMPIRES

The umpires shall be the sole judges of fair and unfair play. If either umpire considers an action, not covered by the Laws, to be unfair, he shall intervene without appeal and, if the ball is in play, shall call and signal Dead ball and implement the procedure as set out in 18 below. Otherwise the umpires shall not interfere with the progress of play, except as required to do so by the Laws.

These two clauses stress the significant responsibilities that the captains and umpires have towards the game. The captains bear the responsibility of ensuring that the game is played within the Spirit of Cricket while the umpires ensure that the Laws are upheld and deal with any cases of unfair play.

This Law allows either umpire to intervene whenever he considers that an act of unfair play has occurred and no appeal is necessary from either side in order for him to take action. Should either umpire wish to intervene in such cases then he will call and signal Dead ball before taking the required remedial action.

During the rest of the game neither umpire must interfere with the progress of the game unless he is required to do so under any of the Laws. The umpires should be silent and unobtrusive participants in the game, becoming involved when required to by Law, or by invitation, by way of an appeal.

3. THE MATCH BALL – CHANGING ITS CONDITION

(a) Any fielder may
- **(i) polish the ball provided that no artificial substance is used and that such polishing wastes no time.**
- **(ii) remove mud from the ball under the supervision of the umpire.**

(iii) dry a wet ball on a towel.

(b) It is unfair for anyone to rub the ball on the ground for any reason, interfere with any of the seams or the surface of the ball, use any implement, or take any other action whatsoever which is likely to alter the condition of the ball, except as permitted in (a) above.

(c) The umpires shall make frequent and irregular inspections of the ball.

(d) In the event of any fielder changing the condition of the ball unfairly, as set out in (b) above, the umpires after consultation shall

   (i)   change the ball forthwith. It shall be for the umpires to decide on the replacement ball, which shall, in their opinion, have had wear comparable with that which the previous ball had received immediately prior to the contravention.

   (ii) inform the batsmen that the ball has been changed.

   (iii) award 5 penalty runs to the batting side. See 17 below.

   (iv) inform the captain of the fielding side that the reason for the action was the unfair interference with the ball.

   (v) inform the captain of the batting side as soon as practicable of what has occurred.

   (vi) report the occurrence as soon as possible to the Executive of the fielding side and any Governing Body responsible for the match, who shall take such action as is considered appropriate against the captain and team concerned.

(e) If there is any further instance of unfairly changing the condition of the ball in that innings, the umpires after consultation shall

   (i)   repeat the procedure in (d)(i), (ii) and (iii) above.

   (ii) inform the captain of the fielding side of the reason for the action taken and direct him to take off forthwith the bowler who delivered the immediately preceding ball. The bowler thus taken off shall not be allowed to bowl again in that innings.

   (iii) inform the captain of the batting side as soon as practicable of what has occurred.

   (iv) report this further occurrence as soon as possible to the Executive of the fielding side and any Governing Body responsible for the match, who shall take such action as is considered appropriate against the captain and team concerned.

It is permissible for any member of the fielding side to:

- **clean** the ball or wipe mud from it using a towel or rag
- **polish** the ball, providing no artificial substance is used to do so
- **dry** the ball either on their clothing, or with a towel.

When wiping or rubbing the ball to clean or dry it the umpire must watch to see that this does not incorporate rubbing it so that one or both sides are 'roughed up', thus giving the bowler an advantage. The fielders can polish or dry the ball as it is passed around the field to get it back to the bowler, but no one should take so long about it that the bowler is left waiting for the ball before he can bowl. Sawdust is not allowed to be used to dry the ball.

Umpires are required to make frequent and irregular inspections of the ball. These inspections can be made at the fall of a wicket, at which time the ball must always be handed back to the umpire, but must not be restricted only to these times. The umpire(s) are entitled to call for the ball at any time should they feel it necessary to inspect it. The more often this is done the less likely it is that the fielding side will attempt to – unfairly – change its condition.

Should an umpire decide that the condition of the ball has been unfairly changed, he must adopt the following procedure:

Fielder unfairly changing condition of the match ball

FIRST occurrence – by ANY fielder	
Action	**Inform**
When ball is dead:	• Batsmen at the crease.
• Consult with colleague.	• Fielding captain.
• If in agreement, immediately replace the ball with one of comparable wear.	*During the next interval when the players leave the field:*
• Award 5 penalty runs to the batting side.	• Batting captain.
	As soon as possible, report the incident to:
	• The Executive of the fielding side.
	• The Governing Body responsible for the match.

Fielder unfairly changing condition of the match ball

ANY subsequent occurrence - by ANY fielder in the same innings	
Action	**Inform**
When ball is dead:	• Batsmen at the crease.
• Consult with colleague.	*During the next interval when the players leave the field:*
• If in agreement, immediately replace the ball with one of comparable wear.	• Batting captain.
• Award 5 penalty runs to the batting side.	*As soon as possible, report the incident to:*
• Direct the captain to immediately **replace the bowler** who bowled the preceding delivery.	• The Executive of the fielding side.
• The suspended bowler cannot bowl again in that innings.	• The Governing Body responsible for the match.

The replacement ball must be one of similar use and wear prior to the offence occurring. It is good practice for the umpires to carry a spare ball each when on the field and also to have readily available a larger selection of spares, just in case they are needed.

An important aspect when replacing the ball is that the fielding captain and the batsmen have no say as to which ball is selected, nor its condition. This is a decision for the umpires alone to make. All the umpires have to do, under Law, is advise the fielding captain and batsmen at the wicket that a replacement has been taken.

4. DELIBERATE ATTEMPT TO DISTRACT STRIKER

It is unfair for any member of the fielding side deliberately to attempt to distract the striker while he is preparing to receive or receiving a delivery.

(a) If either umpire considers that any action by a member of the fielding side is such an attempt, at the first instance he shall

    (i)   immediately call and signal Dead ball.

    (ii) warn the captain of the fielding side that the action is unfair and indicate that this is a first and final warning.

    (iii) inform the other umpire and the batsmen of what has occurred. Neither batsman shall be dismissed from that delivery and the ball shall not count as one of the over.

(b) If there is any further such deliberate attempt in that innings, by any member of the fielding side, the procedures, other than warning, as set out in (a) above shall apply. Additionally, the umpire at the bowler's end shall

    (i)   award 5 penalty runs to the batting side. See 17 below.

    (ii) inform the captain of the fielding side of the reason for this action and, as soon as practicable, inform the captain of the batting side.

    (iii) report the occurrence, together with the other umpire, as soon as possible to the Executive of the fielding side and any Governing Body responsible for the match, who shall take such action as is considered appropriate against the captain and player or players concerned.

Members of the fielding team are not permitted to **deliberately** distract the striker when he is preparing to receive, or receiving, a delivery. This could be by deliberately talking loudly; making noises while the bowler is running in; even movement by close fielders (including movement of shadows on the pitch) would come under this heading.

    If either umpire believes the striker has been distracted by such act(s), he must immediately step in and take the following action:

Deliberate distraction of the striker – prior to ball being received

FIRST occurrence – by ANY fielder	
Action	Inform
• Call and signal Dead ball.	• Colleague.
• Warn the fielding captain	• Batsmen at the crease.
• This is his **first and final warning**.	*During the next interval when the players*
• The warning applies to the whole team.	*leave the field:*
• The warning applies throughout the rest of that innings.	• Batting captain.

Deliberate distraction of the striker – prior to ball being received

ANY subsequent occurrence – by ANY fielder in the same innings

Action	Inform
• Call and signal Dead ball.	• Colleague.
• Award 5 penalty runs .	• Fielding captain.
to the batting side.	• Batsmen at the crease.
	During the next interval when the players leave the field:
	• Batting captain.
	As soon as possible, report the incident to:
	• The Executive of the fielding side.
	• The Governing Body responsible for the match.

Since the call of Dead ball is made before the striker has received the ball, then, as described in Law 22, the delivery is not one of the over.

5. DELIBERATE DISTRACTION OR OBSTRUCTION OF BATSMAN

In addition to 4 above, it is unfair for any member of the fielding side, by word or action, wilfully to attempt to distract or to obstruct either batsman after the striker has received the ball.

(a) It is for either one of the umpires to decide whether any distraction or obstruction is wilful or not.

(b) If either umpire considers that a member of the fielding side has wilfully caused or attempted to cause such a distraction or obstruction he shall

    (i) immediately call and signal Dead ball.

    (ii) inform the captain of the fielding side and the other umpire of the reason for the call.

Additionally,

    (iii) neither batsman shall be dismissed from that delivery.

    (iv) 5 penalty runs shall be awarded to the batting side. See 17 below. In this instance, the run in progress shall be scored, whether or not the batsmen had crossed at the instant of the call. See Law 18.11 (Runs scored when ball becomes dead).

    (v) the umpire at the bowler's end shall inform the captain of the fielding side of the reason for this action and, as soon as practicable, inform the captain of the batting side.

    (vi) the ball shall not count as one of the over

    (vii) the batsmen at the wicket shall decide which of them is to face the next delivery

    (viii) the umpires shall report the occurrence as soon as possible to the Executive of the fielding side and any Governing Body responsible for the match, who shall take such action as is considered appropriate against the captain and player or players concerned.

Batsmen are entitled to expect that, when the ball is in play after the striker has received it, they are not going to be **wilfully** obstructed or distracted by members of the fielding side.

The Law makes it clear that this obstruction or distraction can be effected through a physical act or by word of mouth. In other words the act does not have to be through physical contact alone, it can, for example, be by something said by a fielder.

There will be times, when the batsmen are running and the fielders are fielding the ball, that players will get in each other's way. The umpires must be aware of events that lead up to this obstruction or distraction and be able to decide whether the action, by the fielding side, was deliberate or accidental.

If it was accidental then no action will be taken against them. Where such an obstruction or distraction is deemed to be **deliberate** then the umpire should take the following action:

Deliberate distraction of batsman – after the ball has been received

ANY occurrence – by ANY fielder

Action	Inform
• Call and signal Dead ball.	• Colleague
• Neither batsman can be dismissed.	• Fielding captain.
• Award 5 penalty runs to the batting side.	• Batsmen at the crease.
	During the next interval when the players
• Ensure the scorers understand how many runs are to be recorded.	*leave the field:*
	• Batting captain.
• That delivery does not count as one in the over.	*As soon as possible, report the incident to:*
	• The Executive of the fielding side.
• Batsmen will decide who is to face the next delivery.	• The Governing Body responsible for the match.

The runs scored will depend on how many runs had been completed when the incident took place as well as the run in progress at the time **irrespective of whether the batsmen had crossed or not**.

In cases of deliberate obstruction or distraction of a batsman the fact that a run was being attempted is enough for it to be allowed – and it does not matter whether the batsmen had crossed in that attempt or not.

Following any breach of this Law the batsmen have the right to decide who faces the next delivery.

If this Law is breached, whether from a fair delivery or a Wide or a No ball, that ball does not count as one of the over.

EXAMPLE 1

The 4th ball of the over is a fair delivery and the striker hits it and runs. The batsmen are turning for their 3rd run when the bowler deliberately impedes the non-striker, knocking him off balance.

RUNS SCORED: 2 completed runs + 1 in progress (turning is enough for it to be counted) + 5 penalty runs = 8. These are recorded as 3 to the striker and 5 penalty runs.

The batsmen choose who is to face the next delivery. There are 3 balls left in the over.

EXAMPLE 2

The 5th ball of the over is a Wide and the batsmen run. They turn for their 2nd run when the wicket-keeper deliberately trips up the non-striker.

RUNS SCORED: 1 for the Wide + 2 Wides the batsmen scored by running + 5 penalty runs = 8. These are recorded as 3 Wides and 5 penalty runs.

The batsmen choose who is to face the next delivery. There are 2 balls left in the over.

The penalty runs are recorded in the penalty runs section of the scoring record while the runs scored by the batsmen are credited to the striker if he had hit the ball or to the appropriate extras if he didn't.

6. DANGEROUS AND UNFAIR BOWLING

(a) BOWLING OF FAST SHORT PITCHED BALLS

   (i) The bowling of fast short pitched balls is dangerous and unfair if the umpire at the bowler's end considers that by their repetition and taking into account their length, height and direction they are likely to inflict physical injury on the striker, irrespective of the protective equipment he may be wearing. The relative skill of the striker shall be taken into consideration.

   (ii) Any delivery which, after pitching, passes or would have passed over head height of the striker standing upright at the crease, although not threatening physical injury, shall be included with bowling under (i) both when the umpire is considering whether the bowling of fast short pitched balls has become dangerous and unfair and after he has so decided. The umpire shall call and signal No ball for each such delivery.

(b) BOWLING OF HIGH FULL PITCHED BALLS

   (i) Any delivery, other than a slow paced one, which passes or would have passed on the full above waist height of the striker standing upright at the crease is to be deemed dangerous and unfair, whether or not it is likely to inflict physical injury on the striker.

   (ii) A slow delivery which passes or would have passed on the full above shoulder height of the striker standing upright at the crease is to be deemed dangerous and unfair, whether or not it is likely to inflict physical injury on the striker.

7. DANGEROUS AND UNFAIR BOWLING – ACTION BY THE UMPIRE

(a) As soon as the umpire at the bowler's end decides under 6(a) above that the bowling of fast short pitched balls has become dangerous and unfair, or, except as in 8 below, there is an instance of dangerous and unfair bowling as defined in 6(b) above, he shall call and signal No ball and, when the ball is dead, caution the bowler, inform the other umpire, the captain of the fielding side and the batsman of what has occured. This caution shall continue to apply throughout the innings.

(b) If there is any further instance of dangerous and unfair bowling by the same bowler in the same innings, the umpire at the bowler's end shall repeat the above procedure and indicate to the bowler that this is a final warning.

Both the above caution and final warning shall continue to apply even though the bowler may later change ends.

(c) Should there be any further repetition by the same bowler in that innings, the umpire shall

(i) call and signal No ball.

(ii) direct the captain, when the ball is dead, to take the bowler off forthwith. The over shall be completed by another bowler, who shall neither have bowled the previous over nor be allowed to bowl the next over.

The bowler thus taken off shall not be allowed to bowl again in that innings.

(iii) report the occurrence to the other umpire, the batsmen and, as soon as practicable, the captain of the batting side.

(iv) report the occurrence, with the other umpire, as soon as possible to the Executive of the fielding side and to any Governing Body responsible for the match, who shall take such action as is considered appropriate against the captain and bowler concerned.

These two clauses relate to the use of fast, short pitched deliveries (bouncers) and full pitched deliveries (beamers or full tosses). The Law makes it very clear that while the former may be acceptable, up to a point, the latter are not acceptable at all and, if used, will exact immediate retribution from the umpire.

The Law is also clear to point out that the bowling of either delivery comes under the banner of 'dangerous and unfair' and as such is treated as one and the same offence. Thus if a fast, short pitched delivery is followed by a high, full pitched delivery, they are to be taken as a continuation of the same offence and not taken as two separate offences.

The Law is very clear on the definitions of both types of delivery.

1A. FAST, SHORT PITCHED DELIVERIES (BOUNCERS) –
BELOW HEAD HEIGHT

A bouncer is not, in itself, an illegal delivery. It is a part of a fast bowler's armoury and, when used selectively, a very useful weapon indeed. It is the overuse and its potential for injury that make it dangerous and unfair.

A delivery can be **dangerous** due to its speed, length, height and direction. It becomes **unfair** through repetition. Before he takes action under the Law an umpire must carefully consider each of the following criteria:

- **speed:** this is a relative term to be considered within the context of the game being played. A delivery deemed fast in a school match would not be considered so if bowled in a senior club game or at international level. The ability of the striker must be taken into consideration.
- **length**: in order for it to be classified under this heading the ball must have been a short pitched one. There is no statutory length that governs where the ball has to be pitched in order for it to be considered short pitched. It is for the umpire to decide if the ball was short. The umpire must be careful not to take action against a bowler when the ball is a good length delivery that happens to rise sharply because of the state of the ground.
- **height**: there is no statutory height above which the umpire takes action. However, the umpire should consider that any short pitched delivery that could have hit the striker in the ribs, at the neck/shoulder level, or on the head as being high. This decision must be made in relation to the position of the striker when he is, or would have been, in an upright position at the popping crease.
- **direction**: it is important that the ball is travelling towards the striker's body. If the ball is unlikely to hit the striker, even though it may fulfil the criteria regarding length, speed and height it cannot be termed dangerous and unfair.
- **repetition:** The repetition of this form of bowling, by wearing down the resistance of the batsman, increases the likelihood of an injury. The resistance of batsmen will vary considerably, the better the batsman the longer the sequence. Again, the ability of the batsman must be taken into consideration. The umpire must judge, **for each individual batsman,** when the point has been reached at which the bowling of fast short pitched deliveries has become dangerous.

Only when satisfied on all these five points will the umpire take the actions prescribed in the Law.

EXAMPLE 3

A bouncer rises sharply and passes the striker at chin height, about an arm's length outside the off stump.

This is not going to cause the striker any physical harm since it is wide of him. The umpire would not deem this to be dangerous and unfair.

EXAMPLE 4

The short pitched delivery does not rise very much and reaches the striker just above waist level. Even though it was fast and pitched short, the height at which it reached the striker would not mean that it is dangerous and unfair.

The umpire must also consider the relative ability and skill of the striker. One who has shown that he can cope with these deliveries, even though they fall under the definition above, would not necessarily be considered to be in danger of getting injured, although if this type of delivery is repeated the umpire might consider that the striker's mental fitness to deal with it is being eroded.

If, however, the batsman shows that he cannot handle the deliveries in a manner that gives the umpire confidence in his ability, the umpire may well take action after only one such delivery. If there is a danger that the striker, through his lack of ability, could get hurt then the umpire must act.

The only consideration for the umpire is whether the striker is in danger of being injured from the delivery. The presence of, or lack of, protective equipment is irrelevant when it comes to making this judgement.

ACTION TO BE TAKEN BY THE UMPIRE

This is **discretionary** and will depend on the umpire's judgement of the situation. If he decides that the delivery is dangerous and unfair he will take action. He will call and signal No ball and start, or continue with, the disciplinary procedure outlined on page 268. If he does not consider the bowling to be dangerous and unfair he will do nothing.

1B. SHORT PITCHED DELIVERIES (BOUNCERS) THAT PASS OR WOULD HAVE PASSED ABOVE HEAD HEIGHT OF STRIKER STANDING UPRIGHT AT THE CREASE

The example below illustrates this point of Law. Note that Law 42.6(a)(ii) applies to any ball *WHETHER FAST OR NOT*.

a) Tall batsman: fair delivery

b) Shorter batsman: No ball (above head height)

c) Shorter batsman crouching in front of popping crease: No ball (judged as though upright at crease)

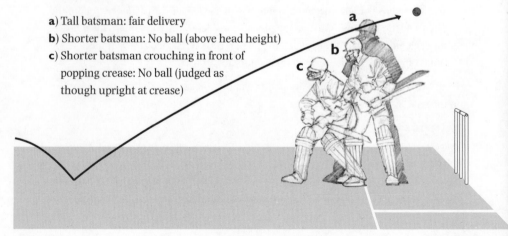

ACTION TO BE TAKEN BY THE UMPIRE

The umpire will call and signal No ball in **every** instance where such a delivery is bowled.

However, the bowling of this type of delivery does not automatically mean that the umpire will start, or continue with, the disciplinary procedure attached to dangerous and unfair bowling. While accepting the fact that such a delivery is unlikely to inflict injury on the striker, it can form part of a systematic attack on his self-confidence and, as such, must be monitored by the umpire. He must consider this type of delivery as part of the repetition sequence, not in the sense that each one is to be counted as a dangerous bouncer but on the basis that it is a general contribution to the striker's growing concern about his own safety.

Once the umpire has decided that the bowler has exceeded what he considers to be fair, either by bowling too many such deliveries or by combining them with other dangerous bouncers, he will start, or continue with, the disciplinary measures detailed under clause 7. Until such time as he considers that this has occurred, having called and signalled No ball, the umpire will take no further action.

Note that the striker's end umpire does not call the No ball – it is not within his jurisdiction. However, he may well give valuable help to his colleague by discreetly signalling that the ball was, in his opinion, above head height. The bowler's end umpire can use this information to back up his judgement if he so desires, but the final decision and call is down to the bowler's end umpire.

2. FULL PITCHED DELIVERIES (BEAMERS OR FULL TOSSES)

Here, the definition is split into two distinct parts according to the speed of the delivery:

- any ball – **other than a slow paced one** – that passes, or would have passed, on the full above **waist** height of the striker when standing upright at the crease is illegal. Even if the striker hits the ball, it is a totally unacceptable delivery and will be dealt with as such.
- any **slow delivery** that passes or would have passed on the full above **shoulder** height of the striker when standing upright at the crease is illegal. Again, it does not matter if the striker hits the ball, it is a totally unacceptable delivery and will be dealt with as such.

Under both definitions, the width of the ball is of no consequence – if it falls under the above criteria then it is not a Wide but will be treated as a totally illegal, unacceptable delivery in its own right.

It must be understood that the Law does not refer to the type of bowler who delivers either of these deliveries, i.e. it is not that a fast bowler can only bowl deliveries under the first definition and that a slow bowler can only bowl those under the second. The wording of the Law clearly states that it is the speed of the **delivery** that is the defining factor. A slow bowler may well bowl a faster ball in which case the first definition would apply.

It must be remembered that the terms, fast, medium fast and slow are all relative and the umpire will have to decide on each delivery in the context of the game he is umpiring.

ACTION TO BE TAKEN BY THE UMPIRE

Any delivery under these two definitions of 'beamer' is illegal and the umpire will call and signal No ball. He will start, or continue with, the disciplinary procedure detailed below. **He has no discretion with this delivery, he must take disciplinary action**.

As stated at the start of these clauses the term 'dangerous and unfair bowling' caters for the bowling of any combination of 'bouncers' and 'beamers'. The immediate action of calling and signalling No ball has been covered within each definition and will apply as stated. It is only when the umpire decides that disciplinary measures need to be taken that he will undertake the following procedure:

Dangerous and unfair bowling

FIRST occurrence

Action	Inform
• Call and signal No ball.	• Colleague.
When the ball is dead:	• Fielding captain.
• **Caution** the bowler.	• Batsmen at the crease.
• The caution shall apply whichever end he bowls from, i.e. he carries the caution around with him.	*During the next interval when the players leave the field:*
	• Batting captain.
• The caution applies throughout the rest of that innings.	

Dangerous and unfair bowling

SECOND occurrence – by SAME bowler in the same innings

Action	Inform
• Call and signal No ball.	• Colleague.
When the ball is dead:	• Fielding captain.
• Issue bowler with a **Final Warning**.	• Batsmen at the crease.
• The final warning shall apply whichever end he bowls from, i.e. he carries the final warning around with him.	*During the next interval when the players leave the field:*
	• Batting captain.
• The final warning applies throughout the rest of that innings.	

Dangerous and unfair bowling

THIRD occurrence – by SAME bowler in the same innings

Action	Inform
• Call and signal No ball.	• Colleague.
When the ball is dead:	• Batsmen at the crease.
• Tell the captain that the bowler is immediately suspended from bowling.	*During the next interval when the players leave the field:*
• Complete the over with another bowler.	• Batting captain.
• Suspended bowler may not bowl again in that innings.	*As soon as possible, report the incident to:*
	• The Executive of the fielding side.
	• The Governing Body responsible for the match.

When the captain is instructed to remove a bowler:

- that bowler may not bowl again in that innings. If the match is of two innings per side and this suspension takes place during the first innings the bowler would be allowed to bowl again in the second innings. He would start with a clean sheet.
- any incomplete over must be completed by another member of the fielding side. The replacement bowler may not bowl in consecutive or part-consecutive overs. In other words the replacement cannot be the bowler who bowled the previous over nor can he go on and bowl the next one.
- the scorers must record the fact that the bowler has been suspended in their scoring record.

8. DELIBERATE BOWLING OF HIGH FULL PITCHED BALLS

If the umpire considers that a high full pitch which is deemed to be dangerous and unfair, as defined in 6(b) above, was deliberately bowled, then the caution and warning prescribed in 7 above shall be dispensed with. The umpire shall

(a) call and signal No ball.

(b) direct the captain, when the ball is dead, to take the bowler off forthwith.

(c) implement the remainder of the procedure as laid down in 7(c) above.

This clause defines the actions the umpire must take should a ball be considered to be a **deliberate** full pitched delivery. This can be of any speed and is not restricted to fast deliveries. It is the fact that it is bowled deliberately that makes it unacceptable, not how fast it is.

If the umpire does decide that the full pitched delivery as defined under clause 6 was bowled deliberately then he must take the following action:

Dangerous and unfair bowling

Bowling of a DELIBERATE full pitch delivery – by ANY bowler	
Action	Inform
• Call and signal No ball.	• Colleague.
When the ball is dead:	• Batsmen at the crease.
• Tell the captain that the bowler is immediately suspended from bowling.	*During the next interval when the players leave the field:*
• Complete the over with another bowler.	• Batting captain.
• Suspended bowler may not bowl again in the innings.	*As soon as possible, report the incident to:*
	• The Executive of the fielding side.
	• The Governing Body responsible for the match.

It is worth noting that should a bowler bowl this type of delivery he will be suspended with immediate effect. It is not necessary for him to have had any previous cautions or final warnings. If a bowler is suspended, the scorers must record the fact in their scoring record.

9. TIME WASTING BY THE FIELDING SIDE

It is unfair for any member of the fielding side to waste time.

(a) If the captain of the fielding side wastes time, or allows any member of his side to waste time, or if the progress of an over is unnecessarily slow, at the first instance the umpire shall call and signal Dead ball if necessary and

    (i) warn the captain, and indicate that this is a first and final warning.

    (ii) inform the other umpire and the batsmen of what has occurred.

(b) If there is any further waste of time in that innings, by any member of the fielding side, the umpire shall

either (i) if the waste of time is not during the course of an over, award 5 penalty runs to the batting side. See 17 below.

or   (ii) if the waste of time is during the course of an over, when the ball is dead, direct the captain to take the bowler off forthwith. If applicable, the over shall be completed by another bowler, who shall neither have bowled the previous over nor be allowed to bowl the next over.

    The bowler thus taken off shall not be allowed to bowl again in that innings.

   (iii) inform the other umpire, the batsmen and, as soon as practicable, the captain of the batting side of what has occurred.

   (iv) report the occurrence, with the other umpire, as soon as possible to the Executive of the fielding side and to any Governing Body responsible for the match, who shall take such action as is considered appropriate against the captain and team concerned.

This is a **team** offence. All procedural actions are channelled through the captain and are cumulative throughout the innings.

It is important to note that, unlike other areas of this Law, the bowler is not treated as a special case. For this clause he is classed as a member of the fielding side and any actions by him are deemed to be as part of the team. In some cases, things done by the fielding side can have a significant effect on an innocent bowler.

The examples of time wasting below are just some of the areas where the umpire must be diligent – generally, umpires must watch out for any event that might have a detrimental effect on the game and in particular the opposing side:

- bowler who has a long follow-through and then walks slowly back to his mark
- bowler waiting at the end of his follow-through for the ball to be given to him before he starts his long slow walk back to his mark
- bowler/fielder unnecessarily cleaning/polishing/drying the ball or taking more time than is reasonable to do so
- fielding side passing the ball round to every member of the team
- bowler and/or captain constantly changing the field after every delivery
- bowler talking with his captain for long periods during the over and then either changing his field or not even making any changes at all
- fielding side taking a long time to get into position ready for a new over
- captain making continual field changes that involve a player(s) having to walk to distant parts of the ground.

All these are examples of the fielding side wasting time, but they are not the only ones and if, in the umpires' opinion, the fielding side are guilty of wasting time they must act.

Sometimes a quiet word to the captain will resolve the situation – letting him know that the umpires are aware of his time wasting tactics may be enough to put a stop to them. It is often the case that if the umpires do nothing the players will continue with what they are doing because they see that no one is bothered by it. However, if they see that the umpires are willing to take action then that is usually enough to make them react in a positive manner.

If the umpire needs to take official action, this is the procedure that he should follow:

Time wasting by the fielding side

FIRST occurrence – at ANY time during the game – by ANY fielder	
Action	**Inform**
When the ball is dead:	• Colleague.
• Warn the fielding captain.	• Batsmen at the crease.
• This is his **first and final warning**.	*During the next interval when the players*
• The warning applies to the whole team.	*leave the field:*
• The warning applies throughout the rest of that innings.	• Batting captain.

Time wasting by the fielding side

ANY repetition – by ANY fielder in the same innings – <u>NOT</u> during an over

Action	Inform
When the ball is dead:	• Colleague.
• Award 5 penalty runs to the batting side.	• Fielding captain.
	• Batsmen at the crease.
	During the next interval when the players leave the field:
	• Batting captain.
	As soon as possible, report the incident to:
	• The Executive of the fielding side.
	• The Governing Body responsible for the match.

Time wasting by the fielding side

ANY repetition – by ANY fielder in the same innings – <u>DURING</u> an over

Action	Inform
When the ball is dead:	• Colleague.
• Tell the captain that the bowler is immediately suspended from bowling.	• Batsmen at the crease.
• Complete the over with another bowler.	*During the next interval when the players leave the field:*
• Suspended bowler may not bowl again in the innings.	• Batting captain.
• Even though the bowler in question may not have caused the delay he is the one who has the action taken against him.	*As soon as possible, report the incident to:*
	• The Executive of the fielding side.
	• The Governing Body responsible for the match.

10. BATSMAN WASTING TIME

It is unfair for a batsman to waste time. In normal circumstances the striker should always be ready to take strike when the bowler is ready to start his run up.

(a) Should either batsman waste time by failing to meet this requirement, or in any other way, the following procedure shall be adopted. At the first instance, either before the bowler starts his run up or when the ball is dead, as appropriate, the umpire shall

    (i) warn the batsman and indicate that this is a first and final warning. This warning shall continue to apply throughout the innings. The umpire shall so inform each incoming batsman.

    (ii) inform the other umpire, the other batsman and the captain of the fielding side of what has occurred.

    (iii) inform the captain of the batting side as soon as practicable.

(b) **if there is any further time wasting by any batsman in that innings, the umpire shall, at the appropriate time while the ball is dead**
  - **(i) award 5 penalty runs to the fielding side. See 17 below.**
  - **(ii) inform the other umpire, the other batsman, the captain of the fielding side and, as soon as practicable, the captain of the batting side of what has occurred.**
  - **(iii) report the occurrence, with the other umpire, as soon as possible to the Executive of the batting side and to any Governing Body responsible for the match, who shall take such action as is considered appropriate against the captain and player or players and, if appropriate, the team concerned.**

This is a **team** offence and all procedural actions are channelled through the captain and are cumulative throughout the innings. Again, it is necessary to look at examples where this could happen so that the umpires can readily identify areas of concern. This list is not exhaustive and umpires must always be alive to the possibility that the batting side is attempting to waste time:

- batsman taking too long over preparing to receive the next delivery
- batsmen holding excessive discussions during an over or before the start of the next over.

The Law clearly states that, barring exceptional circumstances, the striker should be ready to face the next delivery when the bowler has reached his mark and is ready to start his run-up or delivery action. Any undue delay on the part of the striker or his colleague is unacceptable.

As with time wasting by the fielding side, a quiet word to the batsmen will normally put an end to such tactics and the umpire will have achieved his aim without recourse to official action. However, should the umpire need to take official action, this is the procedure that he should follow:

Batsman wasting time

FIRST occurrence – by ANY batsman

Action	Inform
When the ball is dead:	• Colleague.
• Warn the batsman concerned.	• Fielding captain.
• This is his **first and final warning**.	• The other batsman at the crease.
• The warning applies to the whole team.	• Each new batsman at the start of his innings.
• The warning applies throughout the rest of that innings.	*During the next interval when the players leave the field:*
	• Batting captain.

Batsman wasting time

ANY repetition – by ANY batsman in the same innings

Action	Inform
When the ball is dead:	• Colleague.
• Award 5 penalty runs to the fielding side.	• Batsmen at the crease.
	• Fielding captain.
	During the next interval when the players leave the field:
	• Batting captain.
	As soon as possible, report the incident to:
	• The Executive of the batting side.
	• The Governing Body responsible for the match.

11. DAMAGING THE PITCH – AREA TO BE PROTECTED

(a) It is incumbent on all players to avoid unnecessary damage to the pitch. It is unfair for any player to cause deliberate damage to the pitch.

(b) An area of the pitch, to be referred to as 'the protected area', is defined as that area contained within a rectangle bounded at each end by imaginary lines parallel to the popping creases and 5 ft/1.52 m in front of each and on the sides by imaginary lines, one each side of the imaginary line joining the centres of the two middle stumps, each parallel to it and 1 ft/30.48 cm from it.

12. BOWLER RUNNING ON THE PROTECTED AREA AFTER DELIVERING THE BALL

(a) If the bowler, after delivering the ball, runs on the protected area as defined in 11(b) above, the umpire shall at the first instance, and when the ball is dead,

   (i) caution the bowler. This caution shall continue to apply throughout the innings.

   (ii) inform the other umpire, the captain of the fielding side and the batsmen of what has occurred.

(b) If, in that innings, the same bowler runs on the protected area again after delivering the ball, the umpire shall repeat the above procedure, indicating that this is a final warning.

(c) If, in that innings, the same bowler runs on the protected area a third time after delivering the ball, when the ball is dead the umpire shall

   (i) direct the captain of the fielding side to take the bowler off forthwith. If applicable, the over shall be completed by another bowler, who shall neither have bowled the previous over nor be allowed to bowl the next over. The bowler thus taken off shall not be allowed to bowl again in that innings.

(ii) **inform the other umpire, the batsmen and, as soon as practicable, the captain of the batting side of what has occurred.**

(iii) **report the occurrence, with the other umpire, as soon as possible to the Executive of the fielding side and to any Governing Body responsible for the match, who shall take such action as is considered appropriate against the captain and bowler concerned.**

The umpires must protect the **whole** pitch from unnecessary damage. However, there is one area, in particular, that needs special protection and that is known as the **protected area**.

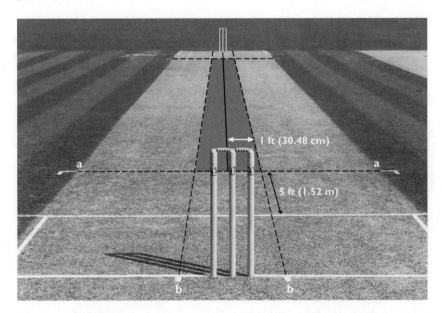

The protected area (shown in green) starts 5 ft (1.52 m) in front of the popping crease at both ends and is 2 ft (60.96 cm) wide, i.e. 1ft (30.48 cm) either side of a line between the middle stumps. In the diagram, the start of the protected area is clearly marked by means of a short line at a) and the width by markings either side of the stumps at b). If these marks are not present (they are not obligatory) the umpire can always make his own marks – with his shoe or other readily available implement – so that he can quickly identify the area concerned. He must not be guilty of damaging the pitch, so any marks he makes must be beside the pitch, not on it.

It is vital that the umpires protect this area since any damage to it will be of great assistance to the bowlers and therefore offer them an unfair advantage. The mere act of the bowler running into this area after he has delivered the ball is enough for the umpire to take action – there does not have to be evidence of any damage having occurred. The whole idea of this Law is to prevent damage from occurring in the first place, not to seek retribution once it has happened.

Once the striker has received the ball, the bowler is allowed to run on to this area provided it is with the sole purpose of fielding the ball. He is not penalised for reacting to the situation placed before him by the action of the striker hitting the ball.

If the bowler does run on to this area unnecessarily after delivery the umpire must take the following action:

Bowler running on the protected area

FIRST occurrence

Action	Inform
When ball is dead:	• Colleague.
• **Caution** the bowler.	• Fielding captain.
• The caution shall apply whichever end he bowls from, i.e. he carries the caution around with him.	• Batsmen at the crease.
	During the next interval when the players leave the field:
• The caution applies throughout the rest of that innings.	• Batting captain.

Bowler running on the protected area

SECOND occurrence – by SAME bowler in the same innings

Action	Inform
When ball is dead:	• Colleague.
• Issue a **Final Warning** to the bowler.	• Fielding captain.
• The final warning shall apply whichever end he bowls from, i.e. he carries the final warning around with him.	• Batsmen at the crease.
	During the next interval when the players leave the field:
• The final warning applies throughout the rest of that innings.	• Batting captain.

Bowler running on the protected area

THIRD occurrence – by SAME bowler in the same innings

Action	Inform
When the ball is dead:	• Colleague.
• Tell the captain that the bowler is immediately suspended from bowling.	• Batsmen at the crease.
• Complete the over with another bowler.	*During the next interval when the players leave the field:*
• Suspended bowler may not bowl again in the innings.	• Batting captain.
	As soon as possible, report the incident to:
	• The Executive of the fielding side.
	• The Governing Body responsible for the match.

13. FIELDER DAMAGING THE PITCH

(a) If any fielder causes avoidable damage to the pitch, other than as in 12(a) above, at the first instance the umpire shall, when the ball is dead,

    (i) caution the captain of the fielding side, indicating that this is a first and final warning. This caution shall continue to apply throughout the innings.

    (ii) inform the other umpire and the batsmen of what has occurred.

(b) If there is any further avoidable damage to the pitch by any fielder in that innings, the umpire shall, when the ball is dead,

    (i) award 5 penalty runs to the batting side. See 17 below.

    (ii) inform the other umpire, the batsmen, the captain of the fielding side and, as soon as practicable, the captain of the batting side of what has occurred.

    (iii) report the occurrence, with the other umpire, as soon as possible to the Executive of the fielding side and any Governing Body responsible for the match, who shall take such action as is considered appropriate against the captain and player or players concerned.

Before looking at the procedures undertaken when this Law is breached it is important to establish the meaning and interpretation of two words that feature in this clause.

DAMAGE

It is important to realise that damage will occur **every time** that anyone places a foot on the pitch. The mere fact that a foot has been placed on the surface will mean that the surface has been changed and that means, within the confines of this Law, damage has occurred.

AVOIDABLE

The use of this word is crucial when deciding if the damage caused is punishable or not. If the damage caused is such that **it could have been avoided** the umpire has reason to take official action. Where damage occurs but the action that caused the damage was unavoidable, no official action can be taken by the umpire. It therefore follows that the umpires must keep a careful eye on the actions of the fielding side and monitor the instances where fielders run on to the pitch.

Fielders will often run on to the pitch to field a ball and provided that this intrusion is as a result of an acceptable act of fielding the ball no official action can be taken. However, if the fielding side run on to the pitch at any other time the umpire will have to consider whether it could have been avoided. Umpires must always be aware of fielders running on to the pitch when celebrating a wicket or when changing ends at the end of an over. These two examples are going to cause damage that could have been avoided and so action must be taken.

ACTION TO BE TAKEN BY THE UMPIRE

The Law allows the umpire to take the official action detailed below but very often the problem can be solved by the umpire quietly reminding the fielding captain of his obligations. Note that the official action taken by the umpires is directed at the whole team and not just at the individual who causes the damage. For this reason all procedural matters have to be channelled through the captain of the fielding side.

Fielder damaging the pitch

FIRST occurrence – by ANY fielder

Action	Inform
When the ball is dead:	• Colleague.
• Caution the captain.	• Batsmen at the crease.
• This is his **first and final warning**.	*During the next interval when the players*
• This caution applies to the whole team	*leave the field:*
• This caution applies throughout the rest of that innings.	• Batting captain.

Fielder damaging the pitch

ANY repetition – by ANY fielder in the same innings

Action	Inform
When the ball is dead:	• Colleague.
• Award 5 penalty runs to the batting side.	• Fielding captain.
	• Batsmen at the crease.
	During the next interval when the players leave the field:
	• Batting captain.
	As soon as possible, report the incident to:
	• The Executive of the fielding side.
	• The Governing Body responsible for the match.

14. BATSMAN DAMAGING THE PITCH

(a) If either batsman causes avoidable damage to the pitch, at the first instance the umpire shall, when the ball is dead,

(i) caution the batsman. This caution shall continue to apply throughout the innings. The umpire shall so inform each incoming batsman.

(ii) inform the other umpire, the other batsman, the captain of the fielding side and, as soon as practicable, the captain of the batting side.

(b) If there is a second instance of avoidable damage to the pitch by any batsman in that innings

   (i)   the umpire shall repeat the above procedure, indicating that this is a final warning.

   (ii) additionally he shall disallow all runs to the batting side from that delivery other than the penalty for a **No** ball or a Wide, if applicable. The batsmen shall return to their original ends.

(c) If there is any further avoidable damage to the pitch by any batsman in that innings, the umpire shall, when the ball is dead,

   (i)   disallow all runs to the batting side from that delivery other than the penalty for a **No** ball or a Wide, if applicable. The batsmen shall return to their original ends.

   (ii) additionally award 5 penalty runs to the fielding side. See 17 below.

   (iii) inform the other umpire, the other batsman, the captain of the fielding side and, as soon as practicable, the captain of the batting side of what has occurred.

   (iv) report the occurrence, with the other umpire, as soon as possible to the Executive of the batting side and any Governing Body responsible for the match, who shall take such action as is considered appropriate against the captain and player or players concerned.

As with the fielding side, the batting side are expected to keep off the pitch as much as possible and not cause avoidable damage to it. The same criteria apply here as they do for the fielding side – the batting side should not cause avoidable damage to **any part** of the pitch. The protected area has no special significance to the batting side in this respect.

The umpires have a responsibility to watch the batsmen and ensure that:

- once the striker starts running he gets off the pitch as soon as possible. It is obvious that he will have to start his run while on the pitch, but he must move to the side of it as soon as he possibly can. It is unacceptable for the striker to continue running in a straight line towards the bowler's end as this causes damage to the pitch. A further danger is that if the striker changes his mind and turns to regain his ground he will either slip, or twist his feet, in turning thus seriously damaging the pitch.
- the non-striker runs along the side of the pitch. He must never run on the pitch itself.
- when completing the run neither batsmen run across the pitch. This is a common practice that can cause damage to the pitch and must be avoided at all times.
- batsmen who wish to have a discussion between overs do so off the pitch, not in the middle if it.
- any minor attention to the state of the pitch by the batsmen must be restricted to prodding down divots and spike marks. They must not beat the pitch with their bats.

ACTION TO BE TAKEN BY THE UMPIRE

Umpires should make every effort to deter the batting side from doing any of these things and a reminder to them at the appropriate moment often solves the problem. Note that the official action taken by the umpires is directed at the whole team and not just at the individual batsman who causes the damage. While it is not necessary to seek out immediately the batting captain when official action needs to be taken, it is paramount that the umpires do tell the batting captain of what happened at the next appropriate interval or interruption.

Batsman damaging the pitch

FIRST occurrence – by ANY batsman

Action	Inform
When ball is dead:	• Colleague.
• **Caution** the batsman.	• The other batsman at the crease.
• The caution applies to the whole team.	• Fielding captain.
• The caution applies throughout the rest of that innings.	• Each new batsman at the start of his innings.
	During the next interval when the players leave the field:
	Batting captain.

Batsman damaging the pitch

SECOND occurrence – by ANY batsman in the same innings

Action	Inform
When ball is dead:	• Colleague.
• Issue a **Final Warning** to the batsman.	• The other batsman at the crease.
• The final warning applies to the whole team.	• The fielding captain.
• The final warning applies throughout the rest of that innings.	• Each new batsman at the start of his innings.
• Disallow all runs scored from that delivery.	*During the next interval when the players leave the field:*
• Allow any penalty for a No ball or Wide to be scored.	• Batting captain.
• Return batsmen to their original ends.	

Batsman damaging the pitch

ANY further occurrence – by ANY batsman in the same innings

Action	Inform
When ball is dead:	• Colleague.
• Disallow all runs scored from that delivery.	• Fielding captain.
	• Batsman at the crease.
• Award 5 penalty runs to the fielding side.	*During the next interval when the players leave the field:*
• Allow any penalty for a No ball or Wide to be scored.	• Batting captain.
	As soon as possible, report the incident to:
• Return batsmen to their original ends	• The Executive of the batting side.
	• The Governing Body responsible for the match.

It is worth noting that the batting side have two 'warnings' before penalty runs are issued whereas the fielding side only have one.

15. BOWLER ATTEMPTING TO RUN OUT NON-STRIKER BEFORE DELIVERY

The bowler is permitted, before entering his delivery stride, to attempt to run out the non-striker. The ball shall not count in the over.

The umpire shall call and signal Dead ball as soon as possible if the bowler fails in the attempt to run out the non-striker.

The non-striker should leave his ground only after the bowler has entered his delivery stride. If he does so any earlier, the bowler is quite entitled to attempt to run him out. No warning is necessary, although the usual custom is for the bowler to mention it to the offending batsman, and tell him that if he does it again he could be out Run out. In Law, this warning is not necessary.

The attempt can be made anytime after the ball comes into play – i.e. when the bowler starts his run-up or, where he has no run-up, his bowling action – up to when he enters his delivery stride. The delivery stride is the last deliberate placement of the bowler's feet during which his arm will swing over to deliver the ball.

Provided that the attempt is made before the back foot lands in the delivery stride it will be allowed. If the bowler attempts the run out after the back foot has landed in this delivery stride the umpire will call and signal Dead ball and the attempt will be disallowed. The bowler **cannot** go through with his bowling action (i.e. swing the arm over as if to bowl the ball), retain hold of it, bring his arm back and run out the non-striker.

Assuming that the attempt at the run out is made prior to the delivery stride, the bowler may

• throw the ball at the wicket, or
• stop in his run up and remove the bail(s) with the ball in his hand.

If the non-striker is out of his ground when either of these methods is used, he will be given out Run out. If any attempt to run out the non-striker fails the umpire will call and signal Dead ball.

When such an attempt is made the ball has not been delivered to the striker and is not counted as one in the over.

16. BATSMEN STEALING A RUN

It is unfair for the batsmen to attempt to steal a run during the bowler's run up. Unless the bowler attempts to run out either batsman – see 15 above and Law 24.4 (Bowler throwing towards striker's end before delivery) – the umpire shall

(i) call and signal Dead ball as soon as the batsmen cross in any such attempt.

(ii) return the batsmen to their original ends.

(iii) award 5 penalty runs to the fielding side. See 17 below.

(iv) inform the other umpire, the batsmen, the captain of the fielding side and, as soon as practicable, the captain of the batting side of the reason for the action taken.

(v) report the occurrence, with the other umpire, as soon as possible to the Executive of the batting side and any Governing Body responsible for the match, who shall take such action as is considered appropriate against the captain and player or players concerned.

Where the batsmen attempt to run while the bowler is running in to bowl, there are two options open to the fielding side (the bowler). Which option he chooses will dictate how the umpire reacts.

OPTION 1

The bowler can attempt to run out either batsman by throwing the ball at either wicket. The attempt must be made prior to him reaching his delivery stride and, provided that he conforms to this, any successful run out of either batsman will be upheld.

If he fails to run out the **non-striker**, the umpire will call and signal Dead ball (as detailed above in clause 15 of this Law).

If he attempts to run out the **striker**, either umpire will call and signal No ball (for illegal arm action) and play continues as it would for any other No ball delivery.

If the ball hits the wicket the striker will be out Run out (see Law 24, page 174, for further details). If the striker hits the ball, or No ball extras are scored, these will be counted.

Since it is a No ball it does not count as one in the over.

OPTION 2

The bowler decides not to take the above action but simply stops in his run up and watches the batsmen run. In this case the umpire will adopt the following procedure:

Batsmen stealing a run

Bowler does not attempt a run out

Action	Inform
• Wait until the batsmen have crossed.	• Colleague.
• Call and signal Dead ball.	• Batsmen at the crease.
• Award 5 penalty runs to the fielding side.	• Fielding captain.
• Return the batsmen to their original ends.	*During the next interval when the players*
• Ensure the scorers do not record any runs for the batting side	*leave the field:*
	• Batting captain.
• Ensure scorers understand how many runs to record to the fielding side.	*As soon as possible, report the incident to:*
	• The Executive of the batting side.
• Ensure this delivery is not counted as one in the over.	• The Governing Body responsible for the match.

17. PENALTY RUNS

(a) When penalty runs are awarded to either side, when the ball is dead the umpire shall signal the penalty runs to the scorers as laid down in Law 3.14 (Signals).

(b) Notwithstanding the provisions of Law 21.6 (Winning hit or extras), penalty runs shall be awarded in each case where the Laws require the award. Note, however, that the restrictions on awarding penalty runs in Laws 26.3 (Leg byes not to be awarded), 34.4(d) (Runs permitted from ball struck lawfully more than once) and Law 41.4 (Penalty runs not to be awarded) will apply.

(c) When 5 penalty runs are awarded to the batting side, under either Law 2.6 (Player returning without permission) or Law 41 (The fielder) or under 3, 4, 5, 9 or 13 above, then

    (i) they shall be scored as penalty extras and shall be in addition to any other penalties.

    (ii) they shall not be regarded as runs scored from either the immediately preceding delivery or the following delivery, and shall be in addition to any runs from those deliveries.

    (iii) the batsmen shall not change ends solely by reason of the 5 run penalty.

(d) When 5 penalty runs are awarded to the fielding side, under Law 18.5(b) (Deliberate short runs), or under 10, 14 or 16 above, they shall be added as penalty extras to that side's total of runs in its most recently completed innings. If the fielding side has not completed an innings, the 5 penalty extras shall be added to its next innings.

This clause summarises all situations where penalty runs are awarded and how they shoud be recorded.

The 5 penalty runs are never deducted from a side's score – in other words they never appear as a minus figure in the scoring record. They are runs given to a side because of an offence committed by the other side. They are never credited to a bats-man nor debited against a bowler. Instead, they are recorded in their own section of the scoring record under penalty runs.

If penalty runs are awarded to the batting side they are recorded in the current innings of that side.

If penalty runs are awarded to the fielding side they are added to the innings that has already taken place for that side. If the fielding side have not batted in the game, they are added to the first innings of that side. So the fielding side might start off their innings with a plus total e.g. 5, 10 or 15 runs.

When penalty runs are awarded following a No ball or Wide, the umpire will ensure that the scorers understand that the two separate awards are acknowledged and recorded as separate entries.

EXAMPLE 5

A Wide is missed by the wicket-keeper and the ball hits the helmet stationed on the ground behind the wicket-keeper.

RUNS SCORED: 1 for the Wide + 5 penalty runs = 6.

EXAMPLE 6

A No ball is hit by the striker and the batsmen complete 3 runs when a fielder illegally fields the ball.

RUNS SCORED: 1 No ball + 3 runs to the striker + 5 penalty runs = 9.

Whenever penalty runs are awarded the batsmen do not automatically return to their original ends if the total runs scored ends up being even. It is the runs scored by the batsmen running that dictate which ends they resume at.

EXAMPLE 7

On the fourth ball of the over, the striker hits a fair delivery and the batsmen complete 3 runs when illegal fielding takes place.

RUNS SCORED: 3 to striker + 5 penalty runs = 8.

The non-striker faces the next delivery because the batsmen actually ran 3 runs. Although the score went up by an even number it does not mean that the batsmen return to their original ends – they ran 3 (an odd number) and so stay at the ends they were at when the illegal act took place. The 5 penalty runs are added after the batsmen have finished their part in the action and they remain where they finished.

Whenever penalty runs are awarded the umpires must follow up the matter by reporting the events which led to the award(s) to the Executive of the side at fault and the Governing Body responsible for the match. The only exceptions to this are when 5 penalty runs are awarded for the ball hitting a helmet placed on the ground behind the wicket-keeper or for the ball **accidentally** coming into contact with a cap, or other article of fielder's clothing, that has been wilfully discarded. If the ball hits this object, the report procedure is not to be implemented.

Scorers' attention is directed to the section on scoring penalty runs in Part 3 of this edition. Because most awards are comparatively rare, it is imperative that scorers know instinctively what to do and where to make their entries.

18. PLAYERS' CONDUCT

If there is any breach of the Spirit of the Game by a player failing to comply with the instructions of an umpire, or criticising his decisions by word or action, or showing dissent, or generally behaving in a manner which might bring the game into disrepute, the umpire concerned shall immediately report the matter to the other umpire. The umpires together shall

(i) **inform the player's captain of the occurrence, instructing the latter to take action.**

(ii) **warn him of the gravity of the offence, and tell him that it will be reported to higher authority.**

(iii) **report the occurrence as soon as possible to the Executive of the player's team and any Governing Body responsible for the match, who shall take such action as is considered appropriate against the captain and player or players, and, if appropriate, the team concerned.**

Players are expected to comply with the decisions and instructions that the umpires make, and should accept them whether they think them correct or not. The Spirit of Cricket also lays down, very concisely, the responsibilities the players and, especially, the captains have within the game.

While one of the captain's roles is to ensure that his team behaves and maintain the traditions of the game, it is up to everyone to ensure that these requirements are met. The umpires have a role to play in this and they should not be slow in coming forward to express their concerns if the captain and/or his players fall short of their expectations.

Human nature being what it is, and especially in today's cultural climate where authority, in whichever guise it may take, is questioned, umpires must expect a certain amount of intolerance. Note the phrase '**expect** a certain amount of intolerance' – NOT condone it, or even ignore it.

It is paramount that umpires have empathy with the players and understand the reasons why they get upset. This is the key to solving most problems encountered by umpires on the field of play.

EXAMPLE 8

A fast bowler is bowling well, but everything is going against him. Slips have dropped two or three catches off him, the batsmen have mastered the skill of hitting everything off the edge of the bat instead of the middle, and, to cap it all, the umpire has just turned down what he, the bowler, thought was a certain LBW. In his frustration, he uses a few expletives.

Before the umpire goes overboard and starts taking official action, he should stop and put himself in the bowler's shoes. Wouldn't he have said something similar in such a situation? It would be best, in this situation, for the umpire to have a quiet but **firm** word with the bowler, showing that he fully understands the bowler's feelings but that he really must try to control himself. This will have a far better result than if he immediately starts taking official action.

By using this method of dealing with things – i.e. by empathising with the player and his frustration rather than immediately taking the officious line – the umpire is more likely to gain the players' respect and acceptance. It is always best when dealing with situations involving bad language, frustration or irritation that the umpires talk to the players in the manner in which, if the roles were reversed, they would like to be spoken to. If treated with respect and courtesy, the players will, in turn, do the same with the umpires. The object of the exercise is to gain the respect and cooperation of the players so that the game proceeds without acrimony.

However, if a situation occurs that the umpires deem to be outside this 'quiet word' situation, they do have a right – indeed, are **expected** – to deal with it officially. The Law lays out clearly what areas the umpires should look at:

- breach of the Spirit of Cricket e.g. directing abusive language towards an opponent or umpire, excessive appealing, excessive noise such as persistent clapping or talking about a batsman and his abilities in a derogatory way, and outright cheating
- failure to comply with an umpire's instructions
- criticism of an umpire's decision(s) either by word or action
- showing dissent
- bringing the game into disrepute.

ACTION TO BE TAKEN BY THE UMPIRE
If the captain cannot or will not control himself or his players in any of the above areas, the following course of action will be taken:

**Breach of The Spirit of Cricket, dissent,
bad behaviour or criticism of an umpire**

Either umpire

Action	Inform
When the ball is dead:	• Captain of the other side.
• Report incident to colleague and acting **together** both umpires will:	*As soon as possible, report the incident to:*
• Tell captain of what occurred.	• The Executive of the offending side.
• Tell him it is not acceptable.	• The Governing Body responsible for the match.
• Tell him to take action to prevent it occurring again.	
• Tell him that the incident will be reported.	

It is worth noting that in cases of disciplinary breakdown the offending side does not get a second chance to behave. The first time either umpire decides that official action needs to be taken, the above procedure is adopted and that means that a report will be issued to the relevant authorities.

Although not required by the Laws, the umpires should ensure that the scorers are made aware of the reasons for any disciplinary action, especially if this results in a bowler being suspended. Scorers will record the reason in the scoring record.

PART 3

Scoring

INTRODUCTION

Scorers are the unseen participants in every game. This does not mean that they are unimportant, indeed their role is just as important as that of the players and the umpires. Without the information recorded by the scorers, how could we identify the batsman who scored the most runs, or the bowler who took the most wickets? More importantly, how could we ascertain the result as required under Law 21? A competent scorer is an important member of a cricket club – who else watches and records every ball in every match played by a team and, hence, writes both the history of the club and a record of the players' achievements as they occur?

A well kept scoring record provides a wealth of information, for players, club officials, league secretaries, the media, selection committees and coaches. They all want, or need, to know the statistics of the match. It is the information recorded by the scorers that permits coaches and selectors to review the strengths and weaknesses of the players.

In earlier times, scorers notched their sticks while sitting within the boundary of the playing area. Each tenth run was cut deeper to match the fingers of their hands and an even deeper notch was cut when twice that was scored. This is thought by many to be the origins of the noun 'score'. As the game progressed the sticks were laid side by side to assess progress and to see if a result was imminent.

Since then, various other methods have been used – the box system designed by Charles Box in 1877, the lineal system developed by Bill Ferguson in 1905 and later refined by Bill Frindall, and now computerisation. To cover the fact that the scorer may not record events on paper, the general term 'scoring record' is now used. This edition does not attempt to explain computerised scoring and will use the box type scoring record in all examples.

Law 4.1 is clear. Two scorers are to be appointed to record the details of the match. Ideally each team has a scorer who knows and can easily recognise the players in the team from his position beyond the boundary. Identification can be difficult, particularly if players are wearing similar caps, hats or helmets. To assist in the identification of players, scorers should meet with the teams prior to the toss and make notes. These could include both batting and fielding, for example left or right handed, fast or slow bowler, clothing, etc. The two scorers must develop a rapport, each respecting the other's abilities and offering help when required. For the duration of the game, their concentration must always be absolute.

Scorers are encouraged to communicate constantly with each other about what is happening on the field of play, thus ensuring nothing is missed and that their records agree.

If only one scorer is available, special care must be taken to record events accurately. No scorer can be expected to complete his duties efficiently and accurately without support. If he finds himself in such circumstances, he may need to let the umpires know he needs a little time to discover the names of players, or balance his scoring record. A mutually acceptable signal can be agreed with the umpires before the match to allow this to happen with a minimum of disruption to the flow of the game. Umpires should be aware of the situation and, as part of the team of officials, should assist whenever possible. In the absence of names, descriptions of players can be entered in pencil and updated later.

The scorers' principal duties are to make entries in the scoring record that accurately reflect the activity on the field of play and to ensure that the scoreboard operator knows and displays the same score on the scoreboard as is in the scoring record.

Duties

Law 4 sets out the four principal duties of scorers: Accept, Acknowledge, Record and Check.

Accept

The scorers must accept the signals that the umpire makes even if they have good reason for believing that a mistake has been made. Discussion should take place at the earliest opportunity about any such events.

If the scorer is uncertain about any incident, perhaps over a method of dismissal, such as Caught or LBW, then he should make a note and ask at the first available opportunity. This would usually be at the next interval or interruption, or at the conclusion of the match. If the uncertainty needs an immediate response, for example the side batting needs 10 runs to win and you are unsure how many overthrows the umpire allowed on the last ball, find out immediately.

Acknowledge

Always acknowledge clearly and promptly – the umpire should not allow play to continue until he is certain that the scorer has seen and understood each and every signal.

Signals to the scorer will be made when the ball is dead. Some signals, for example No Ball, are first made when the ball is in play. This is for the benefit of the players and will be repeated when the ball is dead. The first signal should not be acknowledged, as the umpire will still be watching the action on the field. There may be more than one signal for a ball depending on the sequence of events. The Laws require that each signal should be given and acknowledged separately. For example, when signalling Boundary four Byes, umpires will signal Byes, receive the acknowledgement, then signal Boundary 4 and wait for that to be acknowledged.

Record

The most obvious duty of scorers is to record the events of the match in the scoring record.

The Laws state that the scorers shall record all runs scored, all wickets taken, and, where appropriate, the number of overs bowled. In practice most scorers consider this the minimum amount of information and record much more. A standard system of recommended symbols has been developed for this purpose and some scorers add their own additional symbols.

Check

Regular and frequent checking is essential to ensure that the scoring record balances and that it agrees with the record of the other scorer.

At the end of **each** over the scorer must agree the events of that over with his colleague. This can be done simply by using words like 'Ten off the over, Smith [the bowler] two for twenty three, score seventy five for six off twenty eight overs.' This will reduce the risk of error in the cumulative score.

Checks should also be carried out:

- at the fall of a wicket
- during intervals
- during interruptions
- at the end of an innings
- at the close of each day's play
- at the end of a match
- at any other convenient time.

The checks should ensure that the runs recorded in both the batting and bowling sections agree with the runs crossed off on the cumulative run tally and that the balls bowled and received balance.

There are two checks to balance the runs scored:

- Runs scored by batsmen + Bowling extras (Wide balls and No balls) = Runs scored off all bowlers
- Runs scored off all bowlers + Fielding extras (Byes, Leg byes and penalty extras) = Total runs (Cumulative run tally)

There is one check to balance the balls bowled:

- Balls received by all batsmen + Balls not received by batsmen = Number of Balls Bowled

  Balls not received are: Wide balls; those stopping before reaching the striker and called No ball.

Errors such as crediting runs to the wrong batsman or crediting the batsman with runs which should be extras are important but less so than the constant verification of the cumulative team total. It is the team total from which the result will be determined and not the individual performances.

The Law directs that, at least at every interval other than for drinks, and at the conclusion of the match, the scorers and umpires shall agree the runs scored, wickets taken, and where appropriate the number of overs bowled.

EQUIPMENT

There are a number of items of equipment that scorers must have to enable them to record the score. The list given below is the basic equipment required, however scorers might wish to add to this:

- **Scoring record**: this may take the form of a scorebook, scoresheet or computer. Even when using computers scorers may prefer to keep a written record in addition to that stored on the computer.
- **Pens/pencils/pencil sharpener**: pens should be smudge proof and water resistant with fine tips, the best being 0.3-0.5 mm. If scoring in colour, make sure the colours selected can be photocopied without loss of quality.
- **Eraser and correcting material**
- **Watch or clock:** synchronised with the official timepiece.
- **MCC Laws of Cricket**: a copy of the Laws is a useful reference should an unusual event occur.
- **Experimental Laws:** (if any) from time to time the MCC introduce experimental Laws and scorers must be aware of any that may impact on the entries in the scoring record.
- **Competition Regulations**: every competition, be it league or cup, will have its own set of regulations, many of which detail the method of determining the result or points awarded. These take precedence over the Laws of Cricket and the scorer should always be aware of them.
- **Tom Smith's Cricket Umpiring and Scoring**
- **White/reflective signaller**: ensure that this is clearly visible to the umpires against the background of the scorebox. Some scoreboxes may be equipped with a light for signalling, in which case make sure it works before play begins and after each interval.
- **Notepaper**: useful for recording information that aids scoring, such as descriptions of players, or for recording incidents that need clarification from the umpires.
- **Ruler**
- **Calculator**
- **Binoculars**: useful when trying to identify players.

BEFORE THE MATCH

Most scorers are affiliated to a team or club and as such will be familiar with the league grounds and regulations and of the individual team members. If appointed to an unfamiliar competition or to a match at an unfamiliar ground then this changes.

Appointed scorers should:
- find out where the ground is and how they will get there

- obtain a copy of the competition regulations
- check all points relating to scoring
- check how the result is to be determined – for example, if a match ends with the scores tied will the result be determined by fewest wickets lost, by comparing the scores after a certain number of overs or by some other method as defined in the playing regulations for the competition?

On the match day the scorer has a number of duties to perform, some laid down in Law, others evolving from good practice and experience.

It is the duty of the scorer to be available and ready at the official start time. There are several pre-match duties and the scorer should arrive in time to complete these. The umpires are directed by Law to arrive at least 45 minutes before the start of play, however there is no such stipulation for scorers. As some of the pre-match duties involve agreements with the umpires it makes sense for the scorers to arrive at the same time as the umpires.

A home scorer should aim to arrive earlier and ensure the scorebox is clean and tidy, with tables and chairs. Personal comfort must always be given proper consideration when scoring, for if the location, weather or seating causes discomfort there may be lapses in concentration. If scoring indoors ensure adequate ventilation and shade from the sun; if scoring outdoors, ensure adequate protection from the weather. Welcome the visiting colleague and acquaint him with the amenities.

Scorers arriving late will often find themselves rushing to fulfil their duties, causing them to overlook some important matters.

Both scorers together should meet the umpires before the toss to discuss and confirm:

- the master timepiece to be used during a match. Umpires' and scorers' watches should be synchronised with this timepiece
- the back-up timepiece should the master fail
- the boundary markings and the runs scored should the ball reach the boundary
- whether or not any obstacle, permanent or temporary, within the field of play is to be regarded as a boundary
- where the scorers will be stationed
- method of acknowledgement for all umpires' signals
- the hours of play, the timing and duration of any intervals and if and when any drinks breaks should be taken
- how the scorers will be informed of changes, for example, if lunch is taken early if there is an interruption
- the provision for new balls, if applicable, and where on the scoreboard to record the overs bowled with the new ball
- any special regulations that may apply, particularly if the match has any restrictions of time, the innings is restricted to a maximum number of overs or bowlers are restricted in the number of overs they may bowl

- any local customs which will be applied
- how and when the score will be updated on the scoreboard
- how and when the overs bowled will be updated on the scoreboard
- how and when the overs bowled during the last hour are to be displayed (the recommendation is always that the number of completed overs is displayed starting at 0 and working up to the prescribed number).

In local competitions, this meeting may be a formality as everyone involved is usually familiar with the published playing conditions. However, if appointed to score in unfamiliar competitions the pre-match meeting is particularly important.

The scorers must also know:
- the team winning the toss and which team is to bat first.
- the names of the nominated players. Both captains should, ideally, supply two copies of the team sheet, one for the umpires and one for the scorers. If only one copy is supplied the umpires should make it available to allow the scorers to copy the names.
- the names of the umpires.
- it is also useful to consider the likely batting and bowling orders with descriptions of the bowlers and their actions particularly if the players are not known to either scorer. If there is any doubt the information should be entered in pencil and changed later.

Umpires normally take the field five minutes before the start of play and scorers should be in position and ready to start by then.

It should be noted that there is no requirement in the Laws for scorers to maintain the scoreboard. The updating of the scoreboard should never be permitted to distract scorers from their principal duty, to record the progress of the match. If this happens, scorers should ask others to perform the task.

Scoring alone

The absence of a second scorer places additional and unfair burdens on a sole scorer. Occasionally a team may arrive at a match without a scorer, possibly without a scoring record of any kind, totally ignoring the requirement stated in Law 4 that two scorers must be appointed for each match.

As the umpires are responsible for all Law-related matters, the sole scorer should bring this to their attention during the pre-match conference. The umpires should then make any necessary arrangements to assist the scorer, for example by directing the batting captain to have a player stationed alongside the official scorer at all times.

If possible the sole official scorer should supply a spare scoring record to the player/scorer to enable a record to be kept for that team. A solo scorer should not attempt to keep two scoring records simultaneously.

SCORING SYMBOLS

When completing the record, numerals are used for runs credited to the batsmen while dots are used to denote runs not credited to the batsman. A system of symbols has evolved and the table below shows them.

Action	Fair Ball	No Ball	Wide Ball
No runs scored	●	N/A	N/A
Striker scores runs	l 2 3 etc.	N/A	N/A
Umpire signals No ball or Wide ball and no other runs are scored	N/A	○	+
Umpire signals No ball and striker scores runs	N/A	①②③ etc.	N/A
Batsmen run without striker hitting ball and umpire signals No ball and Bye or Wide ball	N/A	⊙ ⊙ ⊙ etc.	╬ ╬ ╬ etc
Umpire signals Leg byes	▽ ▽ ▽ etc	N/A	N/A
Umpire signals Byes	△ △ △ etc	N/A	N/A
Wicket falls for which bowler gets credit (no runs can be scored other than penalties)	W	N/A	W╪
Wicket falls for which bowler does not get credit (runs may be scored by the batsman or as No balls or Wide balls)	● 1 etc	①②③ ⊙ ⊙ ⊙ etc ○	╬ ╬ ╬ etc +

An underline "_" can be used in conjunction with any of the symbols or numerals if the batsmen finish up at the 'wrong' end. For example:

- The batsmen run 3 but Short run is called
  the batsmen have changed ends
  only 2 runs are scored and this suggests that they are back at their original ends
  the entry would be 2 indicating that they have changed ends
- If the striker is out caught when running and they have crossed to change ends
  the entry will be w.

COMPLETING A BOX SCORING RECORD

Any person experienced in cricket scoring should be able to pick up a scoring record and, while reading through the entries, state what happened on every delivery. To assist this, an accepted convention of entries and symbols has evolved over time, though scorers may use alternatives. Included herein are the recognised and recommended international methods. By adopting these conventions another scorer can take over during an innings and, except for different handwriting, the change should be unnoticed. Consistent entries by scorers, using the same methodology, ensures the regular checking of the scoring record, required during the match, is made easier.

Many scorers use colours in the scoring record, which if used correctly and neatly can make it easier to read and to follow. The recommended method is to use one colour for each bowler and to make all entries during the overs of that bowler in that colour. It is not recommended to use different colours for different events, for example 6 in red and 4 in green, as this can slow down the scoring process as the scorer searches for a pen.

Some entries can be made before play commences; most are made during play; some are made after play finishes. This section sets out to describe the standard entries in as near chronological order as possible.

1. BEFORE PLAY IS CALLED

Before the start of an innings the header can be completed. If scoring in colour, complete these entries in black. Scoring records have space for different combinations of entry, however the basic information should always be present:

- Home team
- Date(s)
- Scorers' names
- Side winning the toss
- Away team
- Batting side
- Type of match
- Weather
- Venue
- Umpires' names
- Start time
- Pitch condition.

Before the final innings of the match the scorer should, in the Cummulative Run Tally, identify the target score. This should be done in pencil to allow a change to be made if penalties are awarded to the batting side.

If the batting side has already fielded, they may have been awarded penalty extras while fielding and these runs must be entered as their starting score. The examples below shows three awards, totalling 15 runs, being entered in the appropriate sections of the scoring record.

Cumulative Run Tally										End of Over					Pen
~~1~~	~~2~~	~~3~~	~~4~~	~~5~~	~~6~~	~~7~~	~~8~~	~~9~~		Ov	Runs	W	B	B	F
~~10~~	~~1~~	~~2~~	~~3~~	~~4~~	~~5~~	6	7	8	9	0	15				
20	1	2	3	4	5	6	7	8	9	1					
30	1	2	3	4	5	6	7	8	9	2					

Batting Sheet

Fielding Extras	Byes	
	Leg Byes	
	Penalties prev inn	15	this inn	

The first row of the **end of over** section has an over number of zero. This is used to record any penalty runs awarded to the side currently batting while fielding in the previous innings. In this example the side batting has been awarded 15 penalty runs and so start their innings with 15 runs. The runs must also be crossed off on the **cumulative run tally** as three separate entries of 5 runs rather than one of 15. To make the identification of penalty extras easier some scorers use a double rather than a single line in the tally when crossing them off. Either is acceptable providing consistency is maintained. The runs should also be recorded in the batting sheet under **penalty extras – previous innings**.

As the first batsman takes guard his name is entered in black, as batsman 1, together with the name of the non-striker as batsman 2. The time of the start of their innings is the time when the umpire first calls Play.

As the opening bowler takes possession of the bowler's marker and paces out his run-up, his name is entered as bowler 1.

2. DURING PLAY

Whenever the bowler delivers the ball an entry should be made in both the batting and bowling sections and in the cumulative run tally when runs are scored. The scorer should always complete the entries in the same order to minimise the risk of errors. The recommended order is:

• Bowling
• Batting – this includes any extras
• Cumulative run tally.

This order is not compulsory – it is for each scorer to adopt his own order, as may be dictated by the layout of the scoring record.

At any time during, or after a match, the **margins** or **note area** should be used to record details of incidents that cannot be recorded elsewhere:

• the time a fielder leaves the field	D Smith left field 2:35
• the time he returns	D Smith returned 3:10
• the names of any substitutes and runners	F Jones substitute for D Smith 2:35 to 3:10

• the times and balls of milestones, for example a batsman or the score reaching 100 runs	100 runs; 135 mins, 245 balls
• incidents where the entries may not be as expected, for example a fairly delivered ball which, because of fielding transgressions, does not count as one of the over	5th Over, 3rd Ball – fielded by D Smith who returned without permission. Ball does not count as one of over

Cumulative run tally

During play a running total of the score is kept by filling in this section. It consists of a grid of numbers crossed off as runs are scored. When doing so, cross off single runs **diagonally**, two or more runs with a **continuous stroke**. Never cross off the runs individually.

Where a single score continues from one line to the next extend the stroke into the margins at the end of the first line and before the start of the next line to indicate the continuation.

Note that this recommended method permits the entries to be converted back – in this example – to the scoring sequence 1, 1, 3, 6.

Identifying runs scored as extras in the tally can aid the reading of the scoring record. The same basic symbols as used in the other sections can be used. For example, continuing the sequence above, 3 No balls were scored next. The circle is used to denote this. Similarly the Wide, Bye and Leg bye symbols could also be used.

Batting section

The batting section of the scoring record is used to record all runs scored, whether they are credited to a batsman or recorded as extras. It also shows the details of a batsman's dismissal.

For each batsman the section contains:
- **Number**: the pre-printed numbers 1 to 11 for the batting order.
- **Name**: the batsman's name should be entered as he commences his innings, i.e. the opening batsmen as numbers 1 and 2 and the others as their innings start.
- **Time in/out**: the time each starts and concludes his innings.
- **Minutes**: the length of the innings of the batsman. This excludes all intervals and interruptions.
- **Details of balls faced**: in this line a symbol is added for every ball faced and these should correspond to the symbols used in the bowling analysis. Note that the Wide symbol is used to show the batsman on strike when the ball was bowled.

- **Balls**: the number of balls received by each batsman. A Wide is not counted as a ball received (faced) as the batsman is unable to hit it. A No ball is a ball received. However, if a ball delivered by the bowler comes to rest in front of the stumps without the striker having made contact, the umpire will call and signal No ball, followed immediately by Dead ball (Law 24.7). Although recorded as a No ball, this will not count as a ball received by the striker.
- **How out**: the method by which the batsman was dismissed, if applicable.
- **Bowler**: the name of the bowler gaining credit for the dismissal, if applicable.
- **Fielder's name credited with the dismissal**
- **Score**: the number of runs scored by that batsman.

As an innings proceeds, a batsman may face a large number of deliveries. A batsman batting for 50 overs and facing the bowling for one third of that time would face 100 deliveries. This will result in a large number of symbols and numerals to be added and balanced at the conclusion of his innings. One method of keeping track of the running totals of a batsman's score and balls faced is that after every ten balls faced:

- an oblique slash is made in a batsman's line. At the end of the innings or when balancing, the number of strokes are counted, multiplied by ten and any additional deliveries added
- alongside this slash the batsman's progressive score is entered. This allows the balancing of runs to be easily completed.

Another method is to do this at the end of each over and record the number of runs as well as the number of balls faced.

The example below shows 21 balls faced. The Wide is recorded to show that the batsman was the striker when it was bowled but it is not a ball received.

| 1 | R | $\ldots 1\,2\,4\,.\,1\,1\,2/^{11}\ldots.+6\,1\ldots1\,4/^{23}\,3$ |
| | FENTON | |

| 1 | R | $\ldots 1/_{4}^{1}\,2\,4\,.\,1\,1/_{9}^{9}\,2\ldots.+6/_{15}^{17}\,1\ldots1\,4\,3/_{21}^{26}$ |
| | FENTON | |

The scorer will find it helps him to quickly balance the score if he notes in the scoring record margin the cumulative runs and cumulative deliveries faced by all the dismissed and/or retired batsmen. When a wicket falls simply update that cumulative total, agree with colleague and then put a line through or erase the old entry. Using this method he has only to add on the details for the two not out batsmen to give him total batsmen's runs and total deliveries faced.

The extras section contains space to record:

- **Bowling extras**: runs scored as No balls or Wides are debited against the bowler

- **Fielding extras**: runs
  scored as Byes, Leg byes
  or penalty runs awarded –
  these are not debited
  against the bowler.

Bowling Extras	No Balls			
	Wides			
Fielding Extras	Byes			
	Leg Byes			
	Penalties	prev inn	this inn	

It is never correct to credit the same runs to both the striker and extras; they are either one or the other.

Bowling section

During play two parts of the bowling section are used; the **analysis**, where each ball is recorded, and the **vertical columns**, where each occurrence of a No ball or a Wide is recorded.

ANALYSIS

One box is used for each over bowled by a bowler. The order in which the balls are entered may vary according to the scoring record layout or the preference of the scorer but must never be changed during a match. If the order is changed the history of the innings is lost.

A	B
1 4	1 2 3
2 5	
3 6	4 5 6

C	D
1 7 4	1 2 3
2 8 5	7 8 9
3 9 6	4 5 6

A standard six-ball over can be recorded in the order 1 to 6 shown in A and B. Space must be left to permit the recording of extra deliveries, as shown in C and D. Throughout this book the order shown in A and C are used.

If less than, or more than, six balls are delivered in an over for whatever reason:

- each delivery must be recorded
- the over as counted and called is a completed over
- if there are more or less than six balls it can still be a maiden over
- never add an extra dot to make up a full over or leave out a delivery. It is the responsibility of the scorer to record accurately the progress of the match.

A **maiden** over is one where no runs are conceded by the bowler, i.e. the striker has not scored any runs and there have been no bowling extras (No balls or Wides). It may include fielding extras (Byes, Leg byes or penalty runs).

Whenever a maiden over occurs, the dots are joined together to form the letter M. If a wicket is taken during a maiden over it becomes a wicket maiden and the letter W is formed. Any symbols entered (wicket, Byes and Leg byes) should not be crossed over by the M or W used, but the line should be broken as shown. Thus it becomes possible to see on which delivery any event occurred.

VERTICAL COLUMNS

These columns are used to record the number of Wides and No balls bowled by each bowler and the only valid entry is 1. Do not use this section to record the runs scored; the extras section in the batting sheet serves that purpose.

The totals obtained from this example show that the bowler has bowled 3 Wides and 2 No balls. This information is used when calculating the number of balls bowled and received.

Number of	
Wides	No Balls
111	11
3	2

If scoring in colour the runs debited to relevant extras can readily be identified in all sections.

Completion of an over

At the end of each over there are a number of entries to be made and checks to be carried out.

ANALYSIS

Beneath each scoring box, there is a smaller box. This is used to keep a running total of:

- the number of runs conceded by the bowler
- the number of wickets for which the bowler gets credit.

1		2	
2	1	1	w
1	.	2	.
.	.	1	4
4 - 0		12 - 1	

Here 4 runs were scored in the first over and 8 in the second giving a running total of 12 runs. The bowler gained credit for a wicket in the second over. These figures may be reversed to show runs then wickets, for example 0–4 and 1–12, but the scorer should use the same method throughout.

It is often useful to show the match over number in the 'smaller' box as an aid to balancing, tracking back, completing a fuller description of events.

END OF OVER SECTION

This section contains columns and rows numbered from zero. The pre-printed number denotes the over and the other columns are completed either at the start of, during or end of an over:

- **Runs**: enter the total score recorded at the end of that over – this is a cumulative entry.
- **Wickets**: if a wicket falls during the over enter the total number of wickets lost at the end of that over – this is a cumulative entry.
- **Bowler**: enter his number taken from the bowling analysis, at the start of that over. Should there be a bowling change mid-over, add a margin note.
- **Penalty runs awarded to the batting side**: always enter 1 for each infringement as it occurs, never 5 which is misleading.

- **Penalty runs awarded to the fielding side**: enter a 1 for each infringement as it occurs, never 5 which is misleading.
- **Time**: there may also be space to record the time the over started.

Penalty runs awarded after the call of Over or Time should always be entered in the next over even if there is no play in that over unless it is the last over of an innings.

Information can be extracted from this section, showing for example:

- at the end of the 4th over the score was 27
- bowler 3 had just taken the 2nd wicket to fall
- 5 runs were scored in the 1st over
- bowler 2 has been replaced with bowler 3 for the 4th over
- during the 4th over 5 penalty runs were awarded to the batting side
- during the 2nd over 5 penalty runs were awarded to the fielding side.

End of Over				Pen	
Ov	Runs	W	B	B	F
0	15				
1	20	1			
2	20	1	2		1
3	22	1			
4	27	2	3	1	
5					

Note that, as with the vertical columns, penalty runs are always shown as 1 to denote that an award has been made. These are then multiplied by 5 when recorded in extras and on the tally and, in the case of fielding penalties, when carried forward or back to their next batting innings.

Change of bowler

During an innings a bowler may be changed for one of four reasons:

- the captain makes a bowling change
- a bowler becomes ill or injured and unable to continue
- the umpire orders the suspension of a bowler for transgression of a Law
- a bowler is called away from the game, perhaps by work or an urgent domestic matter.

Each bowling change, whether enforced or not, must be recorded, if necessary with appropriate margin notes.

END OF SPELL

Bowler 1, White, has ended a spell of bowling as shown by the black vertical line after his last over. Scorers using colours, one for each bowler, are recommended to use the colour to be used for the replacement bowler as this makes it easier to follow the progress of the innings.

	Bowler	1	2	3	4	5
1	J WHITE	M	1 w 2 . . .	. . . . + 1 .	4	
		0 - 0	3 - 1	5 - 1	9 - 1	

ILLNESS OR INJURY TO BOWLER

Bowler 2, Brown, has been injured after 3 balls of his over and bowler 3, Green, has taken over to complete the over. Brown is shown as having completed his spell. Note the positioning of the 3 balls that Green bowls. Brown would be recorded as bowling 2.3 overs and Green 0.3 overs. Such a part over cannot be deemed to be a maiden over. If a bowler is called away, the entries would be shown in the same way.

	Bowler	1		2		3	4	5
2	M BROWN	1 2 . 8 - 1	w 1 4	. . 3 18 - 1	1 2 4	. . 1 19 - 1		
3	P GREEN	w . . 0 - 1						

BOWLER REMOVED BY UMPIRE

Umpires have the authority to prevent a bowler bowling again in that innings. Here bowler 4, Black, has transgressed the Law on the 3rd ball of his 2nd over and has been removed. The end of spell is shown by the vertical line. A thick horizontal line through the remainder of the boxes shows that he cannot bowl again in that innings. Here, another bowler must complete the over – the entries for Grey's 1st over show how the entries would be recorded.

	Bowler	1		2	3	4	5
4	S BLACK	1 . . 2 - 0	. 1 .	M 2 - 0	1 6 4 13 - 0		
5	T GREY	1 1 4 6 - 0					

There is no provision for recording the suspension of a bowler in the scoring record. Should this occur, it is unlikely the scorers will become aware of the reasons until the next interval, when a note should be made in the margin.

Fall of wickets

When a batsman is dismissed several entries must be made:

- runs may be scored as a No ball penalty, a Wide ball penalty, runs credited to the striker, Byes, or Leg byes and should be recorded in the appropriate section of the scoring record.

Batsman	Time In/Out	Mins Balls	Innings of NORTHBROOK CC	4/6	How Out	Bowler	Score
1 T STOKES	2:00 2:24	24 20	+ ..2 ......2 /⁺3 1 ..4 ....w // //	1 -	BOWLED	T BROWN	12
2 W DALL	2:00		1 2 4				

- if the bowler gets credit for the dismissal enter **w** as the symbol in the batting section and the bowler analysis.
- enter two slashes // after the last ball the batsman faced to show that he has been dismissed – if a batsman retires for any reason, enter a single slash / with a symbol to indicate the retirement. At the time of the retirement it is not known whether the batsman's innings will be resumed.
- enter the time of the dismissal in the batting section.
- enter the method of dismissal in the How out column.
- if the bowler is credited for the dismissal enter his name in the bowler's column, otherwise leave the column blank.
- enter the number of runs he scored in the score column.
- enter (as time permits) the number of minutes of his innings in the top box of the Mins Balls column.
- enter (as time permits) the number of balls he faced in the bottom box of the Mins Balls column – Wides are not balls faced.
- complete the fall of wicket section to show the score and the number of the batsman dismissed. There may also be space to record the number of runs scored since the last wicket fell and the details of the partnership.

Wicket	1	2
Score	31	
Bat Out	2	
Partnership	31	

- enter the name of the incoming batsman and the time he crossed the boundary onto the field of play.

Where the bowler does not get the credit for the dismissal the method should be written in the How out column, not across both columns.

4/6	How Out	Bowler	Score	
	RUN	OUT		✘
	RUN OUT			✓

If the striker is dismissed Stumped, the name of the wicket-keeper is entered.

How Out
Stumped Jones
Caught Smith
Caught Sub

If a catch has been taken enter the name of the fielder taking the catch. If the catcher is a substitute fielder, enter Caught Sub. As he is not a member of the nominated side, his name is not officially recorded. However, his name may be recorded in brackets.

How Out
Run Out (Smith)

Where a nominated fielder effects a dismissal his name is recorded in the appropriate section. However, a convention is developing permitting the recording of additional information, such as the name of the fielder who effects a run out. Scorers may wish to record this information if time permits as an aid to players and coaches.

Retirement of batsman

A batsman is permitted to retire at any time during his innings. Depending on the reason for his retirement, as given to the umpire, he may be permitted to resume his innings. As it is unlikely that the scorers will know whether or not he is likely to return, a note should be made at the time of the retirement in the batting section of the scoring record in **pencil** against his name. If he returns, pencil notes can be erased. If he does not return, the correct entry can be determined from the umpires and entered permanently.

How Out	Bowler	Score
Retired, 3:47		

Margin notes should also be used to explain the reason for the retirement as illness, injury or personal reason. Never record personal details although it may be useful to record the incident, such as 'blow to the head' or 'slipped and injured hamstring'.

An entry must be made in the **fall of wickets** section:
- 3 wickets had previously fallen
- the 4th wicket box is split and the retirement shown in the left side
- batsman 4 retires with the score on 49
- the right side will be used when the 4th wicket falls in any other fashion.
- Retirement entries are necessary to calculate partnerships.

				Fall of Wickets	
Wicket	1	2	3	4	5
Score	2	22	29	49	
Bat Out	2	3	1	4	
Partnership	2	20	7	20	

Last hour

The Laws define a last hour during which a **minimum** of 20 overs must be bowled. This is the last hour on the final day of a match.

	Bowler	1	2	3
1	J WHITE	1 1 2 w 4 . 8 - 1	. . . 1 . . 9 - 1	
2	T BROWN	. 1 1 1 2 4 9 - 0		
3				

- the bowler's end umpire signals the start of the last hour to the scorers using the official signal – acknowledge this signal
- show the overs bowled prior to the last hour by drawing a thick line after those overs already bowled. Label this line Last Hour
- include any unused lines in the analysis as it is possible that a new bowler may bowl during the last hour.

The end of overs section should also be ruled off to show the start of the last hour:

End of Over				Pen		
Ov	Runs	W	B	B	F	
0						
1	8	1	1			
2	17		2			
3	18		1			Last Hour
4						6:03

- draw a line under the last over bowled
- note the time in the margin.

Ask the scoreboard attendants to maintain a count of the overs on the scoreboard as agreed with the umpires at the pre-match conference. The scoreboard should record the number of overs bowled starting at 1 up to 20 (or more, as time may permit more than the minimum 20 overs to be bowled).

Interruption in play

If there is an interruption in play for ground, weather or light this must be recorded in either the margin, or the notes or the section provided in some scoring records specifically for recording all interruptions:

Notes
Rain 12:15 after 3rd ball of 21st over. Play resumed 12:40 Play lost: 25 mins, 8 overs

- time the interruption started
- time the interruption ended
- total time lost
- any overs lost – the scoreboard should be adjusted as necessary
- reason/s for the interruption.

Checking with umpires

The Laws of Cricket direct that at every interval (other than the drinks interval) and during every interruption in play, when the players leave the field, the scorers and umpires must agree:

- runs scored
- wickets fallen
- number of overs bowled (where appropriate).

It is during this checking that any other matter requiring clarification can be discussed and entered. The scorers must always have this information recorded on notepaper to hand for the umpires. They should never have to return to the scorebox to get it.

3. After Time called

At the call of Time the umpires will remove the bails. This has no significance as it is the time of the call that identifies the end of the session of play and must be recorded. However this act is a visual signal to the scorers that play has ended. Should the umpire then remove the stumps this may be an indication that:

- play has ceased for the day, or
- the match has concluded, or
- the match is abandoned, or
- weather conditions require the suspension of play and the placing of covers.

At the end of an innings the players and umpires leave the field but there are still entries and calculations to be made in the scoring record, as listed below.

Batting sheet

- Any not out batsman (there can only ever be one or two) should have 'Not Out' entered in the method of dismissal.
- Any batsman who has retired should be recorded 'Retired, not out' or 'Retired out' as appropriate. The umpires will advise the correct entry.

How Out	Bowler
NOT OUT	
RETIRED, OUT	
RETIRED, NOT OUT	
}	
} DID NOT BAT	
}	

- The names of the remaining batsmen should be entered and may be bracketed together with the single entry 'Did Not Bat', which may be abbreviated to 'DNB', against their names.
- Identify the captain by an asterisk *, and the wicket-keeper by an obelisk †.
- Enter the runs scored by the batsmen [111]

- Enter the runs scored as No balls [5] and Wides [2] and total to give bowling extras [7].

				Batsmen Totals		111	
Bowling Extras	No Balls	3 1 1				5	7
	Wides	1 1				2	
Fielding Extras	Byes	4				4	20
	Leg Byes	1				1	
	Penalties	prev inn	15	this inn		15	
		PROVISIONAL SCORE FOR INNINGS				138	for 9 wickets
		Penalties awarded in following innings				10	
		Final Score for Innings				148	for 9 wickets

- Enter the runs scored as Byes [4], Leg byes [1] and awarded as penalties [15] to give total fielding extras [20].
- Add together the batsmen totals [111], bowling extras [7] and fielding extras [20] to the give the provisional score for the innings [138].
- This should agree with the cumulative run tally. If there is an error, complete the bowling section before attempting to locate the error.
- Add up the number of balls received by each batsman and enter the total.
- Enter the number of wickets that have fallen.
- If the batting captain declared show this against the wickets fallen (dec).
- If a captain forfeits an innings, that should be recorded at the top of the batting sheet used for the next innings. There is little point in using up a full sheet for the words 'Innings forfeited'.

Penalties awarded in following innings

This row is used to record penalty extras awarded while fielding **in the next innings**. If the batting side are not fielding again in the match:

- leave this row blank
- transfer the total, wickets and average to the final score row
- this should agree with the final score in the batting section.
- If the batting side will field again:
- leave this row blank
- after they have fielded enter the total of any penalty runs into this row [10]
- complete the final score for innings [148]
- this should agree with the final score in the batting section.

Bowling summary

Bowler				NALYSIS			Number of		Balls	Overs	Mdns	Runs	Wkts	Ave
			1		7	8	Wides	No Balls	Bowled					
1	J WHITE		+.2		2 . 1 . 2 .		1	1	44	7	1	25	1	25
			3		25 - 1		1	1						
2	T BROWN		. . . 4 . .		4 w 4 . . .	W 2 4 6			46	7.4	0	44	5	8.8
			4		32 - 4	44 - 5								

Complete the **summary** for each bowler:

- **Overs**: the number of overs bowled. For a part over, the number of balls are shown. T. Brown has bowled 7 overs 4 balls which is shown as 7.4 (this should not be a decimal: 7.5 is not 7 overs and 3 balls, it is 7 overs and 5 balls).
- **Maidens**: the number of maiden overs bowled taken from the analysis.
- **Runs**: the number of runs conceded by the bowler and taken from the running total.
- **Wickets**: the number of wickets for which the bowler gained credit, taken from the running total.
- **Average**: calculated by dividing the runs by the wickets – normally shown to two decimal places. If no wickets have been taken there can be no average and this is shown by a dash – not zero.
- **Balls bowled**: add the number of Wides and No balls delivered by each bowler. The number of balls bowled can then be calculated as:

(complete overs) x 6 + (number of Wides) + (number of No balls)

Make adjustments for short (5 balls or less) or long (7 balls or more) overs.

Number of		Balls	Overs	Mdns	Runs	Wkts	Ave
Wides	No Balls	Bowled					
1	1	44	7	1	25	1	25.0
1	1						
		46	7.4	0	44	5	8.8
0	0						
2	3	152	24.4	2	118	9	BOWLING TOTALS
less Wides		2			20	0	Extras & other dismissals
Balls Received		150			138	9	PROVISIONAL SCORE
					10		Penalties in following innings
					148	9	FINAL SCORE

- Add up the balls bowled and enter the total [152]. Enter the number of Wide balls bowled [2] and deduct this to give the number of balls received [150]. This should agree with the total calculated in the batting section – Wide deliveries are not balls faced or received by the striker. If necessary, allowance will have to be made for a ball called and signalled No ball followed by Dead ball, but not received by the striker (Law 24.7).
- Add the overs bowled and enter the total [24.4].
- Add the maiden overs and enter the total [2].
- Add the runs scored from the bowlers [118] and add to the fielding extras [20] to give a total of 138. This total should agree with the tally and the batting section.
- Add the wickets credited to bowlers [9]. Enter number of wickets for which bowlers do not gain credit [0], add together to give the total wickets fallen.

End of over

Enter the runs and wickets into the **end of over section** identifying any partial overs. This innings finished after 4 balls of the 25th over.

End of Over				Pen	
Ov	Runs	W	B	B	F
0	15				
1	20		1		
2	20	1	2		1
3	22		1		
4	27	2	2	1	
24	134	9	4		
25	138		2		4 balls
26					

Result

The result of the match should be completed if the innings just concluded was the last. The scores, wickets, overs (where appropriate) and result should be agreed with the umpires. Invite the umpires to initial the final scoring record to confirm their acceptance of the result.

Attention is drawn to Law 21 and its accompanying commentary.

Recording penalty extras

Penalty extras introduce a method by which transgressions by players of either side on the field of play can be punished. The fielding side can be awarded runs, introducing the question, How would runs scored when fielding be added to that side's score?

When awarded to the batting side, penalty runs are:
- added into their current innings as fielding extras
- always recorded as penalty extras in both the row provided and in the End of over section
- never credited to a batsman
- never debited against the bowler.

When awarded to the fielding side they must be added to the runs scored when that side bats. The rule is:

- If the side has already batted the runs are added onto the provisional score of their previous innings. The batting side now requires more runs to win than when they started their innings.
- If the side has not batted the runs are added onto the starting score of their next batting innings. They will commence their innings with runs on the board effectively decreasing the number of runs they need to score to win while batting.

There are three possible scenarios, a one-innings match, a two-innings match and a two-innings match where a side follows on.

1. One-innings match

1st innings	Side A bat	Side B field
	Penalty extras awarded to Side A are added to their batting total at the time of the award.	Penalty extras awarded to Side B are recorded at the time of the award and the total runs are used as the starting score of their batting innings.
2nd innings	Side A field	Side B bat
	Penalty extras awarded to Side A are recorded at the time of the award and, at the end of the innings, the total runs are added to the provisional score of their batting innings.	Penalty extras awarded to Side B are added to their batting total at the time of the award.

2. Two-innings match

1st innings	Side A bat	Side B field
	Penalty extras awarded to Side A are added to their batting total at the time of the award.	Penalty extras awarded to Side B are recorded at the time of the award and the total runs are used as the starting score of their first batting innings.
2nd innings	Side A field	Side B bat
	Penalty extras awarded to Side A are recorded at the time of the award and, at the end of the innings, the total runs are added to the provisional score of their first batting innings.	Penalty extras awarded to Side B are added to their batting total at the time of the award.

3rd innings	Side A bat	Side B field
	Penalty extras awarded to Side A are added to their batting total at the time of the award.	Penalty extras awarded to Side B are recorded at the time of the award and the total runs are used as the starting score of their second batting innings.
4th innings	Side A field	Side B bat
	Penalty extras awarded to Side A are recorded at the time of the award and, at the end of the innings, the total runs are added to the provisional score of their second batting innings.	Penalty extras awarded to Side B are added to their batting total at the time of the award.

3. Two innings-match with follow on

1st innings	Side A bat	Side B field
	Penalty extras awarded to Side A are added to their batting total at the time of the award.	Penalty extras awarded to Side B are recorded at the time of the award and the total runs are used as the starting score of their first batting innings.
2nd innings	Side A field	Side B bat
	Penalty extras awarded to Side A are recorded at the time of the award and, at the end of the innings, the total runs are added to the provisional score of their first batting innings.	Penalty extras awarded to Side B are added to their batting total at the time of the award.
3rd innings	Side A field	Side B bat
	Penalty extras awarded to Side A are recorded at the time of the award and, at the end of the innings, the total runs are added to the provisional score of their first batting innings.	Penalty extras awarded to Side B are added to their batting total at the time of the award.
4th innings	Side A bat	Side B field
	Penalty extras awarded to Side A are added to their batting total at the time of the award.	Penalty extras awarded to Side B are recorded at the time of the award and, at the end of the innings, the total runs are added to the provisional score of their second batting innings.

SCORING RECORD ENTRIES

End of Over				Pen	
Ov	Runs	W	B	B	F
0	15				
1	20		1		
2	20	1	2		1
3	22		1		
4	27	2	2	1	
5					

Awards of penalties are recorded as they happen in the Penalty section of the End of Over section.

Here an award has been made to the fielding side in the 2nd over. There are no other entries to be made at this time. An award has also been made to the batting side in the 4th over. These runs would also be recorded in the batting sheet and in the cumulative run tally.

The entries required to add runs awarded while fielding at the start of the batting innings, in this case three awards making 15 runs:

Cumulative Run Tally										End of Over				Pen	
1	2	3	4	5	6	7	8	9		Ov	Runs	W	B	B	F
10	1	2	3	4	5	6	7	8	9	0	15				
20	1	2	3	4	5	6	7	8	9	1					
30	1	2	3	4	5	6	7	8	9	2					

Fielding Extras	Byes					
	Leg Byes					
	Penalties	prev inn	15	this inn		

The entry required when runs awarded when fielding are to be added to the provisional score of a previous innings. In this example 10 runs are added into both the bowling and batting sections:

118	9		BOWLING TOTALS
20	0		Extras & other dismissals
138	9		PROVISIONAL SCORE
10			Penalties in other innings
148	9		FINAL SCORE

PROVISIONAL SCORE FOR INNINGS	138	for 9 wickets
Penalties awarded in following innings	10	
FINAL SCORE FOR INNINGS	148	for 9 wickets

Ball Not to Count as One of the Over

The Laws of Cricket (2000 Code 2nd Edition – 2003) introduced balls that shall not be counted as one of the six of the over but which are not called No ball or Wide ball. There are three which the scorer must be aware of as entries need to be made to explain the action. They must also be taken into consideration when counting balls bowled as it will appear that an over of more than six balls has been bowled.

Balls do not count as one of the over when:

- a fielder who has returned without permission comes into contact with the ball while it is in play
- a fielder illegally fields the ball
- either batsman is wilfully distracted after a delivery has been received by the striker.

In all cases the striker will have received the delivery and so there will be entries in both the batting and bowling section. A margin note should be made to explain that the ball does not count as one of the over.

Conclusion of match

As the match is nearing its conclusion, players and others may be tempted to interrupt scorers to request information. Provided they cause no distraction, they should be permitted to look over the scorers' shoulders to glean the information they seek. If this is not possible, or if distractions occur, they should politely be discouraged as concentration must be maintained until the scoring record is balanced and the result is confirmed to the umpires.

Other duties scorers may be asked to complete may include:

- compiling match statistics
- completing match reports.

Scorers should ensure they leave their scorebox as they would hope to find it – clean and tidy.

MAIN CAUSES OF INACCURACIES

Inaccuracies, errors or mistakes can occur because of:

- lack of regular checks within the scoring record and with the other scorer
- poor signalling by umpires
- umpire failing to wait for scorers' acknowledgement and continuing play
- failure to consult with umpires on doubtful matters
- lack of knowledge of the laws and of scoring techniques
- personal discomfort, location etc. causing distractions
- interruptions by players, officials, etc.
- updating the scoreboard while play is in progress
- only one scorer appointed.

The importance of regular checking cannot be overstated: it ensures that mistakes are quickly identified and corrected. If a mistake is not easily identified then one scorer should continue recording the events while the other searches for the error.

WELLSTED	CC	versus	NORTHBROOK

In a **25 OVER, ONE INNINGS** Match — Played at **WELLSTED PARK**

	Batsman	Time In/Out	Mins Balls	Innings of **NORTH-BROOK**	CC
1	T. STONES	17.00 / 17.19	19 / 18	......+..11/² .. 4 ....w //	
2	W. BELL	17.00 / 17.34	34 / 33	....4...../⁴.1...☉...2/⁷2......44./¹⁷..w //	
3	G. HARRIS	17.20 / 17.27	7 / 5	..41w //	
4	C. WELLS ✳	17.28 / 17.53	25 / 25	.....241.../⁷.2○...4.../¹³.12.w //	
5	S. PEARCE	17.35 / 18.15	40 / 17	13△ ..../⁴143211w //	
6	T. BARTON	17.54 / 18.04	10 / 14	..1..4.③▽2/¹⁰...w //	
7	P. MOORE †	18.05 / 18.09	4 / 4	....⁻ʷ //	
8	B. JARVIS	18.10 / 18.35	25 / 22	....4...../⁴4........2./¹⁰..	
9	R. FOWLER	18.16 / 18.26	10 / 7	.1144.w //	
10	H BROWN	18.27 / 18.32	5 / 3	21w //	
11	D. SOUTH	18.33 / 18.35	2 / 3	462	
			151	Total balls received	Total boundaries scored

Fall of wicket; score & No of Batsman out

Wicket	1	2	3	4	5	6	7	8	9	10
Score	25	34	42	72	97	101	106	125	130	
Bat out	1	3	2	4	6	7	5	9	10	
Partnership **B**	15	9	8	30	25	4	5	19	5	

O Underlining to show that the batsmen cross before the catch
P Batsmen run 3 but only the 2 runs needed to win are scored

	Bowler	BOWLING ANALYSIS									
		1	**C** 2	3 **D**	4	**E** 5	6	7	8	9	10
1	J. WILLIAMS	M / 0	+ . 1 / . . / . . / 2	. . ☉ / . . / . . / 5	2 . / 2 . / . . / 9	w / . . / W / 9–1	2 1 / 4 1 / 1 . / 17–1				
2	T. JACKSON	. . / 4 / . . / 4	1 1 / . . / . . / 6	4 . / . . / w / 10–1	. 1 / 4 . / . . / 15–1	4 . / 4 . / . w / 23–2					
3	F. BARKER **F**	3 . ○ / 2 . / 6	4 . / . . / . 1 / 11	. . ③ / 4 **H** / 4 . / 19	4 . / 3 . / w . / 26–1			**O**	**P**		
4	M.GREEN **G**	△M / . . / 0	2 . / . . / w 1 / 3–1	▽**I** / 1 . / 2 . / 6–1	2 ⁻ᵂ / 1 . / . . / 10–2	w . / . . / 1 . / 11–3	4 w / 4 . / . . / 19–4	w 2 / 4 . / 6 . / 31–5			
5	W. SMITH **L**	1 4 / . . / . . / 5	1 . . / 4 . / . . / 10	2 . / 1 . / 2 . / 15	. **J** **K**						

J Moore stumped off a Wide. Score 1 wide extra before the fall of the wicket
K Umpire calls over after only 5 balls that count in the over
L Leg byes not awarded – no runs scored
M Deliberate short running – runs disallowed. 5 Penalty runs to the fielding side. Amend the Wellstead score in the cumulative run tally. An explanation side note is needed

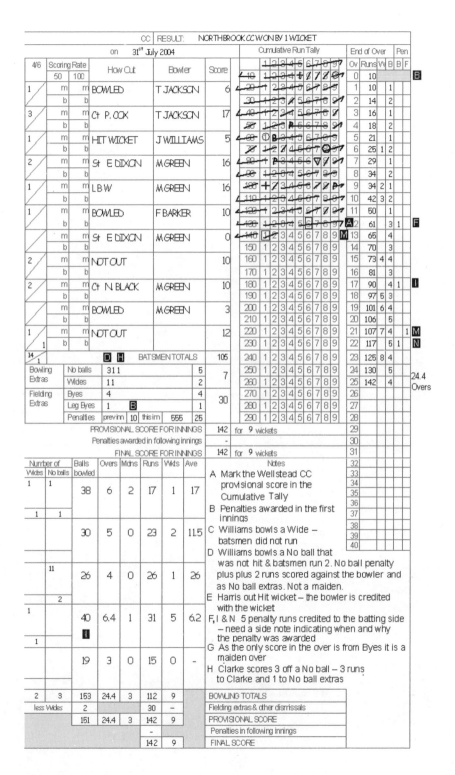

	CC	RESULT:	NORTHBROOK CC WON BY 1 WICKET

The scorebook shows a completed cricket scoresheet dated **31st July 2004**.

Batting (How Out / Bowler / Score)

4/6	Scoring Rate 50 / 100	How Out	Bowler	Score
1	m / b	BOWLED	T JACKSON	6
3	m / b	Ct P. COX	T JACKSON	17
1	m / b	HIT WICKET	J WILLIAMS	5
2	m / b	St E DIXON	M GREEN	16
1	m / b	LBW	M GREEN	16
1	m / b	BOWLED	F BARKER	10
	m / b	St E DIXON	M GREEN	0
2	m / b	NOT OUT		10
2	m / b	Ct N BLACK	M GREEN	10
	m / b	BOWLED	M GREEN	3
1 (1)	m / b	NOT OUT		12
14 (1)			BATSMEN TOTALS	105

Extras

Bowling Extras	No balls	3 1 1		5	7
	Wides	1 1		2	
Fielding Extras	Byes	4		4	30
	Leg Byes	1		1	
	Penalties	prev inn 10	this inn 555	25	

PROVISIONAL SCORE FOR INNINGS 142 for 9 wickets
Penalties awarded in following innings -
FINAL SCORE FOR INNINGS 142 for 9 wickets

Cumulative Run Tally / End of Over

Ov	Runs	W	B	B	F
0	10				
1	10	1			
2	14	2			
3	16	1			
4	18	2			
5	21	1			
6	25	1	2		
7	29	1			
8	34	2			
9	34	2	1		
10	42	3	2		
11	50	1			
12	61		3	1	
13	65	4			
14	70	4			
15	73	4	4		
16	81	4			
17	90	4	1		
18	97	5	3		
19	101	6	4		
20	106	5			
21	107	7	4	1	
22	117		5	1	
23	125	8	4		
24	130	5			
25	142	4			24.4 Overs

Bowling

Number of Wides	No balls	Balls bowled	Overs	Mdns	Runs	Wkts	Ave
1	1	38	6	2	17	1	17
1	1	30	5	0	23	2	11.5
	11	26	4	0	26	1	26
1	2	40	6.4	1	31	5	6.2
1		19	3	0	15	0	-
2	3	153	24.4	3	112	9	BOWLING TOTALS
less Wides		2			30	-	Fielding extras & other dismissals
		151	24.4	3	142	9	PROVISIONAL SCORE
					-		Penalties in following innings
					142	9	FINAL SCORE

Notes

A Mark the Wellstead CC provisional score in the Cumulative Tally
B Penalties awarded in the first innings
C Williams bowls a Wide – batsmen did not run
D Williams bowls a No ball that was not hit & batsmen run 2. No ball penalty plus plus 2 runs scored against the bowler and as No ball extras. Not a maiden.
E Harris out Hit wicket – the bowler is credited with the wicket
F,I & N 5 penalty runs credited to the batting side – need a side note indicating when and why the penalty was awarded
G As the only score in the over is from Byes it is a maiden over
H Clarke scores 3 off a No ball – 3 runs to Clarke and 1 to No ball extras

The story of the innings of Northbrook CC in the match Wellsted CC v Northbrook CC
A 25 over, one-innings match played at Wellsted Park on 31 July 2004
Wellsted batted first and their provisional score is 136 all out

Over	Bowler	Delivery		Incident
0			A	Highlight the provisional score of Wellsted CC
			B	Enter 10 penalty runs awarded in the first innings
1	J Williams			T Stones facing
		1st		Batsmen do not run. No signal
		2nd		Batsmen do not run. No signal
		3rd		Batsmen do not run. No signal
		4th		Batsmen do not run. No signal
		5th		Batsmen do not run. No signal
		6th		Batsmen do not run. No signal
2	T Jackson			W Bell facing
		1st		Batsmen do not run. No signal
		2nd		Batsmen do not run. No signal
		3rd		Batsmen do not run. No signal
		4th		Batsmen do not run. No signal
		5th		Umpire signals **Boundary 4**
		6th		Batsmen do not run. No signal
3	J Williams			T Stones facing
		1st	C	Batsmen do not run. Umpire signals **Wide ball**
		2nd		Batsmen do not run. No signal
		3rd		Batsmen do not run. No signal
		4th		Batsmen run 1. No signal
		5th		Batsmen do not run. No signal
		6th		Batsmen do not run. No signal
		7th		Batsmen do not run. No signal
4	T Jackson			T Stones facing
		1st		Batsmen run 1. No signal
		2nd		Batsmen do not run. No signal
		3rd		Batsmen do not run. No signal
		4th		Batsmen run 1. No signal
		5th		Batsmen do not run. No signal
		6th		Batsmen do not run. No signal
5	J Williams			W Bell facing
		1st		Batsmen do not run. No signal
		2nd		Batsmen do not run. No signal
		3rd		Batsmen do not run. No signal
		4th	D	Batsmen run 2. The umpire signals **No ball** and then gives the **Bye** signal
		5th		Batsmen do not run. No signal
		6th		Batsmen do not run. No signal
		7th		Batsmen do not run. No signal
6	T Jackson			T Stones facing
		1st		Batsmen run 2, stop and return to their original ends.
				The umpire signals **Boundary 4**
		2nd		Batsmen do not run. No signal
		3rd		Batsmen do not run. No signal
		4th		Batsmen do not run. No signal
		5th		Batsmen do not run. No signal
		6th		T Stones **out – Bowled**
				The new batsman is G Harris

Over	Bowler	Delivery		Incident
7	J Williams			W Bell facing
		1st		Batsmen run 2. No signal
		2nd		Batsmen run 2. No signal
		3rd		Batsmen do not run. No signal
		4th		Batsmen do not run. No signal
		5th		Batsmen do not run. No signal
		6th		Batsmen do not run. No signal
8	T Jackson			G Harris facing
		1st		Batsmen do not run. No signal
		2nd		Batsmen do not run. No signal
		3rd		The umpire signals **Boundary 4**
		4th		Batsmen run 1. No signal
		5th		Batsmen do not run. No signal
		6th		Batsmen do not run. No signal
9	J Williams			G Harris facing
		1st	E	As he plays a shot the bails fall from his wicket.
				On appeal the striker's end umpire gives him **out – Hit Wicket**
				The new batsman is C Wells (Capt)
		2nd		Batsmen do not run. No signal
		3rd		Batsmen do not run. No signal
		4th		Batsmen do not run. No signal
		5th		Batsmen do not run. No signal
		6th		Batsmen do not run. No signal
10	T Jackson			W Bell facing
		1st		The umpire signals **Boundary 4**
		2nd		The umpire signals **Boundary 4**
		3rd		Batsmen do not run. No signal
		4th		Batsmen do not run. No signal
		5th		Batsmen do not run. No signal
		6th		The batsman hits the ball which is caught P Cox
				The bowler's end umpire gives Bell **out**
				The new batsman is S Pearce
11	J Williams			C Wells facing
		1st		Batsmen run 2. No signal
		2nd		The umpire signals **Boundary 4**
		3rd		Batsmen run 1. No signal
		4th		Batsmen run 1. No signal
		5th		Batsmen do not run. No signal
		6th		Batsmen do not run. No signal
12	F Barker			S Pearce facing
		1st		Batsmen run 3. No signal
		2nd		The ball runs through the legs of the wicket-keeper and strikes
				a helmet on the ground behind him. No runs attempted.
			F	The umpire signals **five penalty runs to the batting side**
		3rd		Batsmen run 2. No signal
		4th		Batsmen do not run. The umpire signals **No ball**
		5th		Batsmen do not run. No signal
		6th		Batsmen do not run. No signal
		7th		Batsmen do not run. No signal
13	M Green			S Pearce facing
		1st	G	The umpire signals **Bye** and then signals **Boundary 4**
		2nd		Batsmen do not run. No signal
		3rd		Batsmen do not run. No signal
		4th		Batsmen do not run. No signal
		5th		Batsmen do not run. No signal
		6th		Batsmen do not run. No signal

Over	Bowler	Delivery	Incident
14	F Barker		C Wells facing
		1st	The umpire signals **Boundary 4**
		2nd	Batsmen do not run. No signal
		3rd	Batsmen do not run. No signal
		4th	Batsmen do not run. No signal
		5th	Batsmen do not run. No signal
		6th	Batsmen run 1. No signal
15	M Green		C Wells facing
		1st	Batsmen run 2. No signal
		2nd	Batsmen do not run. No signal
		3rd	The ball goes through to the wicket-keeper, E Dixon, who breaks the wicket. The striker's end umpire gives the batsman **out – Stumped** The new batsman is T Barton
		4th	Batsmen do not run. No signal
		5th	Batsmen do not run. No signal
		6th	Batsmen run 1. No signal
16	F Barker		T Barton facing
		1st	Batsmen do not run. No signal
		2nd	Batsmen do not run. No signal
		3rd	The umpire signals **Boundary 4**
		4th	Batsmen do not run. No signal
		5th H	Batsmen run 3. The umpire signals **No ball**
		6th	Batsmen do not run. No signal
		7th	Batsmen do not run. No signal
17	M Green	I	Following discussion with his colleague the umpire signals five penalty runs to the batting side. (Later he informs the scorers that this was for pitch damage) T Barton facing
		1st	Batsmen run 1. The umpire signals **Leg bye**
		2nd	Batsmen run 1. No signal
		3rd	Batsmen run 2. No signal
		4th	Batsmen do not run. No signal
		5th	Batsmen do not run. No signal
		6th	Batsmen do not run. No signal
18	F Barker		S Pearce facing
		1st	The umpire signals **Boundary 4**
		2nd	Batsmen run 3. No signal
		3rd	T Barton **out – Bowled** The new batsman is P Moore (Wicket-keeper)
		4th	Batsmen do not run. No signal
		5th	Batsmen do not run. No signal
		6th	Batsmen do not run. No signal
19	M Green		S Pearce facing
		1st	Batsmen run 2. No signal
		2nd	Batsmen run 1. No signal
		3rd	Batsmen do not run. No signal
		4th J	The ball goes to the wicket-keeper, E Dixon, who removes the bails. The bowler's end umpire signals **Wide ball.** The striker's end umpire gives the batsman **out – Stumped** The incoming batsman is B Jarvis
		5th	Batsmen do not run. No signal
		6th	Batsmen do not run. No signal
		K	The umpire calls Over

Over	Bowler	Delivery		Incident
20	W Smith			S Pearce facing
		1st		Batsmen run 1. No signal
		2nd		Batsmen do not run. No signal
		3rd		Batsmen do not run. No signal
		4th		The umpire signals **Boundary 4**
		5th		Batsmen do not run. No signal
		6th	L	After the ball hits the striker's pad the batsmen complete one run. The bowler's end umpire signals **Dead ball** and the batsmen return to their original ends
21	M Green			S Pearce facing
		1st		Pearce is hit on the pads. The bowler's end umpire gives him **out – LBW** The new batsman is R Fowler
		2nd	M	Batsmen run 2. Having previously warned the batting side for deliberate short running the umpire considers they have again deliberately run short and signals **five penalty runs to the fielding side**
		3rd		Batsmen run 1. No signal
		4th		Batsmen do not run. No signal
		5th		Batsmen do not run. No signal
		6th		Batsmen do not run. No signal
22	W Smith			R Fowler facing
		1st	N	Batsmen run 1. No signal. The umpire signals **five penalty runs to the batting side** for deliberate obstruction of the batsman
		2nd		The umpire signals **Boundary 4**
		3rd		Batsmen do not run. No signal
		4th		Batsmen do not run. No signal
		5th		Batsmen do not run. No signal
		6th		Batsmen do not run. No signal
		7th		Batsmen do not run. No signal
23	M Green			R Fowler facing
		1st		The umpire signals **Boundary 4**
		2nd		The umpire signals **Boundary 4**
		3rd		Batsmen do not run. No signal
		4th		The batsman hits the ball in the air; the batsmen cross before N Black catches the ball
			O	The new batsman is H Brown. Jarvis is facing
		5th		Batsmen do not run. No signal
		6th		Batsmen do not run. No signal
24	W Smith			H Brown facing
		1st		Batsmen run 2. No signal
		2nd		Batsmen run 1. No signal
		3rd		Batsmen run 2. No signal
		4th		Batsmen do not run. No signal
		5th		Batsmen do not run. No signal
		6th		Batsmen do not run. No signal
25	M Green			H Brown facing
		1st		Brown **out – Bowled** The new batsman is D South
		2nd		The umpire signals **Boundary 4**
		3rd		The umpire signals **Boundary 6**
		4th	P	The batsmen run 3. No signal The umpire calls Time and removes the bails

PART 4

Appendices

APPENDIX A
Law 8 (The wickets)

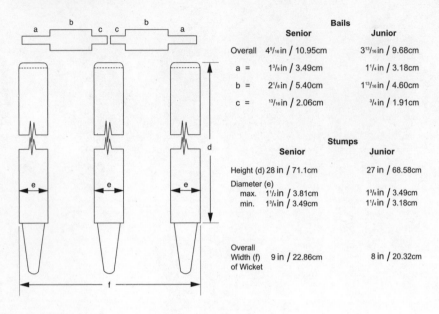

	Bails	
	Senior	**Junior**
Overall	4^{5}/$_{16}$ in / 10.95cm	3^{13}/$_{16}$ in / 9.68cm
a =	1^{3}/$_{8}$ in / 3.49cm	1^{1}/$_{4}$ in / 3.18cm
b =	2^{1}/$_{8}$ in / 5.40cm	1^{13}/$_{16}$ in / 4.60cm
c =	^{13}/$_{16}$ in / 2.06cm	^{3}/$_{4}$ in / 1.91cm

	Stumps	
	Senior	**Junior**
Height (d)	28 in / 71.1cm	27 in / 68.58cm
Diameter (e)		
max.	1^{1}/$_{2}$ in / 3.81cm	1^{3}/$_{8}$ in / 3.49cm
min.	1^{3}/$_{8}$ in / 3.49cm	1^{1}/$_{4}$ in / 3.18cm
Overall Width (f) of Wicket	9 in / 22.86cm	8 in / 20.32cm

APPENDIX B
Laws 7 (The pitch) and 9 (The bowling, popping and return creases)

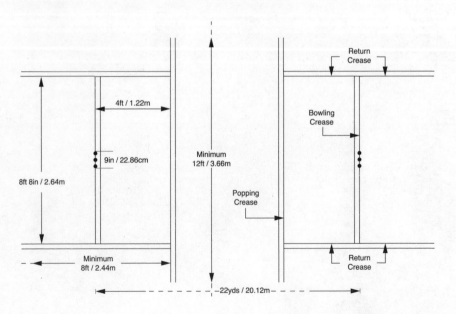